BEYOND
GOOD and EVIL

BEYOND GOOD and EVIL

*Prelude
to a
Philosophy of the Future*

by
FRIEDRICH NIETZSCHE

Translated, with Commentary,
by
WALTER KAUFMANN

VINTAGE BOOKS
A Division of Random House
NEW YORK

for DAVID

CONTENTS

TRANSLATOR'S PREFACE *ix*

BIBLIOGRAPHICAL NOTE *xxi*

NIETZSCHE'S PREFACE 2

On the Prejudices of Philosophers 7

The Free Spirit 33

What Is Religious 57

Epigrams and Interludes 77

Natural History of Morals 95

We Scholars 119

Our Virtues 143

Peoples and Fatherlands 171

What Is Noble 199

From High Mountains: *Aftersong* 238

INDEX 247

Translator's Preface

Nietzsche was controversial to the marrow. He sought controversy and is still controversial. But the area of agreement about him is growing. What the Germans and the French have known for some time is gradually being recognized in the English-speaking world as well: Nietzsche was one of the greatest German writers and philosophers of all time and one of the most interesting and influential Europeans of the nineteenth century. *Beyond Good and Evil* is one of his most important books, and its nine parts with their descriptive subtitles are designed to give the reader a comprehensive idea of Nietzsche's thought and style.

For all that, the book, like all of Nietzsche's best volumes, is easily misunderstood. For readers who come to it with no previous knowledge of Nietzsche or with erroneous preconceptions about him, I have ventured to offer something of a commentary in the form of copious footnotes. *All of the footnotes are mine; none are Nietzsche's.*

I have chosen to use notes for elucidation of major and minor points in the text rather than a long introduction or interlarded commentaries because such notes can provide immediate clarification or interpretation for the reader who requires such assistance. On the other hand, the reader can skip the notes if he wishes, and read Nietzsche straight through without the intrusion of the editor's commentaries.

Another possibility would have been to offer the commentary on facing pages, as I myself have done in the case of Hegel's long Preface to the *Phenomenology*. But Nietzsche's book is not *that* difficult: one can read it like an ordinary book, and many pages require no elucidation. Everything considered, then, it seemed best to offer the commentary in the form of notes—none on some pages, several on others.

To keep down the length of the commentary and to avoid excessive repetition of material available elsewhere, I have referred to detailed discussion of many points in my own *Nietzsche* volume.

2

A word about the text: it was originally published in 1886, following *Thus Spoke Zarathustra,* which is generally and rightly regarded as Nietzsche's first attempt to present his whole philosophy. All of his previous works had been stages in his development: with *Zarathustra* the final phase begins; a comprehensive vision has been attained but is far from easy to communicate. *Zarathustra,* though much of the work consists of apparently direct preaching, is a form of "indirect communication," to use Kierkegaard's term: the form is literary and there is an abundance of symbolism. For those who know the author well, the book is a stunning epitome of his thought; for those who do not, some other approach is needed. It was with this in mind that Nietzsche wrote *Beyond Good and Evil.* And on September 22, 1886, he wrote Jacob Burckhardt: "Please read this book (although it says the same things as my *Zarathustra,* but differently, very differently—)."

The first edition was the only one that Nietzsche himself supervised. In a letter to his friend Franz Overbeck, he wrote: "I am making the experiment of having something published at *my* expense: assuming 300 copies will be sold, my expenses will be covered and I might be able to repeat the experiment some time. The firm of C. G. Naumann permits the use of its highly respectable name. This between us. The neglect by Schm.[1] was monstrous: for ten years now no copies distributed to bookstores; neither any review copies . . . no promotion—in short, my writings beginning with *Human, All-Too-Human* are 'anecdota.' Of *Zarathustra* 60–70 copies each[2] have been sold, etc., etc."[3]

---

[1] Ernst Schmeitzner had been Nietzsche's publisher.

[2] The reference is to the first three parts, published separately in 1883 and 1884. Of Part Four, only forty copies had been printed privately, and only seven were distributed among friends.

[3] Written from Sils Maria, summer 1886; Number 255 in *Friedrich Nietzsches Briefwechsel mit Franz Overbeck* (Friedrich Nietzsche's correspondence with Franz Overbeck), Leipzig, 1916, p. 341.

The book of which Nietzsche had hoped to sell 300 copies was *Beyond Good and Evil*, but a year later, June 8, 1887, he writes Peter Gast: "This time, for *Bey. G. & E.,* everything necessary (and even a little more than that) has been done as far as the book trade is concerned: so Herr Schmeitzner cannot be blamed any more, as I had done so far. *In spite of all this*—the result is the same as with Schmeitzner: rather, it is still worse! Altogether only 114 copies have been sold (while 66 copies have been given away to newspapers and journals).

"Instructive! Namely, one simply does not want my literature; and I—may no longer afford the luxury of print."[4]

By 1903, 17,000 copies were in print; by 1906, 36,000. Since then new editions and translations into other languages have mushroomed.

The first edition has become a great rarity and has never been reprinted exactly as published in 1886. All subsequent editions contain a few very minor deviations. Karl Schlechta's edition of Nietzsche's works in three volumes[5] is widely considered vastly superior to all previous editions, at least philologically, although it contains much less of Nietzsche's *Nachlass*[6] than some earlier editions; and Schlechta claims unequivocally that he has followed the original edition, published by C. G. Naumann (Leipzig, 1886),[7] but he has not. Where the standard editions differ from the original edition, he follows the later editions.[8] No matter of philosophical substance is involved; the deviations are very small; but the fact remains astonishing. Notwithstanding all sorts of sensational claims, none of the scholarly corrections of the older editions of Nietzsche's writings, published since World War II, are important philosophi-

---

[4] *Friedrich Nietzsches Briefe an Peter Gast* (Friedrich Nietzsche's letters to Peter Gast), Leipzig, 1908.

[5] *Werke in drei Bänden,* Munich, 1954–56; *Nietzsche–Index,* Munich, 1965.

[6] The notes, fragments, lectures, and drafts he had not published himself. Moreover, the three volumes include only 278 of Nietzsche's thousands of published letters and none of his early scholarly articles.

[7] "Philological Postscript," in Vol. III, p. 1,387.

[8] Sections 65a, 73a, 186, 237, 247, 269, and 270.

cally, and it is ironical that the editions of Schlechta and Podach[9] are by no means models of belated philological soundness.[10] This translation follows the first edition. In my footnote commentary, deviations of the later editions are pointed out.

I have taken two liberties. Nietzsche occasionally uses dots, usually four, as a punctuation mark; for example, but by no means there alone, at the end of sections 62 and 227. In serious works in the English-speaking world dots are so generally taken to indicate omissions that it did not seem advisable to follow Nietzsche's usage. Dashes have therefore been used instead. Moreover, Nietzsche often employs dots or dashes in the middle of lengthy paragraphs. In such cases I have often begun a new paragraph to mark the break; and beyond that, I have generally broken up long paragraphs. The reader may always assume that in the original a numbered section constitutes a single paragraph; even if it is as long as the whole Preface or sections 25, 26, and 28.

3

Beyond Good and Evil has been translated into English twice before. The first translator, Helen Zimmern, was an English writer who had met Nietzsche in Sils Maria in the summer of 1886—the period when the book was completed, printed, and published. Indeed, Nietzsche mentions her in the margin of the letter to Franz Overbeck previously cited: "Till the middle of September I shall stay here. There is no dearth of old acquaintances . . . Miss Helen Zimmern . . ."

In the index of names at the end of Nietzsche's *Briefe an Peter Gast,* Helen Zimmern is identified as an "English writer"; in the index to *Briefe an Mutter und Schwester* (letters to mother and sister, Leipzig, 1909), as "engl. Litteratin," which is less respectful. Neither volume mentions that she translated *Beyond Good and Evil.* What Nietzsche wrote (September 19, 1886) about her to his

---

mother or sister was: "I had the privilege of introducing this 'champion of women's rights' (Frl. von Salis) to another 'champion' who is my neighbor at meals, Miss Helen Zimmern, who is extremely clever, incidentally not an Englishwoman—but Jewish. May heaven have mercy on the European intellect if one wanted to subtract the Jewish intellect from it."[11] In 1885, the year before, Nietzsche's sister had married Bernhard Förster, one of the leaders of the German anti-Semitic movement.[12]

Helen Zimmern (1846–1934), two years Nietzsche's junior, had published *Arthur Schopenhauer: His Life and His Philosophy* (1876) and *Gotthold Ephraim Lessing: His Life and His Works* (1878); she also published many other books and translations, including several from the Italian. About her version of *Beyond Good and Evil,* Dr. Oscar Levy reported in 1913 in a short essay on "The Nietzsche Movement in England" (in the last volume, the eighteenth, of his edition of *The Complete Works*): "But in 1907 the party had somewhat recovered its spirit, and as a last experiment brought out a translation of *Beyond Good and Evil*—this time at private risk, for no publisher could be induced to take up an author twice repudiated. This translation was one which had been made nearly ten years ago, but until then had never seen, and was never expected to see, the light of publicity. It turned out to be a success —a half-hearted success perhaps, but one that at last told the few inmates of the Nietzschean ark that the waters of democracy had diminished, and that at least some higher peaks of humanity were free from the appalling deluge. The success encouraged them once more to take up their old project of the publication of the complete works. . . ."

---

[11] Cf. the similar remarks about her in letters to Gast, July 20, 1886, and January 6, 1888: "Of course Jewish:—it is terrific to what extent this race now holds the 'spirit [Geistigkeit]' in Europe in its hands," and, "the clever Englishwoman (resp., Jewess) who introduced Schopenhauer to the English. . . . (Summer before last she was in Sils Maria, sitting next to me at meals)."

[12] Cf. Kaufmann, *Nietzsche: Philosopher, Psychologist, Antichrist,* Chapter 1, section III, where Nietzsche's letters about the marriage and his opposition to anti-Semitism are quoted. For full-length portraits of the Försters see E. F. Podach, *Gestalten um Nietzsche* (persons around Nietzsche, Weimar, 1932), Chapter 4.

The "inmates" in England were a very different lot from those who were by then writing about Nietzsche in Germany and France: English professional *philosophers,* for example, had developed curious versions of Hegelianism after Hegel had gone into eclipse on the continent, and at the beginning of the twentieth century the young G. E. Moore and Bertrand Russell were trying to emancipate philosophy from the influence of the leading Idealists, F. H. Bradley and J. M. E. McTaggart. The tone of the English Nietzscheans, in turn, helped to create a public image of Nietzsche that did not attract philosophers to him.

It was over fifty years after *Beyond Good and Evil* had originally appeared in 1886 that professional philosophers began to publish studies of Nietzsche's philosophy in English.

Meanwhile, the Zimmern translation of *Beyond Good and Evil* found its way into the Modern Library, and it was until 1955 the only version through which myriads of readers knew the book. In preparing the present edition, I hoped at first that I might merely revise her version, modernizing her somewhat Victorian prose and correcting mistakes; but I soon gave up. The mistakes were too numerous, and in Nietzsche's case nuances are so important that it would be difficult to say at what point an infelicitous rendering becomes downright wrong.

The second translator, Marianne Cowan, is not a philosopher either. Her version is modern and very readable. But the merits are somewhat offset by errors of understanding, and therefore I have pointed out a few such instances in my notes.

Often it seems helpful to call the reader's attention to crucial passages in some of Nietzsche's other works. These are cited in each instance according to sections, to enable the reader to find them in any edition; but in the case of material included in a volume of Nietzsche translations that I published in 1954 [13] I have also given the page numbers in parentheses.

---

[13] *The Portable Nietzsche,* which contains complete versions of *Zarathustra, Twilight of the Idols, Antichrist,* and *Nietzsche contra Wagner,* as well as selections from Nietzsche's other books, his notes, and his letters.

4

About the title of the book: like many of Nietzsche's titles, phrases, and coinages, it is brilliant, unforgettable, and usually misconstrued. The following sections of the book are relevant to an understanding of what Nietzsche meant by "beyond good and evil": the author's Preface and sections 2, 4, 32, 33, 56, 153, 164, 202, 212, the end of 241, 260, and 284. This is not to say that the other sections are not relevant nor that the reader would be best advised to look up these passages first. Rather, it would be well to read the book with an open mind and a readiness to distinguish the many connotations of its striking title. And it might be helpful to read the editor's note for section 250 at the start.

To an extent at least it may help many readers to relate several themes of the book to other great writers, and some such comparisons will be found in the notes. One theme, however, should be stated here at the outset. Ibsen's Dr. Thomas Stockmann says at the end of *An Enemy of the People*: "*He* is the strongest man in the world that stands alone." This leitmotif of the play illustrates Kierkegaard's influence on Ibsen, to which Georg Brandes referred in a letter to Nietzsche, March 7, 1888: "Intellectually, he has been very dependent on Kierkegaard." We may recall Kierkegaard's remarks on "That Individual"[14] with its refrain "The crowd is untruth." The fourth act of Ibsen's play could almost be subtitled "Variations on a Theme by Kierkegaard." Witness Dr. Stockmann's words:

> The most dangerous enemy of truth and freedom among us—is the compact majority. Yes, the damned, compact, liberal majority . . .
>
> The majority has *might*—unfortunately—but *right* it is not. Right—are I and a few others. The minority is always right. . . .
>
> I have a mind to make a revolution against the lie that the majority is in the possession of truth. What kind of truths

---

[14] Included in *Existentialism from Dostoevsky to Sartre*, ed. Walter Kaufmann (New York, Meridian Books, 1956), pp. 92–99.

are those around which the majority usually gathers? They are truths that have become so old that they are on the way toward becoming shaky. But once a truth has become that old, it is also on the way toward becoming a lie . . . A normally constituted truth lives, let us say, as a rule seventeen or eighteen years; at most twenty, rarely more. But such aged truths are always exceedingly thin. Nevertheless it is only at that stage that the majority makes their acquaintance . . . All these majority truths . . . are rather like rancid, spoiled . . . hams. And that is the source of the moral scurvy that rages all around us. . . ."

A generation later, Freud said on the second page of his autobiographical *Selbstdarstellung* (Leipzig, 1925) that, as a Jew at an anti-Semitic university, "I learned early to know the lot of standing in opposition and being placed under a ban by the 'compact majority.' Thus the ground was laid for a certain independence of judgment."

One reasonable perspective for *Beyond Good and Evil* is to see it somewhere between Kierkegaard and Ibsen on the one hand and Freud and Sartre on the other. And considering how much Nietzsche has to say about "nobility" in this book, it is good to recall that the old Freud said in a letter about Nietzsche: "In my youth he signified a nobility which I could not attain." [15]

Such sections as 212 and 296, to name only two among a great many, invite comparison with some of the phrases cited here. But it would be pointless to attempt a long list, for what is at stake is not just a verbal similarity here or there but rather one way of seeing the whole book. There are many others.

It would be foolish for a translator, and even for a commentator, to attempt to foist his own estimate of a book with which he has been living for some time on those who will henceforth share his experience to some extent. But in the spirit of Zarathustra's

---

[15] Included by Ernest Jones in his *Life and Work of Sigmund Freud* (New York, Basic Books, 1957), III, 460. For details of the image of Nietzsche communicated to Freud in the early eighteen-eighties by his friend Dr. Paneth who met Nietzsche in Nice, see Kaufmann, *From Shakespeare to Existentialism* (Garden City, N. Y., Anchor Books, 1960), pp. 323f.

"This is *my* way; where is yours?" [16] I shall venture a suggestion.

This is one of the great books of the nineteenth century, indeed of any century, despite much with which the modern reader might disagree. There is much in it with which I too do not agree; but that is also true of Plato's and Aristotle's writings, of all great philosophical works and, making due allowances for the different genre, of Dante's and Dostoevsky's ideas and of the Bible. There are some passages that strike me as blemishes without which the book would be better; for example, the tedious remarks about women, the mercifully briefer comments on the English, and the poem at the end.

It is possible to say briefly what makes the book great: the prophetic independence of its spirit; the hundreds of doors it opens for the mind, revealing new vistas, problems, and relationships; and what it contributes to our understanding of much of recent thought and literature and history. Readers might ask, for example, about the relation of various passages to psychoanalysis, to analytical philosophy, or to existentialism. But even a far longer list would not do justice to the book. There remains another dimension. This is one of those rare books in which one encounters not only a great thinker but also a fascinating human being of exceptional complexity and integrity.

One final caution. *Beyond Good and Evil* is not a collection of aphorisms for browsing. Each of the nine major parts, with the possible exception of part four, is meant to be read straight through. Each pursues one complex of problems, and what is said in one section is frequently qualified decisively in the next, or a few pages later. The often surprising developments of an idea constitute one of the major charms of this work. And it is in part on their account that this book, like all great books—for this is part of their definition or, as Nietzsche might say, a criterion for the order of rank—needs to be read more than once. It is a book to reread and live with.

September 1965

                                                          W. K.

---

[16] End of the chapter "On the Spirit of Gravity" in Part III (*Portable Nietzsche*, p. 307).

Acknowledgments

But for Jason Epstein, this volume would never have come into being. He urged me for years to make more new translations of Nietzsche, before I finally consented to go over some of the old versions to eliminate outright errors. This proved to be a thankless, endless, and all but impossible undertaking. So I gave up and began some more new translations, of which this is the first to appear. The commentary, not anticipated, took form as the translation progressed.

But for Berenice Hoffman, this volume would be much less satisfactory. As an editor, she went far beyond the call of duty, putting me in mind of my not altogether literal translation of the conclusion of Goethe's *Faust:*

> *The Eternal-Feminine*
> *Lures to perfection.*

As for the Index, almost all of the work on that was done by Stephen Watson. Sonia Volochova made many additions to the Index and greatly increased its value.

It was often extremely difficult to decide what phrases in the text required notes. Mr. Watson, as a University Scholar at Princeton University, called to my attention many points on which he thought students needed help, and he also helped me with the proofs. I am grateful to him and to Princeton's excellent program of undergraduate research assistantships.

WALTER KAUFMANN

Bibliographical Note

Nietzsche's works are generally cited by section numbers, as these are the same in all editions. But *Thus Spoke Zarathustra, Twilight of the Idols,* and *Nietzsche contra Wagner* are not composed of consecutively numbered sections; on the other hand they are available in a single volume, along with *The Antichrist* and selections from Nietzsche's other books, from his notes, and from his letters: *The Portable Nietzsche,* selected and translated, with an introduction, prefaces, and notes, by Walter Kaufmann, The Viking Press, New York, 1954. Page numbers refer to this volume. The same translation of *Zarathustra,* with preface and notes, is also available separately as a Compass Book paperback, The Viking Press, New York, 1966.

Walter Kaufmann, *Nietzsche: Philosopher, Psychologist, Antichrist* (originally published by the Princeton University Press, 1950; revised paperback edition with different pagination, published by Meridian Books, New York, 1956), is cited by chapters and sections to facilitate ready reference.

Jenseits

von Gut und Böse.

Vorspiel

einer

Philosophie der Zukunft.

Von

Friedrich Nietzsche.

Leipzig

Druck und Verlag von C. G. Naumann.

1886.

Preface

Supposing truth is a woman—what then? Are there not grounds for the suspicion that all philosophers, insofar as they were dogmatists, have been very inexpert about women? That the gruesome seriousness, the clumsy obtrusiveness with which they have usually approached truth so far[1] have been awkward and very improper methods for winning a woman's heart? What is certain is that she has not allowed herself to be won—and today every kind of dogmatism is left standing dispirited and discouraged. *If* it is left standing at all! For there are scoffers who claim that it has fallen, that all dogmatism lies on the ground—even more, that all dogmatism is dying.

Speaking seriously, there are good reasons why all philosophical dogmatizing, however solemn and definitive its airs used to be, may nevertheless have been no more than a noble childishness and tyronism. And perhaps the time is at hand when it will be comprehended again and again *how little* used to be sufficient to furnish the cornerstone for such sublime and unconditional philosophers' edifices as the dogmatists have built so far: any old popular superstition from time immemorial (like the soul superstition which, in the form of the subject and ego superstition, has not even yet ceased to do mischief); some play on words perhaps, a seduction by grammar, or an audacious generalization of very narrow, very personal, very human, all too human facts.

The dogmatists' philosophy was, let us hope, only a promise across millennia—as astrology was in still earlier times when perhaps more work, money, acuteness, and patience were lavished in its service than for any real science so far: to astrology and its "supra-terrestrial" claims we owe the grand style of architecture in Asia and Egypt. It seems that all great things first have to bestride

---

[1] *Bisher* (so far) is a word that recurs constantly throughout *Beyond Good and Evil*. It helps to color the word "beyond" in the title.

the earth in monstrous and frightening masks in order to inscribe themselves in the hearts of humanity with eternal demands: dogmatic philosophy was such a mask; for example, the Vedanta doctrine in Asia and Platonism in Europe.

Let us not be ungrateful to it, although it must certainly be conceded that the worst, most durable, and most dangerous of all errors so far was a dogmatist's error—namely, Plato's invention of the pure spirit and the good as such. But now that it is overcome, now that Europe is breathing freely again after this nightmare and at least can enjoy a healthier—sleep, we, *whose task is wakefulness itself,* are the heirs of all that strength which has been fostered [2] by the fight against this error. To be sure, it meant standing truth on her head and denying *perspective,* the basic condition of all life, when one spoke of spirit and the good as Plato did. Indeed, as a physician one might ask: "How could the most beautiful growth of antiquity, Plato, contract such a disease? Did the wicked Socrates corrupt him after all? Could Socrates have been the corrupter of youth after all? And did he deserve his hemlock?"

But the fight against Plato or, to speak more clearly and for "the people," the fight against the Christian-ecclesiastical pressure of millennia—for Christianity is Platonism for "the people"—has created in Europe a magnificent tension of the spirit the like of which had never yet existed on earth: with so tense a bow we can now shoot for the most distant goals. To be sure, European man experiences this tension as need and distress; twice already attempts have been made in the grand style to unbend the bow—once by means of Jesuitism, the second time by means of the democratic enlightenment which, with the aid of freedom of the press and newspaper-reading, might indeed bring it about that the spirit would no longer experience itself so easily as a "need." (The Germans have invented gunpowder—all due respect for that!—but then they made up for that: they invented the press.) [3] But we who

---

[2] *Grossgezüchtet: züchten* means to breed, grow, or cultivate animals, plants, or qualities. Nietzsche uses the word frequently, and in these pages it is most often rendered by "cultivate." In his usage the connotation is generally spiritual.

[3] Cf. the Preface to *The Antichrist:* "One must be skilled in living on moun-

are neither Jesuits nor democrats, nor even German enough, we *good Europeans*[4] and free, *very* free spirits—we still feel it, the whole need of the spirit and the whole tension of its bow. And perhaps also the arrow, the task, and—who knows?—the *goal*——

Sils Maria, Upper Engadine,
June 1885.[5]

---

tains—seeing the wretched ephemeral babble of politics and national self-seeking *beneath* oneself" (*Portable Nietzsche,* p. 568). In the daily newspaper the concern with ephemeral matters is institutionalized and cultivated at the expense of genuine "spirituality."

[4] Nietzsche's coinage, initially introduced by him in *Human, All-Too-Human* (1878), section 475 (*Portable Nietzsche,* pp. 61-63).

[5] The book was written "summer 1885 in the Upper Engadine and the following winter in Nizza" (letter to Georg Brandes, April 10, 1888). This is borne out by other letters, except that additions and revisions were made until June 1886. The book was printed in June and July and published the beginning of August 1886.

CONTENTS [1]

On the Prejudices of Philosophers   7

The Free Spirit   33

What Is Religious   57

Epigrams and Interludes   77

Natural History of Morals   95

We Scholars   119

Our Virtues   143

Peoples and Fatherlands   171

What Is Noble   199

From High Mountains: *Aftersong*   238

---

[1] The Table of Contents appears here in the original edition, but not in the later standard editions or in Schlechta.

PART ONE

ON THE PREJUDICES
OF PHILOSOPHERS

Part[1] One

1

The will to truth which will still tempt us to many a venture, that famous truthfulness of which all philosophers so far have spoken with respect—what questions has this will to truth not laid before us! What strange, wicked, questionable questions! That is a long story even now—and yet it seems as if it had scarcely begun. Is it any wonder that we should finally become suspicious, lose patience, and turn away impatiently? that we should finally learn from this Sphinx to ask questions, too? *Who* is it really that puts questions to us here? *What* in us really wants "truth"?

Indeed we came to a long halt at the question about the cause of this will—until we finally came to a complete stop before a still more basic question. We asked about the *value* of this will. Suppose we want truth: *why not rather* untruth? and uncertainty? even ignorance?

The problem of the value of truth came before us—or was it we who came before the problem? Who of us is Oedipus here? Who the Sphinx? It is a rendezvous, it seems, of questions and question marks.

And though it scarcely seems credible, it finally almost seems to us as if the problem had never even been put so far—as if we were the first to see it, fix it with our eyes, and *risk* it. For it does involve a risk, and perhaps there is none that is greater.

2

"How *could* anything originate out of its opposite? for example, truth out of error? or the will to truth out of the will to

---

[1] Marianne Cowan has suggested in the preface to her translation that Nietzsche divided this book "into 'articles' like articles of faith," and she sees "irony in this." But there is no warrant for rendering *Hauptstück* as "article": it means "major part." Kant's *Critique of Pure Reason* and *Critique of Practical Reason* are both divided into *Hauptstücke*. So is Nietzsche's own *Human, All-Too-Human.* The term is obviously particularly appropriate for books subdivided into many short sections.

deception? or selfless deeds out of selfishness? or the pure and sunlike gaze of the sage out of lust? Such origins are impossible; whoever dreams of them is a fool, indeed worse; the things of the highest value must have another, *peculiar* origin—they cannot be derived from this transitory, seductive, deceptive, paltry world, from this turmoil of delusion and lust. Rather from the lap of Being, the intransitory, the hidden god, the 'thing-in-itself'—there must be their basis, and nowhere else."

This way of judging constitutes the typical prejudgment and prejudice which give away the metaphysicians of all ages; this kind of valuation looms in the background of all their logical proce-dures; it is on account of this "faith" that they trouble themselves about "knowledge," about something that is finally baptized sol-emnly as "the truth." The fundamental faith of the metaphysicians is *the faith in opposite values.*[2] It has not even occurred to the most cautious among them that one might have a doubt right here at the threshold where it was surely most necessary—even if they vowed to themselves, *"de omnibus dubitandum."* [3]

For one may doubt, first, whether there are any opposites at all, and secondly whether these popular valuations and opposite values on which the metaphysicians put their seal, are not perhaps merely foreground estimates, only provisional perspectives, per-haps even from some nook, perhaps from below, frog perspectives, as it were, to borrow an expression painters use. For all the value that the true, the truthful, the selfless may deserve, it would still be possible that a higher and more fundamental value for life might have to be ascribed to deception, selfishness, and lust. It might even be possible that what constitutes the value of these good and re-vered things is precisely that they are insidiously related, tied to, and involved with these wicked, seemingly opposite things—maybe even one with them in essence. Maybe!

But who has the will to concern himself with such dangerous maybes? For that, one really has to wait for the advent of a new

---

2 Nietzsche's attack on this faith is prefigured in the title of the book. This aphorism invites comparison with the first aphorism of *Human, All-Too-Human.*

3 "All is to be doubted." Descartes.

species of philosophers, such as have somehow another and converse taste and propensity from those we have known so far—
philosophers of the dangerous "maybe" in every sense.

And in all seriousness: I see such new philosophers coming
up.

3   *the understanding is no dry
      light - but then all "logic"
      is accused*

After having looked long enough between the philosopher's
lines and fingers, I say to myself: by far the greater part of conscious thinking must still be included among instinctive activities,
and that goes even for philosophical thinking. We have to relearn
here, as one has had to relearn about heredity and what is "innate."
As the act of birth deserves no consideration in the whole process
and procedure of heredity, so "being conscious" is not in any decisive sense the *opposite* of what is instinctive: most of the conscious
thinking of a philosopher is secretly guided and forced into certain
channels by his instincts.

Behind all logic and its seeming sovereignty of movement, too,
there stand valuations or, more clearly, physiological demands for
the preservation of a certain type of life. For example, that the definite should be worth more than the indefinite, and mere appearance worth less than "truth"—such estimates might be, in spite of
their regulative importance for *us,* nevertheless mere foreground
estimates, a certain kind of *niaiserie*[4] which may be necessary for
the preservation of just such beings as we are. Supposing, that is,
that not just man is the "measure of things" [5]—

4

The falseness of a judgment is for us not necessarily an objection to a judgment; in this respect our new language may sound
strangest. The question is to what extent it is life-promoting, life-
preserving, species-preserving, perhaps even species-cultivating.

---

[4] Folly, stupidity, silliness: one of Nietzsche's favorite French words.
[5] "Man is the measure of all things." Protagoras, born about 480 B.C.

And we are fundamentally inclined to claim that the falsest judgments (which include the synthetic judgments *a priori*)[6] are the most indispensable for us; that without accepting the fictions of logic, without measuring reality against the purely invented world of the unconditional and self-identical, without a constant falsification of the world by means of numbers, man could not live—that renouncing false judgments would mean renouncing life and a denial of life. To recognize untruth as a condition of life—that certainly means resisting accustomed value feelings in a dangerous way; and a philosophy that risks this would by that token alone place itself beyond good and evil.

5

What provokes one to look at all philosophers half suspiciously, half mockingly, is not that one discovers again and again how innocent they are—how often and how easily they make mistakes and go astray; in short, their childishness and childlikeness— but that they are not honest enough in their work, although they all make a lot of virtuous noise when the problem of truthfulness is touched even remotely. They all pose as if they had discovered and reached their real opinions through the self-development of a cold, pure, divinely unconcerned dialectic (as opposed to the mystics of every rank, who are more honest and doltish—and talk of "inspiration"); while at bottom it is an assumption, a hunch, indeed a kind of "inspiration"—most often a desire of the heart that has been filtered and made abstract—that they defend with reasons they have sought after the fact. They are all advocates who resent that name, and for the most part even wily spokesmen for

---

[6] One of Kant's central questions was, "How are synthetic judgments *a priori* possible?" He meant judgments that are known for certain to be true, independently of experience, but not by definition. His examples include the judgment that every event has a cause. Hans Vaihinger, a leading Kant scholar who published a book on *Nietzsche als Philosoph* (1902; 4th ed. 1916), later published his own theory of necessary fictions under the title, *Die Philosophie des Als-Ob* (1911; English tr. by C. K. Ogden, 1924: *The Philosophy of "As If"*), devoting the final chapter to a detailed discussion of Nietzsche's similar ideas. Cf. section 11 below.

their prejudices which they baptize "truths"—and *very* far from having the courage of the conscience that admits this, precisely this, to itself; very far from having the good taste of the courage which also lets this be known, whether to warn an enemy or friend, or, from exuberance, to mock itself.

The equally stiff and decorous Tartuffery of the old Kant as he lures us on the dialectical bypaths that lead to his "categorical imperative"—really lead astray and seduce—this spectacle makes us smile, as we are fastidious and find it quite amusing to watch closely the subtle tricks of old moralists and preachers of morals. Or consider the hocus-pocus of mathematical form with which Spinoza clad his philosophy—really "the love of *his* wisdom," to render that word fairly and squarely—in mail and mask, to strike terror at the very outset into the heart of any assailant who should dare to glance at that invincible maiden and Pallas Athena: how much personal timidity and vulnerability this masquerade of a sick hermit betrays!

6

Gradually it has become clear to me what every great philosophy so far has been: namely, the personal confession of its author and a kind of involuntary and unconscious memoir; also that the moral (or immoral) intentions in every philosophy constituted the real germ of life from which the whole plant had grown.

Indeed, if one would explain how the abstrusest metaphysical claims of a philosopher really came about, it is always well (and wise) to ask first: at what morality does all this (does *he*) aim? Accordingly, I do not believe that a "drive to knowledge" is the father of philosophy; but rather that another drive has, here as elsewhere, employed understanding (and misunderstanding) as a mere instrument. But anyone who considers the basic drives of man to see to what extent they may have been at play just here as *inspiring* spirits (or demons and kobolds) will find that all of them have done philosophy at some time—and that every single one of them would like only too well to represent just *itself* as the ultimate purpose of existence and the legitimate *master* of all the other drives. For every drive wants to be master—and it attempts to philosophize in *that spirit*.

To be sure: among scholars who are really scientific men, things may be different—"better," if you like—there you may really find something like a drive for knowledge, some small, independent clockwork that, once well wound, works on vigorously *without* any essential participation from all the other drives of the scholar. The real "interests" of the scholar therefore lie usually somewhere else—say, in his family, or in making money, or in politics. Indeed, it is almost a matter of total indifference whether his little machine is placed at this or that spot in science, and whether the "promising" young worker turns himself into a good philologist or an expert on fungi or a chemist: it does not *characterize* him that he becomes this or that. In the philosopher, conversely, there is nothing whatever that is impersonal;[7] and above all, his morality bears decided and decisive witness to *who he is*— that is, in what order of rank the innermost drives of his nature stand in relation to each other.

7

How malicious philosophers can be! I know of nothing more venomous than the joke Epicurus permitted himself against Plato and the Platonists; he called them *Dionysiokolakes*. That means literally—and this is the foreground meaning—"flatterers of Dionysius," in other words, tyrant's baggage and lickspittles; but in addition to this he also wants to say, "they are all *actors*, there is nothing genuine about them" (for *Dionysokolax* was a popular name for an actor).[8] And the latter is really the malice that Epicurus aimed at Plato: he was peeved by the grandiose manner, the *mise en scène*[9] at which Plato and his disciples were so expert—at

---

[7] Nietzsche is thinking of the "great" philosophers. Now that there are literally thousands of "philosophers," these tend to be more akin to their colleagues in other departments than to the men discussed here.

[8] The reference is to Epicurus' fragment 238, and the ambiguity is due to the fact that Dionysius was the name of the Sicilian tyrant whom Plato had tried for several years to convert to his own philosophy.

[9] Staging.

which Epicurus was not an expert—he, that old schoolmaster from Samos, who sat, hidden away, in his little garden at Athens and wrote three hundred books—who knows? perhaps from rage and ambition against Plato?

It took a hundred years until Greece found out who this garden god, Epicurus, had been.— Did they find out?—

8

There is a point in every philosophy when the philosopher's "conviction" appears on the stage—or to use the language of an ancient Mystery:

Adventavit asinus,
Pulcher et fortissimus. [10]

9

"According to nature" you want to *live?* O you noble Stoics, what deceptive words these are! Imagine a being like nature, wasteful beyond measure, indifferent beyond measure, without purposes and consideration, without mercy and justice, fertile and desolate and uncertain at the same time; imagine indifference itself as a power—how *could* you live according to this indifference? Living—is that not precisely wanting to be other than this nature? Is not living—estimating, preferring, being unjust, being limited, wanting to be different? And supposing your imperative "live according to nature" meant at bottom as much as "live according to life"—how could you *not* do that? Why make a principle of what you yourselves are and must be?

In truth, the matter is altogether different: while you pretend rapturously to read the canon of your law in nature, you want something opposite, you strange actors and self-deceivers! Your pride wants to impose your morality, your ideal, on nature—even on nature—and incorporate them in her; you demand that she should be nature "according to the Stoa," and you would like all

---

[10] "The ass arrived, beautiful and most brave."

existence to exist only after your own image—as an immense eternal glorification and generalization of Stoicism. For all your love of truth, you have forced yourselves so long, so persistently, so rigidly-hypnotically to see nature the wrong way, namely Stoically, that you are no longer able to see her differently. And some abysmal arrogance finally still inspires you with the insane hope that *because* you know how to tyrannize yourselves—Stoicism is self-tyranny—nature, too, lets herself be tyrannized: is not the Stoic—a *piece* of nature?

But this is an ancient, eternal story: what formerly happened with the Stoics still happens today, too, as soon as any philosophy begins to believe in itself. It always creates the world in its own image; it cannot do otherwise. Philosophy is this tyrannical drive itself, the most spiritual will to power, to the "creation of the world," to the *causa prima*.[11]

10

The eagerness and subtlety—I might even say, shrewdness—with which the problem of "the real and the apparent world" is today attacked all over Europe makes one think and wonder; and anyone who hears nothing in the background except a "will to truth," certainly does not have the best of ears. In rare and isolated instances it may really be the case that such a will to truth, some extravagant and adventurous courage, a metaphysician's ambition to hold a hopeless position, may participate and ultimately prefer even a handful of "certainty" to a whole carload of beautiful possibilities; there may actually be puritanical fanatics of conscience who prefer even a certain nothing to an uncertain something to lie down on—and die. But this is nihilism and the sign of a despairing, mortally weary soul—however courageous the gestures of such a virtue may look.

It seems, however, to be otherwise with stronger and livelier thinkers who are still eager for life. When they side *against* appearance, and speak of "perspective," with a new arrogance; when they

---

[11] First cause.

rank the credibility of their own bodies about as low as the credibility of the visual evidence that "the earth stands still," and thus, apparently in good humor, let their securest possession go (for in what does one at present believe more firmly than in one's body?) —who knows if they are not trying at bottom to win back something that was formerly an even *securer* possession, something of the ancient domain of the faith of former times, perhaps the "immortal soul," perhaps "the old God," in short, ideas by which one could live better, that is to say, more vigorously and cheerfully, than by "modern ideas"? There is *mistrust* of these modern ideas in this attitude, a disbelief in all that has been constructed yesterday and today; there is perhaps some slight admixture of satiety and scorn, unable to endure any longer the *bric-a-brac* of concepts of the most diverse origin, which is the form in which so-called positivism offers itself on the market today; a disgust of the more fastidious taste at the village-fair motleyness and patchiness of all these reality-philosophasters in whom there is nothing new or genuine, except this motleyness. In this, it seems to me, we should agree with these skeptical anti-realists and knowledge-microscopists of today: their instinct, which repels them from *modern* reality, is unrefuted—what do their retrograde bypaths concern us! The main thing about them is *not* that they wish to go "back," but that they wish to get—*away*. A little *more* strength, flight, courage, and artistic power, and they would want to *rise*— not return!

11

It seems to me that today attempts are made everywhere to divert attention from the actual influence Kant exerted on German philosophy, and especially to ignore prudently the value he set upon himself. Kant was first and foremost proud of his table of categories; with that in his hand he said: "This is the most difficult thing that could ever be undertaken on behalf of metaphysics."

Let us only understand this "could be"! He was proud of having *discovered* a new faculty in man, the faculty for synthetic judgments, *a priori*. Suppose he deceived himself in this matter; the de-

velopment and rapid flourishing of German philosophy depended
nevertheless on his pride, and on the eager rivalry of the younger
generation to discover, if possible, something still prouder—at all
events "new faculties"!

But let us reflect; it is high time to do so. "How are synthetic
judgments *a priori possible?*" Kant asked himself—and what really
is his answer? *"By virtue of a faculty"* [12]—but unfortunately not in
five words, but so circumstantially, venerably, and with such a display of German profundity and curlicues that people simply failed
to note the comical *niaiserie allemande*[13] involved in such an answer. People were actually beside themselves with delight over this
new faculty, and the jubilation reached its climax when Kant further discovered a moral faculty in man—for at that time the Germans were still moral and not yet addicted to *Realpolitik*.

The honeymoon of German philosophy arrived. All the
young theologians of the Tübingen seminary went into the bushes
—all looking for "faculties." And what did they not find—in that
innocent, rich, and still youthful period of the German spirit, to
which romanticism, the malignant fairy, piped and sang, when one
could not yet distinguish between "finding" and "inventing"! [14]
Above all, a faculty for the "suprasensible": Schelling christened it
intellectual intuition, and thus gratified the most heartfelt cravings
of the Germans, whose cravings were at bottom pious. One can do
no greater wrong to the whole of this exuberant and enthusiastic
movement, which was really youthfulness, however boldly it disguised itself in hoary and senile concepts, than to take it seriously,
or worse, to treat it with moral indignation. Enough, one grew
older and the dream vanished. A time came when people scratched
their heads, and they still scratch them today. One had been
dreaming, and first and foremost—old Kant. "By virtue of a faculty"—he had said, or at least meant. But is that—an answer? An
explanation? Or is it not rather merely a repetition of the ques-

---

12 *Vermöge eines Vermögens:* by virtue of some virtue, or by means of a
means.
13 German foolishness.
14 *"Finden"* und *"erfinden."*

tion? How does opium induce sleep? "By virtue of a faculty,"
namely the *virtus dormitiva,* replies the doctor in Molière,

> *Quia est in eo virtus dormitiva,*
> *Cujus est natura sensus assoupire.*[15]

But such replies belong in comedy, and it is high time to re-
place the Kantian question, "How are synthetic judgments *a priori*
possible?" by another question, "Why is belief in such judgments
necessary?"—and to comprehend that such judgments must be *believed* to be true, for the sake of the preservation of creatures like
ourselves; though they might, of course, be *false* judgments for all
that! Or to speak more clearly and coarsely: synthetic judgments
a priori should not "be possible" at all; we have no right to them; in
our mouths they are nothing but false judgments. Only, of course,
the belief in their truth is necessary, as a foreground belief and visual evidence belonging to the perspective optics of life.

Finally, to call to mind the enormous influence that "German
philosophy"—I hope you understand its right to quotation marks—
has exercised throughout the whole of Europe, there is no doubt
that a certain *virtus dormitiva* had a share in it: it was a delight to
the noble idlers, the virtuous, the mystics, artists, three-quarter
Christians, and political obscurantists of all nations, to find, thanks
to German philosophy, an antidote to the still predominant sensualism which overflowed from the last century into this, in short—
"sensus assoupire."

12

As for materialistic atomism, it is one of the best refuted
theories there are, and in Europe perhaps no one in the learned
world is now so unscholarly as to attach serious significance to it,
except for convenient household use (as an abbreviation of the
means of expression)—thanks chiefly to the Dalmatian Boscovich:
he and the Pole Corpernicus have been the greatest and most successful opponents of visual evidence so far. For while Copernicus

---

[15] "Because it contains a sleepy faculty whose nature it is to put the senses
to sleep."

has persuaded us to believe, contrary to all the senses, that the earth does *not* stand fast, Boscovich has taught us to abjure the belief in the last part of the earth that "stood fast"—the belief in "substance," in "matter," in the earth-residuum and particle-atom:[16] it is the greatest triumph over the senses that has been gained on earth so far.

One must, however, go still further, and also declare war, relentless war unto death, against the "atomistic need" which still leads a dangerous afterlife in places where no one suspects it, just like the more celebrated "metaphysical need": one must also, first of all, give the finishing stroke to that other and more calamitous atomism which Christianity has taught best and longest, the *soul atomism*. Let it be permitted to designate by this expression the belief which regards the soul as something indestructible, eternal, indivisible, as a monad, as an *atomon*: this belief ought to be expelled from science! Between ourselves, it is not at all necessary to get rid of "the soul" at the same time, and thus to renounce one of the most ancient and venerable hypotheses—as happens frequently to clumsy naturalists who can hardly touch on "the soul" without immediately losing it. But the way is open for new versions and refinements of the soul-hypothesis; and such conceptions as "mortal soul," and "soul as subjective multiplicity," and "soul as social structure of the drives and affects," [17] want henceforth to

---

16 "Boscovich, an eighteenth-century Jesuit philosopher somewhat out of the main stream of science . . . had defined atoms only as centers of force, and not as particles of matter in which powers somehow inhere" (Charles Coulston Gillispie, *The Edge of Objectivity: An Essay in the History of Scientific Ideas*, Princeton, N.J., Princeton University Press, 1960, p. 455).

17 *Affekt:* I have rendered this term consistently as "affect": good dictionaries include the relevant meanings. "Feeling" comes close to Nietzsche's meaning but fails to suggest the fact that the term is somewhat technical and carries overtones of Spinoza's *affectus* and a long philosophical tradition. Moreover, "feeling" is needed to render *Gefühl*, which occurs several times in this section.

In his discussion of Spinoza's *affectus*, Stuart Hampshire uses "affection" and places the word in quotation marks (*Spinoza*, Baltimore, Penguin Books, 1951, pp. 135f.). In James Mark Baldwin's *Dictionary of Philosophy and Psychology*, vol. I (1901), "affect" is defined as "A stimulus or motive to action which is AFFECTIVE (q.v.) or felt, not presented as an end," a usage "suggested by Baldwin," while "affection" is suggested to

have citizens' rights in science. When the *new* psychologist puts an end to the superstitions which have so far flourished with almost tropical luxuriance around the idea of the soul, he practically exiles himself into a new desert and a new suspicion—it is possible that the older psychologists had a merrier and more comfortable time of it; eventually, however, he finds that precisely thereby he also condemns himself to *invention*—and—who knows?—perhaps to discovery.

13

Physiologists should think before putting down the instinct of self-preservation as the cardinal instinct of an organic being. A living thing seeks above all to *discharge* its strength—life itself is *will to power;* self-preservation is only one of the indirect and most frequent *results.*

In short, here as everywhere else, let us beware of *superfluous* teleological principles—one of which is the instinct of self-preservation (we owe it to Spinoza's inconsistency).[18] Thus method, which must be essentially economy of principles, demands it.

14

It is perhaps just dawning on five or six minds that physics, too, is only an interpretation and exegesis of the world (to suit us, if I may say so!) and *not* a world-explanation; but insofar as it is

---

an equivalent of the German *Affekt,* which is defined as "passing emotional states . . . The best writers distinguish it from passion, as having less vehemence, and as less distinctly, if at all, connected with a sensuous basis. . . . St. Augustine, as quoted and adopted by Aquinas, says: 'Those mental states (*motus animi*) which the Greeks call *pathē,* and Cicero *perturbationes,* are by some called *affectus,* or *affectiones* by others, keeping to the literal rendering of the Greek *passiones.*' "

My reason for preferring "affect" to "affection" is that the former is readily recognized as a technical term, while the latter is very apt to be misunderstood as suggesting a mild form of love.

[18] Nietzsche admired Spinoza for, among other things, his critique of teleology.

based on belief in the senses, it is regarded as more, and for a long time to come must be regarded as more—namely, as an explanation. Eyes and fingers speak in its favor, visual evidence and palpableness do, too: this strikes an age with fundamentally plebeian tastes as fascinating, persuasive, and *convincing*—after all, it follows instinctively the canon of truth of eternally popular sensualism. What is clear, what is "explained"? Only what can be seen and felt—every problem has to be pursued to that point. Conversely, the charm of the Platonic way of thinking, which was a *noble* way of thinking, consisted precisely in *resistance* to obvious sense-evidence—perhaps among men who enjoyed even stronger and more demanding senses than our contemporaries, but who knew how to find a higher triumph in remaining masters of their senses—and this by means of pale, cold, gray concept nets which they threw over the motley whirl of the senses—the mob of the senses, as Plato said. In this overcoming of the world, and interpreting of the world in the manner of Plato, there was an *enjoyment* different from that which the physicists of today offer us—and also the Darwinists and anti-teleologists among the workers in physiology, with their principle of the "smallest possible force" and the greatest possible stupidity. "Where man cannot find anything to see or to grasp, he has no further business"—that is certainly an imperative different from the Platonic one, but it may be the right imperative for a tough, industrious race of machinists and bridge-builders of the future, who have nothing but *rough* work to do.

15

To study physiology with a clear conscience, one must insist that the sense organs are *not* phenomena in the sense of idealistic philosophy; as such they could not be causes! Sensualism, therefore, at least as a regulative hypothesis, if not as a heuristic principle.

What? And others even say that the external world is the work of our organs? But then our body, as a part of this external world, would be the work of our organs! But then our organs themselves would be—the work of our organs! It seems to me that this is a complete *reductio ad absurdum*,[19] assuming that the concept of a *causa sui*[20] is something fundamentally absurd. Consequently, the external world is *not* the work of our organs—?

16

There are still harmless self-observers who believe that there are "immediate certainties"; for example, "I think," or as the superstition of Schopenhauer put it, "I will"; as though knowledge here got hold of its object purely and nakedly as "the thing in itself," without any falsification on the part of either the subject or the object. But that "immediate certainty," as well as "absolute knowledge" and the "thing in itself," involve a *contradictio in adjecto*,[21] I shall repeat a hundred times; we really ought to free ourselves from the seduction of words!

Let the people suppose that knowledge means knowing things entirely; the philosopher must say to himself: When I analyze the process that is expressed in the sentence, "I think," I find a whole series of daring assertions that would be difficult, perhaps impossible, to prove; for example, that it is *I* who think, that there must necessarily be something that thinks, that thinking is an activity and operation on the part of a being who is thought of as a cause, that there is an "ego," and, finally, that it is already determined what is to be designated by thinking—that I *know* what thinking is. For if I had not already decided within myself what it is, by what standard could I determine whether that which is just happening is not perhaps "willing" or "feeling"? In short, the assertion "I think" assumes that I *compare* my state at the present moment with other states of myself which I know, in order to determine what it is; on account of this retrospective connection with further "knowledge," it has, at any rate, no immediate certainty for me.

In place of the "immediate certainty" in which the people may believe in the case at hand, the philosopher thus finds a series of

---

[19] Reduction to the absurd.
[20] Something that is its own cause—a term traditionally applied to God.
[21] Contradiction between the noun and the adjective.

metaphysical questions presented to him, truly searching questions of the intellect; to wit: "From where do I get the concept of thinking? Why do I believe in cause and effect? What gives me the right to speak of an ego, and even of an ego as cause, and finally of an ego as the cause of thought?" Whoever ventures to answer these metaphysical questions at once by an appeal to a sort of *intuitive* perception, like the person who says, "I think, and know that this, at least, is true, actual, and certain"—will encounter a smile and two question marks from a philosopher nowadays. "Sir," the philosopher will perhaps give him to understand, "it is improbable that you are not mistaken; but why insist on the truth?"—

17

With regard to the superstitions of logicians, I shall never tire of emphasizing a small terse fact, which these superstitious minds hate to concede—namely, that a thought comes when "it" wishes, and not when "I" wish, so that it is a falsification of the facts of the case to say that the subject "I" is the condition of the predicate "think." *It* thinks; but that this "it" is precisely the famous old "ego" is, to put it mildly, only a supposition, an assertion, and assuredly not an "immediate certainty." After all, one has even gone too far with this "it thinks"—even the "it" contains an *interpretation* of the process, and does not belong to the process itself. One infers here according to the grammatical habit: "Thinking is an activity; every activity requires an agent; consequently—"

It was pretty much according to the same schema that the older atomism sought, besides the operating "power," that lump of matter in which it resides and out of which it operates—the atom. More rigorous minds, however, learned at last to get along without this "earth-residuum," and perhaps some day we shall accustom ourselves, including the logicians, to get along without the little "it" (which is all that is left of the honest little old ego).

18

It is certainly not the least charm of a theory that it is refutable; it is precisely thereby that it attracts subtler minds. It seems that the hundred-times-refuted theory of a "free will" owes its persistence to this charm alone; again and again someone comes along who feels he is strong enough to refute it.

19

Philosophers are accustomed to speak of the will as if it were the best-known thing in the world; indeed, Schopenhauer has given us to understand that the will alone is really known to us, absolutely and completely known, without subtraction or addition. But again and again it seems to me that in this case, too, Schopenhauer only did what philosophers are in the habit of doing—he adopted a *popular prejudice* and exaggerated it. Willing seems to me to be above all something *complicated,* something that is a unit only as a word—and it is precisely in this one word that the popular prejudice lurks, which has defeated the always inadequate caution of philosophers. So let us for once be more cautious, let us be "unphilosophical": let us say that in all willing there is, first, a plurality of sensations, namely, the sensation of the state *"away from which,"* the sensation of the state *"towards which,"* the sensations of this *"from"* and *"towards"* themselves, and then also an accompanying muscular sensation, which, even without our putting into motion "arms and legs," begins its action by force of habit as soon as we "will" anything.

Therefore, just as sensations (and indeed many kinds of sensations) are to be recognized as ingredients of the will, so, secondly, should thinking also: in every act of the will there is a ruling thought—let us not imagine it possible to sever this thought from the "willing," as if any will would then remain over!

Third, the will is not only a complex of sensation and thinking, but it is above all an *affect,* and specifically the affect of the command. That which is termed "freedom of the will" is essentially the affect of superiority in relation to him who must obey: "I am free, 'he' must obey"—this consciousness is inherent in every will; and equally so the straining of the attention, the straight look that fixes itself exclusively on one aim, the unconditional evaluation that "this and nothing else is necessary now," the inward certainty that obedience will be rendered—and whatever else belongs to the position of the commander. A man who *wills* commands something within himself that renders obedience, or that he believes renders obedience.

But now let us notice what is strangest about the will—this manifold thing for which the people have only one word: inasmuch as in the given circumstances we are at the same time the commanding *and* the obeying parties, and as the obeying party we know the sensations of constraint, impulsion, pressure, resistance, and motion, which usually begin immediately after the act of will; inasmuch as, on the other hand, we are accustomed to disregard this duality, and to deceive ourselves about it by means of the synthetic concept "I," a whole series of erroneous conclusions, and consequently of false evaluations of the will itself, has become attached to the act of willing—to such a degree that he who wills believes sincerely that willing *suffices* for action. Since in the great majority of cases there has been exercise of will only when the effect of the command—that is, obedience; that is, the action—was to be *expected,* the *appearance* has translated itself into the feeling, as if there were *a necessity of effect.* In short, he who wills believes with a fair amount of certainty that will and action are somehow one; he ascribes the success, the carrying out of the willing, to the will itself, and thereby enjoys an increase of the sensation of power which accompanies all success.

"Freedom of the will"—that is the expression for the complex state of delight of the person exercising volition, who commands and at the same time identifies himself with the executor of the order—who, as such, enjoys also the triumph over obstacles, but thinks within himself that it was really his will itself that overcame them. In this way the person exercising volition adds the feelings of delight of his successful executive instruments, the useful "underwills" or under-souls—indeed, our body is but a social structure composed of many souls—to his feelings of delight as commander. *L'effet c'est moi:*[22] what happens here is what happens in every well-constructed and happy commonwealth; namely, the governing

---

[22] "*I* am the effect."

class identifies itself with the successes of the commonwealth. In all willing it is absolutely a question of commanding and obeying, on the basis, as already said, of a social structure composed of many "souls." Hence a philosopher should claim the right to include willing as such within the sphere of morals—morals being understood as the doctrine of the relations of supremacy under which the phenomenon of "life" comes to be.

20

That individual philosophical concepts are not anything capricious or autonomously evolving, but grow up in connection and relationship with each other; that, however suddenly and arbitrarily they seem to appear in the history of thought, they nevertheless belong just as much to a system as all the members of the fauna of a continent—is betrayed in the end also by the fact that the most diverse philosophers keep filling in a definite fundamental scheme of possible philosophies. Under an invisible spell, they always revolve once more in the same orbit; however independent of each other they may feel themselves with their critical or systematic wills, something within them leads them, something impels them in a definite order, one after the other—to wit, the innate systematic structure and relationship of their concepts. Their thinking is, in fact, far less a discovery than a recognition, a remembering, a return and a homecoming to a remote, primordial, and inclusive household of the soul, out of which those concepts grew originally: philosophizing is to this extent a kind of atavism of the highest order.

The strange family resemblance of all Indian, Greek, and German philosophizing is explained easily enough. Where there is affinity of languages, it cannot fail, owing to the common philosophy of grammar—I mean, owing to the unconscious domination and guidance by similar grammatical functions—that everything is prepared at the outset for a similar development and sequence of philosophical systems; just as the way seems barred against certain other possibilities of world-interpretation. It is highly probable that philosophers within the domain of the Ural-Altaic languages (where the concept of the subject is least developed) look otherwise "into the world," and will be found on paths of thought different from those of the Indo-Germanic peoples and the Muslims: the spell of certain grammatical functions is ultimately also the spell of *physiological* valuations and racial conditions.

So much by way of rejecting Locke's superficiality regarding the origin of ideas.

21

The *causa sui* is the best self-contradiction that has been conceived so far, it is a sort of rape and perversion of logic; but the extravagant pride of man has managed to entangle itself profoundly and frightfully with just this nonsense. The desire for "freedom of the will" in the superlative metaphysical sense, which still holds sway, unfortunately, in the minds of the half-educated; the desire to bear the entire and ultimate responsibility for one's actions oneself, and to absolve God, the world, ancestors, chance, and society involves nothing less than to be precisely this *causa sui* and, with more than Münchhausen's audacity, to pull oneself up into existence by the hair, out of the swamps of nothingness.[23] Sup-

---

[23] Cf. Sartre's famous dictum: "If man as the existentialist sees him is not definable, it is because to begin with he is nothing. He will not be anything until later, and then he will be what he makes of himself. . . . Man simply is. Not that he is simply what he conceives himself to be, but he is what he wills . . . Man is nothing else but that which he makes of himself. That is the first principle of existentialism. . . . Before that projection of the self nothing exists . . . Man is responsible for what he is. Thus, the first effect of existentialism is that it puts every man in possession of himself as he is, and places the entire responsibility for his existence squarely upon his own shoulders" ("Existentialism Is a Humanism," included in *Existentialism from Dostoevsky to Sartre*, ed. Walter Kaufmann, pp. 290f.).

Reading this without knowing that *Beyond Good and Evil* was published in 1886 and Sartre's lecture in 1946, one would scarcely guess at Nietzsche's immense influence on existentialism in general and Sartre in particular; one might even suppose that Nietzsche was here polemicizing against Sartre. Cf. also section 8 of "The Four Great Errors" in *Twilight of the Idols* (*Portable Nietzsche*, p. 500), where some implications of the above passage in *Beyond Good and Evil* are developed briefly.

pose someone were thus to see through the boorish simplicity of this celebrated concept of "free will" and put it out of his head altogether, I beg of him to carry his "enlightenment" a step further, and also put out of his head the contrary of this monstrous conception of "free will": I mean "unfree will," which amounts to a misuse of cause and effect. One should not wrongly reify "cause" and "effect," as the natural scientists do (and whoever, like them, now "naturalizes" in his thinking), according to the prevailing mechanical doltishness which makes the cause press and push until it "effects" its end; one should use "cause" and "effect" only as pure concepts, that is to say, as conventional fictions for the purpose of designation and communication—*not* for explanation. In the "in-itself" there is nothing of "causal connections," of "necessity," or of "psychological non-freedom"; there the effect does *not* follow the cause, there is no rule of "law." It is *we* alone who have devised cause, sequence, for-each-other, relativity, constraint, number, law, freedom, motive, and purpose; and when we project and mix this symbol world into things as if it existed "in itself," we act once more as we have always acted—*mythologically.* The "unfree will" is mythology; in real life it is only a matter of *strong* and *weak* wills.

It is almost always a symptom of what is lacking in himself when a thinker senses in every "causal connection" and "psychological necessity" something of constraint, need, compulsion to obey, pressure, and unfreedom; it is suspicious to have such feelings —the person betrays himself. And in general, if I have observed correctly, the "unfreedom of the will" is regarded as a problem from two entirely opposite standpoints, but always in a profoundly *personal* manner: some will not give up their "responsibility," their belief in *themselves,* the personal right to *their* merits at any price (the vain races belong to this class). Others, on the contrary, do not wish to be answerable for anything, or blamed for anything, and owing to an inward self-contempt, seek to *lay the blame for themselves somewhere else.* The latter, when they write books, are in the habit today of taking the side of criminals; a sort of socialist pity is their most attractive disguise. And as a matter of fact, the fatalism of the weak-willed embellishes itself surprisingly when it can pose as *"la religion de la souffrance humaine"*;[24] that is *its* "good taste."

22

Forgive me as an old philologist who cannot desist from the malice of putting his finger on bad modes of interpretation: but "nature's conformity to law," of which you physicists talk so proudly, as though—why, it exists only owing to your interpretation and bad "philology." It is no matter of fact, no "text," but rather only a naïvely humanitarian emendation and perversion of meaning, with which you make abundant concessions to the democratic instincts of the modern soul! "Everywhere equality before the law; nature is no different in that respect, no better off than we are"—a fine instance of ulterior motivation, in which the plebeian antagonism to everything privileged and autocratic as well as a second and more refined atheism are disguised once more. *"Ni Dieu, ni maître"* [25]—that is what you, too, want; and therefore "cheers for the law of nature!"—is it not so? But as said above, that is interpretation, not text; and somebody might come along who, with opposite intentions and modes of interpretation, could read out of the same "nature," and with regard to the same phenomena, rather the tyrannically inconsiderate and relentless enforcement of claims of power—an interpreter who would picture the unexceptional and unconditional aspects of all "will to power" so vividly that almost every word, even the word "tyranny" itself, would eventually seem unsuitable, or a weakening and attenuating metaphor—being too human—but he might, nevertheless, end by asserting the same about this world as you do, namely, that it has a "necessary" and "calculable" course, *not* because laws obtain in it, but because they are absolutely *lacking*, and every power draws its ultimate consequences at every moment. Supposing that this also is only in-

---

[24] "The religion of human suffering."
[25] "Neither God nor master."

terpretation—and you will be eager enough to make this objection?—well, so much the better.

23

All psychology so far has got stuck in moral prejudices and fears; it has not dared to descend into the depths. To understand it as morphology and *the doctrine of the development of the will to power,* as I do—nobody has yet come close to doing this even in thought—insofar as it is permissible to recognize in what has been written so far a symptom of what has so far been kept silent. The power of moral prejudices has penetrated deeply into the most spiritual world, which would seem to be the coldest and most devoid of presuppositions, and has obviously operated in an injurious, inhibiting, blinding, and distorting manner. A proper physio-psychology has to contend with unconscious resistance in the heart of the investigator, it has "the heart" against it: even a doctrine of the reciprocal dependence of the "good" and the "wicked" drives, causes (as refined immorality) distress and aversion in a still hale and hearty conscience—still more so, a doctrine of the derivation of all good impulses from wicked ones. If, however, a person should regard even the affects of hatred, envy, covetousness, and the lust to rule as conditions of life, as factors which, fundamentally and essentially, must be present in the general economy of life (and must, therefore, be further enhanced if life is to be further enhanced)—he will suffer from such a view of things as from seasickness. And yet even this hypothesis is far from being the strangest and most painful in this immense and almost new domain of dangerous insights; and there are in fact a hundred good reasons why everyone should keep away from it who—*can.*

On the other hand, if one has once drifted there with one's bark, well! all right! let us clench our teeth! let us open our eyes and keep our hand firm on the helm! We sail right *over* morality, we crush, we destroy perhaps the remains of our own morality by daring to make our voyage there—but what matter are *we!* Never yet did a *profounder* world of insight reveal itself to daring travelers and adventurers, and the psychologist who thus "makes a sacrifice"—it is *not* the *sacrifizio dell' intelletto*,[26] on the contrary! —will at least be entitled to demand in return that psychology shall be recognized again[27] as the queen of the sciences, for whose service and preparation the other sciences exist. For psychology is now again the path to the fundamental problems.

---

[26] Sacrifice of the intellect.
[27] "Again" is surely open to objections.

PART TWO

THE FREE SPIRIT

Part Two

24

O sancta simplicitas! [1] In what strange simplification and falsification man lives! One can never cease wondering once one has acquired eyes for this marvel! How we have made everything around us clear and free and easy and simple! how we have been able to give our senses a passport to everything superficial, our thoughts a divine desire for wanton leaps and wrong inferences! how from the beginning we have contrived to retain our ignorance in order to enjoy an almost inconceivable freedom, lack of scruple and caution, heartiness, and gaiety of life—in order to enjoy life! And only on this now solid, granite foundation of ignorance could knowledge rise so far—the will to knowledge on the foundation of a far more powerful will: the will to ignorance, to the uncertain, to the untrue! Not as its opposite, but—as its refinement!

Even if *language,* here as elsewhere, will not get over its awkwardness, and will continue to talk of opposites where there are only degrees and many subtleties of gradation; even if the inveterate Tartuffery of morals, which now belongs to our unconquerable "flesh and blood," infects the words even of those of us who know better—here and there we understand it and laugh at the way in which precisely science at its best seeks most to keep us in this *simplified,* thoroughly artificial, suitably constructed and suitably falsified world—at the way in which, willy-nilly, it loves error, because, being alive, it loves life.

25

After such a cheerful commencement, a serious word would like to be heard; it appeals to the most serious. Take care, philosophers and friends, of knowledge, and beware of martyrdom! Of

---

[1] Holy simplicity!

suffering "for the truth's sake"! Even of defending yourselves! It spoils all the innocence and fine neutrality of your conscience; it makes you headstrong against objections and red rags; it stupefies, animalizes, and brutalizes when in the struggle with danger, slander, suspicion, expulsion, and even worse consequences of hostility, you have to pose as protectors of truth upon earth—as though "the truth" were such an innocuous and incompetent creature as to require protectors! and you of all people, you knights of the most sorrowful countenance,[2] dear loafers and cobweb-spinners of the spirit! After all, you know well enough that it cannot be of any consequence if *you* of all people are proved right; you know that no philosopher so far has been proved right, and that there might be a more laudable truthfulness in every little question mark that you place after your special words and favorite doctrines (and occasionally after yourselves) than in all the solemn gestures and trumps before accusers and law courts.[3] Rather, go away. Flee into concealment. And have your masks and subtlety,[4] that you may be mistaken for what you are not, or feared a little. And don't forget the garden, the garden with golden trelliswork. And have people around you who are as a garden—or as music on the waters in the evening, when the day is turning into memories. Choose the *good* solitude, the free, playful, light solitude that gives you, too, the right to remain good in some sense. How poisonous, how crafty, how bad, does every long war make one, that cannot be waged openly by means of force! How *personal* does a long fear make one, a long watching of enemies, of possible enemies! These outcasts of society, these long-pursued, wickedly persecuted ones—also the compulsory recluses, the Spinozas or Giordano Brunos—always become in the end, even under the most spiritual masquerade, and

---

[2] For the role of Don Quixote, alluded to above, in Nietzsche's thought, see Kaufmann, *Nietzsche*, Chapter 1, note 40.

[3] Compare Nietzsche's splendid formulation in a note of the 1880's: "A very popular error: having the courage of one's convictions; rather it is a matter of having the courage for an *attack* on one's convictions!!!" (*Werke*, Musarion edition, Munich, 1920-29, XVI, p. 318.

[4] *Feinheit* (subtlety) can also mean fineness or, depending on the context, delicacy, sensitivity, nicety, elegance, purity. In this translation it has been generally rendered as "subtlety" and sometimes as "refinement."

perhaps without being themselves aware of it, sophisticated vengeance-seekers and poison-brewers (let someone lay bare the foundation of Spinoza's ethics and theology!), not to speak of the stupidity of moral indignation, which is the unfailing sign in a philosopher that his philosophical sense of humor has left him. The martyrdom of the philosopher, his "sacrifice for the sake of truth," forces into the light whatever of the agitator and actor lurks in him; and if one has so far contemplated him only with artistic curiosity, with regard to many a philosopher it is easy to understand the dangerous desire to see him also in his degeneration (degenerated into a "martyr," into a stage- and platform-bawler). Only, that it is necessary with such a desire to be clear *what* spectacle one will see in any case—merely a satyr play, merely an epilogue farce, merely the continued proof that the long, real tragedy *is at an end,* assuming that every philosophy was in its genesis a long tragedy.

26

Every choice human being strives instinctively for a citadel and a secrecy where he is saved from the crowd, the many, the great majority—where he may forget "men who are the rule," being their exception—excepting only the one case in which he is pushed straight to such men by a still stronger instinct, as a seeker after knowledge in the great and exceptional sense. Anyone who, in intercourse with men, does not occasionally glisten in all the colors of distress, green and gray with disgust, satiety, sympathy, gloominess, and loneliness, is certainly not a man of elevated tastes; supposing, however, that he does not take all this burden and disgust upon himself voluntarily, that he persistently avoids it, and remains, as I said, quietly and proudly hidden in his citadel, one thing is certain: he was not made, he was not predestined, for knowledge. If he were, he would one day have to say to himself: "The devil take my good taste! but the rule is more interesting than the exception—than myself, the exception!" And he would go *down,*[5] and above all, he would go "inside."

---

[5] An echo of the Prologue to *Zarathustra.*

The long and serious study of the *average* man, and consequently much disguise, self-overcoming, familiarity, and bad contact (all contact is bad contact except with one's equals)—this constitutes a necessary part of the life-history of every philosopher, perhaps the most disagreeable, odious, and disappointing part. If he is fortunate, however, as a favorite child of knowledge should be, he will encounter suitable shortcuts and helps for his task; I mean so-called cynics, those who simply recognize the animal, the commonplace, and "the rule" in themselves, and at the same time still have that degree of spirituality and that itch which makes them talk of themselves and their likes *before witnesses*—sometimes they even wallow in books, as on their own dung.

Cynicism is the only form in which base souls approach honesty; and the higher man must listen closely to every coarse or subtle cynicism, and congratulate himself when a clown without shame or a scientific satyr speaks out precisely in front of him.

There are even cases where enchantment mixes with the disgust—namely, where by a freak of nature genius is tied to some such indiscreet billygoat and ape, as in the case of the Abbé Galiani,[6] the profoundest, most clear-sighted, and perhaps also filthiest man of his century—he was far profounder than Voltaire and consequently also a good deal more taciturn. It happens more frequently, as has been hinted, that a scientific head is placed on an ape's body, a subtle exceptional understanding in a base soul, an occurrence by no means rare, especially among doctors and physiologists of morality. And whenever anyone speaks without bitterness, quite innocently, of man as a belly with two requirements, and a head with one; whenever anyone sees, seeks, and *wants* to see only hunger, sexual lust, and vanity as the real and only mo-

---

[6] Abbé Ferdinand Galiani (1728-87) is characterized in *The Oxford Companion to French Literature* (Oxford, Clarendon Press, 1959) as "a Neapolitan, of diminutive size, secretary at the embassy in Paris from 1759 . . . of considerable learning and originality of views, somewhat of a buffoon, much appreciated in the literary and philosophical society of the day . . . His *Dialogues sur les blés,* a work remarkable for lively wit as well as force of argument, combating the doctrines of the more extreme physiocrats, appeared in 1770, after his departure from Paris in 1769." His letters to Mme d'Épinay, Mme Geoffrin, and Mme Necker have also been published.

tives of human actions; in short, when anyone speaks "badly"—
and not even *"wickedly"*—of man, the lover of knowledge should
listen subtly and diligently; he should altogether have an open ear
wherever people talk without indignation. For the indignant and
whoever perpetually tears and lacerates with his own teeth himself (or as a substitute, the world, or God, or society) may indeed,
morally speaking, stand higher than the laughing and self-satisfied
satyr, but in every other sense they are a more ordinary, more indifferent, and less instructive case. And no one *lies* as much as the
indignant do.

27

It is hard to be understood, especially when one thinks and
lives *gāngāsrotagati*[7] among men who think and live differently—
namely, *kūrmagati,*[8] or at best "the way frogs walk," *mandūkagati*[9] (I obviously do everything to be "hard to understand" myself!)—and one should be cordially grateful for the good will to
some subtlety of interpretation. As regards "the good friends,"
however, who are always too lazy and think that as friends they

———

[7] In the original edition: gangasrotogati. Although the second "o" is clearly
a misprint, it has not been corrected in later editions or in the English translations. *Gati* means gait; *srota,* the current of a river, and *ganga* is the river
Ganges. So the word means: as the current of the Ganges moves. (For the
information about the Sanskrit words, also in the two following notes, I
am indebted to Professor Samuel D. Atkins.)

[8] As the tortoise moves. In the original edition and in subsequent editions
and translations the diacritical mark is missing.

[9] In the original edition: mandeikagati, without diacritical marks. The "ei"
is a misprint, perhaps due to the misreading of a handwritten "u"—but has
been perpetuated in subsequent editions and translations.

Far from being *merely* playful or concerned with style to the exclusion
of philosophy, this section touches on a crucial problem: Nietzsche's *tempo*
is a major reason for the long delay in his reception as a philosopher; and
three quarters of a century after the appearance of *Beyond Good and Evil*
the *tempo* of articles in British and American philosophical journals had
slowed down to the point where many philosophers were bound to feel that
anything written *gāngāsrotagati* simply could not be philosophy. Even Wittgenstein, though he had never followed the fashion of moving like the tortoise, had at least proceeded *mandūkagati.* For this whole question of philosophical style and *tempo* see Kaufmann, *Critique of Religion and Philosophy* (Garden City, N.Y., Anchor Books), sections 3-10.

have a right to relax, one does well to grant them from the outset some leeway and romping place for misunderstanding: then one can even laugh—or get rid of them altogether, these good friends —and also laugh.

28

What is most difficult to render from one language into another is the *tempo* of its style, which has its basis in the character of the race, or to speak more physiologically, in the average *tempo* of its metabolism. There are honestly meant translations that, as involuntary vulgarizations, are almost falsifications of the original, merely because its bold and merry *tempo* (which leaps over and obviates all dangers in things and words) could not be translated. A German is almost incapable of *presto*[10] in his language; thus also, as may be reasonably inferred, of many of the most delightful and daring *nuances* of free, free-spirited thought. And just as the buffoon and satyr are foreign to him in body and conscience, so Aristophanes and Petronius are untranslatable for him. Everything ponderous, viscous, and solemnly clumsy, all long-winded and boring types of style are developed in profuse variety among Germans —forgive me the fact that even Goethe's prose, in its mixture of stiffness and elegance, is no exception, being a reflection of the "good old time" to which it belongs, and a reflection of German taste at a time when there still was a "German taste"—a rococo taste *in moribus et artibus*.[11]

Lessing is an exception, owing to his histrionic nature which understood much and understood how to do many things. He was not the translator of Bayle for nothing and liked to flee to the neighborhood of Diderot and Voltaire, and better yet that of the Roman comedy writers. In *tempo,* too, Lessing loved free thinking and escape from Germany. But how could the German language, even in the prose of a Lessing, imitate the *tempo* of Machia-

---

[10] Rapid tempo.
[11] In morals and arts.

velli,[12] who in his *Principe* [*The Prince*] lets us breathe the dry, refined air of Florence and cannot help presenting the most serious matters in a boisterous *allegrissimo*,[13] perhaps not without a malicious artistic sense of the contrast he risks—long, difficult, hard, dangerous thoughts and the *tempo* of the gallop and the very best, most capricious humor?

Who, finally, could venture on a German translation of Petronius, who, more than any great musician so far, was a master of *presto* in invention, ideas, and words? What do the swamps of the sick, wicked world, even the "ancient world," matter in the end, when one has the feet of a wind as he did, the rush, the breath, the liberating scorn of a wind that makes everything healthy by making everything *run!* And as for Aristophanes—that transfiguring, complementary spirit for whose sake one *forgives* everything Hellenic for having existed, provided one has understood in its full profundity *all* that needs to be forgiven and transfigured here— there is nothing that has caused me to meditate more on *Plato's* secrecy and sphinx nature than the happily preserved *petit fait*[14] that under the pillow of his deathbed there was found no "Bible," nor anything Egyptian, Pythagorean, or Platonic—but a volume of Aristophanes. How could even Plato have endured life—a Greek life he repudiated—without an Aristophanes?

29

Independence is for the very few; it is a privilege of the strong. And whoever attempts it even with the best right but without inner constraint proves that he is probably not only strong, but also daring to the point of recklessness. He enters into a labyrinth, he multiplies a thousandfold the dangers which life brings with it in any case, not the least of which is that no one can see how and where he loses his way, becomes lonely, and is torn piecemeal by

---

[12] In the original edition and in the standard editions; Macchiavelli.

[13] Extremely brisk and lively manner.

[14] Small fact.

some minotaur of conscience. Supposing one like that comes to grief, this happens so far from the comprehension of men that they neither feel it nor sympathize. And he cannot go back any longer. Nor can he go back to the pity of men.—

30

Our highest insights must—and should—sound like follies and sometimes like crimes when they are heard without permission by those who are not predisposed and predestined for them.[15] The difference between the exoteric and the esoteric, formerly known to philosophers—among the Indians as among the Greeks, Persians, and Muslims, in short, wherever one believed in an order of rank and *not* in equality and equal rights—does not so much consist in this, that the exoteric approach comes from outside and sees, estimates, measures, and judges from the outside, not the inside: what is much more essential is that the exoteric approach sees things from below, the esoteric looks *down from above*. There are heights of the soul from which even tragedy ceases to look tragic; and rolling together all the woe of the world—who could dare to decide whether its sight would *necessarily* seduce us and compel us to feel pity and thus double this woe?

What serves the higher type of men as nourishment or delectation must almost be poison for a very different and inferior type. The virtues of the common man might perhaps signify vices and weaknesses in a philosopher. It could be possible that a man of a high type, when degenerating and perishing, might only at that point acquire qualities that would require those in the lower sphere into which he had sunk to begin to venerate him like a saint. There are books that have opposite values for soul and health, depending on whether the lower soul, the lower vitality, or the higher and more vigorous ones turn to them: in the former case, these books are dangerous and lead to crumbling and disintegration; in the latter, heralds' cries that call the bravest to *their*

---

[15] This theme is taken up again in several later sections, where the concept of the mask is discussed; e.g., section 40.

courage. Books for all the world are always foul-smelling books: the smell of small people clings to them. Where the people eat and drink, even where they venerate, it usually stinks. One should not go to church if one wants to breathe *pure* air.

31

When one is young, one venerates and despises without that art of nuances which constitutes the best gain of life, and it is only fair that one has to pay dearly for having assaulted men and things in this manner with Yes and No. Everything is arranged so that the worst of tastes, the taste for the unconditional, should be cruelly fooled and abused until a man learns to put a little art into his feelings and rather to risk trying even what is artificial—as the real artists of life do.

The wrathful and reverent attitudes characteristic of youth do not seem to permit themselves any rest until they have forged men and things in such a way that these attitudes may be vented on them—after all, youth in itself has something of forgery and deception. Later, when the young soul, tortured by all kinds of disappointments, finally turns suspiciously against itself, still hot and wild, even in its suspicion and pangs of conscience—how wroth it is with itself now! how it tears itself to pieces, impatiently! how it takes revenge for its long self-delusion, just as if it had been a deliberate blindness! In this transition one punishes oneself with mistrust against one's own feelings; one tortures one's own enthusiasm with doubts; indeed, one experiences even a good conscience as a danger, as if it were a way of wrapping oneself in veils and the exhaustion of subtler honesty—and above all one takes sides, takes sides on principle, *against* "youth."— Ten years later one comprehends that all this, too—was still youth.

32

During the longest part of human history—so-called prehistorical times—the value or disvalue of an action was derived from its consequences. The action itself was considered as little as its origin. It was rather the way a distinction or disgrace still reaches back today from a child to its parents, in China: it was the retroactive force of success or failure that led men to think well or ill of an action. Let us call this period the *pre-moral* period of mankind: the imperative "know thyself!" was as yet unknown.

In the last ten thousand years, however, one has reached the point, step by step, in a few large regions on the earth, where it is no longer the consequences but the origin of an action that one allows to decide its value. On the whole this is a great event which involves a considerable refinement of vision and standards; it is the unconscious aftereffect of the rule of aristocratic values and the faith in "descent"—the sign of a period that one may call *moral* in the narrower sense. It involves the first attempt at self-knowledge. Instead of the consequences, the origin: indeed a reversal of perspective! Surely, a reversal achieved only after long struggles and vacillations. To be sure, a calamitous new superstition, an odd narrowness of interpretation, thus become dominant: the origin of an action was interpreted in the most definite sense as origin in an *intention;* one came to agree that the value of an action lay in the value of the intention. The intention as the whole origin and prehistory of an action—almost to the present day this prejudice dominated moral praise, blame, judgment, and philosophy on earth.

But today—shouldn't we have reached the necessity of once more resolving on a reversal and fundamental shift in values, owing to another self-examination of man, another growth in profundity? Don't we stand at the threshold of a period which should be designated negatively, to begin with, as *extra-moral?* After all, today at least we immoralists have the suspicion that the decisive value of an action lies precisely in what is *unintentional* in it, while everything about it that is intentional, everything about it that can be seen, known, "conscious," still belongs to its surface and skin—which, like every skin, betrays something but *conceals* even more. In short, we believe that the intention is merely a sign and symptom that still requires interpretation—moreover, a sign that means too much and therefore, taken by itself alone, almost nothing. We believe that morality in the traditional sense, the morality of intentions, was a prejudice, precipitate and perhaps provisional

—something on the order of astrology and alchemy—but in any case something that must be overcome. The overcoming of morality, in a certain sense even the self-overcoming of morality—let this be the name for that long secret work which has been saved up for the finest and most honest, also the most malicious, consciences of today, as living touchstones of the soul.

33

There is no other way: the feelings of devotion, self-sacrifice for one's neighbor, the whole morality of self-denial must be questioned mercilessly and taken to court—no less than the aesthetics of "contemplation devoid of all interest" which is used today as a seductive guise for the emasculation of art, to give it a good conscience. There is too much charm and sugar in these feelings of "for others," "*not* for myself," for us not to need to become doubly suspicious at this point and to ask: "are these not perhaps—*seductions?*"

That they *please*—those who have them and those who enjoy their fruits, and also the mere spectator—this does not yet constitute an argument in their *favor* but rather invites caution. So let us be cautious.

34

Whatever philosophical standpoint one may adopt today, from every point of view the *erroneousness* of the world in which we think we live is the surest and firmest fact that we can lay eyes on: we find reasons upon reasons for it which would like to lure us to hypotheses concerning a deceptive principle in "the essence of things." But whoever holds our thinking itself, "the spirit," in other words, responsible for the falseness of the world—an honorable way out which is chosen by every conscious or unconscious *advocatus dei*[16]—whoever takes this world, along with space, time,

---

[16] Advocate of God: Nietzsche's coinage, modeled after *advocatus diaboli*, devil's advocate.

form, movement, to be falsely *inferred*—anyone like that would at least have ample reason to learn to be suspicious at long last of all thinking. Wouldn't thinking have put over on us the biggest hoax yet? And what warrant would there be that it would not continue to do what it has always done?

In all seriousness: the innocence of our thinkers is somehow touching and evokes reverence, when today they still step before consciousness with the request that it should please give them *honest* answers; for example, whether it is "real," and why it so resolutely keeps the external world at a distance, and other questions of that kind. The faith in "immediate certainties" is a *moral* naïveté that reflects honor on us philosophers; but—after all we should not be *"merely* moral" men. Apart from morality, this faith is a stupidity that reflects little honor on us. In bourgeois life ever-present suspicion may be considered a sign of "bad character" and hence belong among things imprudent; here, among us, beyond the bourgeois world and its Yes and No—what should prevent us from being imprudent and saying: a philosopher has nothing less than a *right* to "bad character," as the being who has so far always been fooled best on earth; he has a *duty* to suspicion today, to squint maliciously out of every abyss of suspicion.

Forgive me the joke of this gloomy grimace and trope; for I myself have learned long ago to think differently, to estimate differently with regard to deceiving and being deceived, and I keep in reserve at least a couple of jostles for the blind rage with which the philosophers resist being deceived. Why *not?* It is no more than a moral prejudice that truth is worth more than mere appearance; it is even the worst proved assumption there is in the world. Let at least this much be admitted: there would be no life at all if not on the basis of perspective estimates and appearances; and if, with the virtuous enthusiasm and clumsiness of some philosophers, one wanted to abolish the "apparent world" altogether—well, supposing *you* could do that, at least nothing would be left of your "truth" either. Indeed, what forces us at all to suppose that there is an essential opposition of "true" and "false"? Is it not sufficient to assume degrees of apparentness and, as it were, lighter and darker shadows and shades of appearance—different "values," to use the language of painters? Why couldn't the world *that concerns us*— be a fiction? And if somebody asked, "but to a fiction there surely belongs an author?"—couldn't one answer simply: *why?* Doesn't this "belongs" perhaps belong to the fiction, too? Is it not permitted to be a bit ironical about the subject no less than the predicate and object? Shouldn't philosophers be permitted to rise above faith in grammar? All due respect for governesses—but hasn't the time come for philosophy to renounce the faith of governesses? [17]

35

O Voltaire! O humaneness! O nonsense! There is something about "truth," about the *search* for truth; and when a human being is too human about it—*"il ne cherche le vrai que pour faire le bien"* [18]—I bet he finds nothing.

36

Suppose nothing else were "given" as real except our world of desires and passions, and we could not get down, or up, to any other "reality" besides the reality of our drives—for thinking is merely a relation of these drives to each other: is it not permitted to make the experiment and to ask the question whether this "given" would not be *sufficient* for also understanding on the basis of this kind of thing the so-called mechanistic (or "material") world? I mean, not as a deception, as "mere appearance," an "idea" (in the sense of Berkeley and Schopenhauer) but as holding the same rank of reality as our affect—as a more primitive form of the world of affects in which everything still lies contained in a powerful unity

---

[17] Cf.: "It might be amusing, perhaps even instructive, to compare Ryle on ordinary language with W. D. Ross on *prima facie* duties. There is a close resemblance between Oxford deontology and Oxford linguisticism, not least in the assumption that duties, like verbal habits, are 'learnt in the nursery' [Ryle's phrase], and that what nurse has told us goes for the rest of the world, too" (John Passmore. "Professor Ryle's Use of 'Use' and 'Usage.' " *The Philosophical Review*, LXIII [January 1954], 62).

[18] "He seeks the true only to do the good."

before it undergoes ramifications and developments in the organic process (and, as is only fair, also becomes tenderer and weaker) —as a kind of instinctive life in which all organic functions are still synthetically intertwined along with self-regulation, assimilation, nourishment, excretion, and metabolism—as a *pre-form* of life.

In the end not only is it permitted to make this experiment; the conscience of *method* demands it. Not to assume several kinds of causality until the experiment of making do with a single one has been pushed to its utmost limit (to the point of nonsense, if I may say so)—that is a moral of method which one may not shirk today —it follows "from its definition," as a mathematician would say. The question is in the end whether we really recognize the will as *efficient*, whether we believe in the causality of the will: if we do —and at bottom our faith in this is nothing less than our faith in causality itself—then we have to make the experiment of positing the causality of the will hypothetically as the only one. "Will," of course, can affect only "will"—and not "matter" (not "nerves," for example). In short, one has to risk the hypothesis whether will does not affect will wherever "effects" are recognized—and whether all mechanical occurrences are not, insofar as a force is active in them, will force, effects of will.

Suppose, finally, we succeeded in explaining our entire instinctive life as the development and ramification of *one* basic form of the will—namely, of the will to power, as *my* proposition has it; suppose all organic functions could be traced back to this will to power and one could also find in it the solution of the problem of procreation and nourishment—it is *one* problem—then one would have gained the right to determine *all* efficient force univocally as —*will to power*. The world viewed from inside, the world defined and determined according to its "intelligible character"—it would be "will to power" and nothing else.—

37

"What? Doesn't this mean, to speak with the vulgar: God is refuted, but the devil is not?" On the contrary! On the contrary, my friends. And, the devil—who forces you to speak with the vulgar?

38

What happened most recently in the broad daylight of modern times in the case of the French Revolution—that gruesome farce which, considered closely, was quite superfluous, though noble and enthusiastic spectators from all over Europe contemplated it from a distance and interpreted it according to their own indignations and enthusiasms for so long, and so passionately, that *the text finally disappeared under the interpretation*—could happen once more as a noble posterity might misunderstand the whole past and in that way alone make it tolerable to look at.

Or rather: isn't this what has happened even now? haven't we ourselves been this "noble posterity"? And isn't now precisely the moment when, insofar as we comprehend this, it is all over?

39

Nobody is very likely to consider a doctrine true merely because it makes people happy or virtuous—except perhaps the lovely "idealists" who become effusive about the good, the true, and the beautiful and allow all kinds of motley, clumsy, and benevolent desiderata to swim around in utter confusion in their pond. Happiness and virtue are no arguments. But people like to forget— even sober spirits—that making unhappy and evil are no counter-arguments. Something might be true while being harmful and dangerous in the highest degree. Indeed, it might be a basic characteristic of existence that those who would know it completely would perish, in which case the strength of a spirit should be measured according to how much of the "truth" one could still barely endure— or to put it more clearly, to what degree one would *require* it to be thinned down, shrouded, sweetened, blunted, falsified.[19]

But there is no doubt at all that the evil and unhappy are more favored when it comes to the discovery of certain *parts* of truth,

---

[19] This is relevant to Nietzsche's conception of an order of rank and the themes of Part IX below.

and that the probability of their success here is greater—not to speak of the evil who are happy, a species the moralists bury in silence. Perhaps hardness and cunning furnish more favorable conditions for the origin of the strong, independent spirit and philosopher than that gentle, fine, conciliatory good-naturedness and art of taking things lightly which people prize, and prize rightly, in a scholar. Assuming first of all that the concept "philosopher" is not restricted to the philosopher who writes books—or makes books of *his* philosophy.

A final trait for the image of the free-spirited philosopher is contributed by Stendhal whom, considering German taste, I do not want to fail to stress—for he goes against the German taste. *"Pour être bon philosophe,"* says this last great psychologist, *"il faut être sec, clair, sans illusion. Un banquier, qui a fait fortune, a une partie du caractère requis pour faire des découvertes en philosophie, c'est-à-dire pour voir clair dans ce qui est."* [20]

40

Whatever is profound loves masks; what is most profound even hates image and parable. Might not nothing less than the *opposite* be the proper disguise for the shame of a god? [21] A questionable question: it would be odd if some mystic had not risked something to that effect in his mind. There are occurrences of such a delicate nature that one does well to cover them up with some rudeness to conceal them; there are actions of love and extravagant generosity after which nothing is more advisable than to take a stick and give any eyewitness a sound thrashing: that would muddle his memory. Some know how to muddle and abuse their own memory in order to have their revenge at least against this only witness: shame is inventive.

It is not the worst things that cause the worst shame: there is

---

[20] "To be a good philosopher, one must be dry, clear, without illusion. A banker who has made a fortune has one character trait that is needed for making discoveries in philosophy, that is to say, for seeing clearly into what is."

[21] Cf. section 30 above.

not only guile behind a mask—there is so much graciousness in cunning. I could imagine that a human being who had to guard something precious and vulnerable might roll through life, rude and round as an old green wine cask with heavy hoops: the refinement of his shame would want it that way.

A man whose sense of shame has some profundity encounters his destinies and delicate decisions, too, on paths which few ever reach and of whose mere existence his closest intimates must not know: his mortal danger is concealed from their eyes, and so is his regained sureness of life. Such a concealed man who instinctively needs speech for silence and for burial in silence and who is inexhaustible in his evasion of communication, *wants* and sees to it that a mask of him roams in his place through the hearts and heads of his friends. And supposing he did not want it, he would still realize some day that in spite of that a mask of him is there—and that this is well. Every profound spirit needs a mask: even more, around every profound spirit a mask is growing continually, owing to the constantly false, namely *shallow*, interpretation of every word, every step, every sign of life he gives.[22]—

41

One has to test oneself to see that one is destined for independence and command—and do it at the right time. One should not dodge one's tests, though they may be the most dangerous

---

[22] This section is obviously of great importance for the student of Nietzsche: it suggests plainly that the surface meaning noted by superficial browsers often masks Nietzsche's real meaning, which in extreme cases may approximate the opposite of what the words might suggest to hasty readers. In this sense "beyond good and evil" and "will to power," "master morality" and "hardness" and "cruelty" may be masks that elicit reactions quite inappropriate to what lies behind them. Specific examples will be found on later pages.

Karl Jaspers has called attention to the similarity between Nietzsche and Kierkegaard at this point, in his lecture on Kierkegaard and Nietzsche (*Existentialism from Dostoevsky to Sartre*, ed. Kaufmann, New York, Meridian Books, 1956, p. 165). See also Jaspers' *Nietzsche* (1936, pp. 358ff.; pp. 405ff. of the English version, Tucson, University of Arizona Press, 1965, which unfortunately omits the references for the quotations).

game one could play and are tests that are taken in the end before no witness or judge but ourselves.

Not to remain stuck to a person—not even the most loved— every person is a prison, also a nook.[23] Not to remain stuck to a fatherland—not even if it suffers most and needs help most—it is less difficult to sever one's heart from a victorious fatherland. Not to remain stuck to some pity—not even for higher men into whose rare torture and helplessness some accident allowed us to look.[24] Not to remain stuck to a science—even if it should lure us with the most precious finds that seem to have been saved up precisely for us.[25] Not to remain stuck to one's own detachment, to that voluptuous remoteness and strangeness of the bird who flees ever higher to see ever more below him—the danger of the flier. Not to remain stuck to our own virtues and become as a whole the victim of some detail in us, such as our hospitality, which is the danger of dangers for superior and rich souls who spend themselves lavishly, almost indifferently, and exaggerate the virtue of generosity into a vice. One must know how *to conserve oneself:* the hardest test of independence.

42

A new species of philosophers is coming up: I venture to baptize them with a name that is not free of danger. As I unriddle them, insofar as they allow themselves to be unriddled—for it belongs to their nature to *want* to remain riddles at some point— these philosophers of the future may have a right—it might also be a wrong—to be called *attempters.*[26] This name itself is in the end a mere attempt and, if you will, a temptation.

---

[23] *Winkel* has been translated here and elsewhere as "nook"; but it can also mean angle, which would make sense here though not in many of the other passages.

[24] This might be an allusion to Richard Wagner; but this is a point Nietzsche considered important generally, and it is developed at length in Part IV of *Zarathustra.*

[25] In German usage, classical philology, which Nietzsche had given up in order to devote himself entirely to his own writing, is a science.

[26] *Versucher* could also mean tempters (which does not seem intended here,

43

Are these coming philosophers new friends of "truth"? That is probable enough, for all philosophers so far have loved their truths. But they will certainly not be dogmatists. It must offend their pride, also their taste, if their truth is supposed to be a truth for everyman —which has so far been the secret wish and hidden meaning of all dogmatic aspirations. "My judgment is *my* judgment": no one else is easily entitled to it—that is what such a philosopher of the future may perhaps say of himself.

One must shed the bad taste of wanting to agree with many. "Good" is no longer good when one's neighbor mouths it. And how should there be a "common good"! The term contradicts itself: whatever can be common always has little value. In the end it must be as it is and always has been: great things remain for the great, abysses for the profound, nuances and shudders for the refined, and, in brief, all that is rare for the rare.[27]—

44

Need I still say expressly after all this that they, too, will be free, *very* free spirits, these philosophers of the future—though just as certainly they will not be merely free spirits but something more, higher, greater, and thoroughly different that does not want to be misunderstood and mistaken for something else. But saying this I

---

at least as the primary meaning) or experimenters (which is meant but would spoil the triple play on words): *Versuch* (attempt or experiment) and *Versuchung* (temptation). For some discussion of Nietzsche's "experimentalism" see Kaufmann's *Nietzsche*, Chapter 2, section III. See also section 210 below.

[27] It is interesting to compare this critique of dogmatism with Hegel's. Hegel had insisted that dogmatism is wrong in supposing that an isolated proposition can be the form of the truth; nothing is accomplished by repeating such formulations: their significance depends on the meaning assigned to the terms and on the context; hence only the system can be the form of the truth. For a comparison of Hegel's and Nietzsche's views of systems see Kaufmann's *Nietzsche*, Chapter 2, section II; the remainder of the chapter deals with Nietzsche's "experimentalism" and its "existential" quality.

feel an *obligation*—almost as much to them as to ourselves who are their heralds and precursors, we free spirits—to sweep away a stupid old prejudice and misunderstanding about the lot of us: all too long it has clouded the concept "free spirit" like a fog.

In all the countries of Europe, and in America, too, there now is something that abuses this name: a very narrow, imprisoned, chained type of spirits who want just about the opposite of what accords with our intentions and instincts—not to speak of the fact that regarding the *new* philosophers who are coming up they must assuredly be closed windows and bolted doors. They belong, briefly and sadly, among the *levelers*—these falsely so-called "free spirits"—being eloquent and prolifically scribbling slaves of the democratic taste and its "modern ideas"; they are all human beings without solitude, without their own solitude, clumsy good fellows whom one should not deny either courage or respectable decency —only they are unfree and ridiculously superficial, above all in their basic inclination to find in the forms of the old society as it has existed so far just about the cause of *all* human misery and failure —which is a way of standing truth happily upon her head! What they would like to strive for with all their powers is the universal green-pasture happiness of the herd, with security, lack of danger, comfort, and an easier life for everyone; the two songs and doctrines which they repeat most often are "equality of rights" and "sympathy for all that suffers"—and suffering itself they take for something that must be *abolished*.

We opposite men, having opened our eyes and conscience to the question where and how the plant "man" has so far grown most vigorously to a height—we think that this has happened every time under the opposite conditions, that to this end the dangerousness of his situation must first grow to the point of enormity, his power of invention and simulation (his "spirit") had to develop under prolonged pressure and constraint into refinement and audacity, his life-will had to be enhanced into an unconditional power-will. We think that hardness, forcefulness, slavery, danger in the alley and the heart, life in hiding, stoicism, the art of experiment and devilry of every kind, that everything evil, terrible, tyrannical in man, everything in him that is kin to beasts of prey and serpents, serves the enhancement of the species "man" as much as its opposite does. Indeed, we do not even say enough when we say only that much; and at any rate we are at this point, in what we say and keep silent about, at the *other* end from all modern ideology and herd desiderata—as their antipodes perhaps?

Is it any wonder that we "free spirits" are not exactly the most communicative spirits? that we do not want to betray in every particular *from what* a spirit can liberate himself and *to what* he may then be driven? And as for the meaning of the dangerous formula "beyond good and evil," with which we at least guard against being mistaken for others: we *are* something different from *"libres-penseurs," "liberi pensatori," "Freidenker,"* [28] and whatever else all these goodly advocates of "modern ideas" like to call themselves.

At home, or at least having been guests, in many countries of the spirit; having escaped again and again from the musty agreeable nooks into which preference and prejudice, youth, origin, the accidents of people and books or even exhaustion from wandering seemed to have banished us; full of malice against the lures of dependence that lie hidden in honors, or money, or offices, or enthusiasms of the senses; grateful even to need and vacillating sickness because they always rid us from some rule and its "prejudice," grateful to god, devil, sheep, and worm in us; curious to a vice, investigators to the point of cruelty, with uninhibited fingers for the unfathomable, with teeth and stomachs for the most indigestible, ready for every feat that requires a sense of acuteness and acute senses, ready for every venture, thanks to an excess of "free will," with fore- and back-souls into whose ultimate intentions nobody can look so easily, with fore- and backgrounds which no foot is likely to explore to the end; concealed under cloaks of light, conquerors even if we look like heirs and prodigals, arrangers and collectors from morning till late, misers of our riches and our crammed drawers, economical in learning and forgetting, inventive in schemas, occasionally proud of tables of categories, occasionally pedants, occasionally night owls of work even in broad daylight;

---

[28] Free-thinkers.

yes, when it is necessary even scarecrows—and today it is necessary; namely, insofar as we are born, sworn, jealous friends of *solitude*, of our own most profound, most midnightly, most middaily solitude: that is the type of man we are, we free spirits! And perhaps *you* have something of this, too, you that are coming? you *new* philosophers?—

PART THREE

WHAT IS RELIGIOUS[1]

---

[1] The German title is *Das religiöse Wesen*. The word *Wesen* is not easy to translate. In philosophical prose it is most often rendered by "essence," but in many contexts "being" is called for; e.g., a natural being, a human being. Above, either "the religious nature" or "the religious being" might do. But in section 47 Nietzsche speaks of "the religious neurosis—or what I call *'das religiöse Wesen'*"; and this puts one in mind of contexts in which *Wesen* means character, conduct, manners, airs, and even ado: *viel Wesen* means much ado. *Finanzwesen* means financial affairs, or the financial establishment, or finances. *Bankwesen*, banks or banking in general; *Minenwesen*, mining; and *Kriegswesen*, military art—these last examples come from a dictionary.

Part Three

45

The human soul and its limits, the range of inner human experiences reached so far, the heights, depths, and distances of these experiences, the whole history of the soul *so far* and its as yet unexhausted possibilities—that is the predestined hunting ground for a born psychologist and lover of the "great hunt." But how often he has to say to himself in despair: "One hunter! alas, only a single one! and look at this huge forest, this primeval forest!" And then he wishes he had a few hundred helpers and good, well-trained hounds that he could drive into the history of the human soul to round up *his* game. In vain: it is proved to him again and again, thoroughly and bitterly, how helpers and hounds for all the things that excite his curiosity cannot be found. What is wrong with sending scholars into new and dangerous hunting grounds, where courage, sense, and subtlety in every way are required, is that they cease to be of any use precisely where the *"great hunt,"* but also the great danger, begins: precisely there they lose their keen eye and nose.

To figure out and determine, for example, what kind of a history the problem of *science and conscience*[2] has so far had in the soul of *homines religiosi*,[3] one might perhaps have to be as profound, as wounded, as monstrous as Pascal's intellectual conscience was—and then one would still need that vaulting heaven of bright, malicious spirituality that would be capable of surveying from above, arranging, and forcing into formulas this swarm of dangerous and painful experiences.

But who would do me this service? But who would have time to wait for such servants? They obviously grow too rarely; they are so improbable in any age. In the end one has to do everything one-

---

[2] *Wissen und Gewissen:* literally, knowledge and conscience.
[3] Religious men.

self in order to know a few things oneself: that is, one has *a lot* to do.

But a curiosity of my type remains after all the most agreeable of all vices—sorry, I meant to say: the love of truth has its reward in heaven and even on earth.—

46

The faith demanded, and not infrequently attained, by original Christianity, in the midst of a skeptical and southern free-spirited world that looked back on, and still contained, a centuries-long fight between philosophical schools, besides the education for tolerance given by the *imperium Romanum*[4]—this faith is *not* that ingenuous and bearlike subalterns' faith with which, say, a Luther or a Cromwell, or some other northern barbarian of the spirit, clung to his god and to Christianity. It is much closer to the faith of Pascal, which resembles in a gruesome manner a continual suicide of reason—a tough, long-lived, wormlike reason that cannot be killed all at once and with a single stroke.

From the start, the Christian faith is a sacrifice: a sacrifice of all freedom, all pride, all self-confidence of the spirit; at the same time, enslavement and self-mockery, self-mutilation. There is cruelty and religious Phoenicianism in this faith which is expected of an over-ripe, multiple, and much-spoiled conscience: it presupposes that the subjection of the spirit *hurts* indescribably; that the whole past and the habits of such a spirit resist the *absurdissimum*[5] which "faith" represents to it.

Modern men, obtuse to all Christian nomenclature, no longer feel the gruesome superlative that struck a classical taste in the paradoxical formula "god on the cross." Never yet and nowhere has there been an equal boldness in inversion, anything as horrible, questioning, and questionable as this formula: it promised a revaluation of all the values of antiquity.

It is the Orient, *deep* Orient, it is the Oriental slave who re-

---

[4] Roman Empire.
[5] Height of absurdity.

venged himself in this way on Rome and its noble and frivolous tolerance, on the Roman "catholicity" of faith. It has always been not faith but the freedom from faith, that half-stoical and smiling unconcern with the seriousness of faith, that enraged slaves in their masters—against their masters. "Enlightenment" enrages: for the slave wants the unconditional; he understands only what is tyrannical, in morals, too; he loves as he hates, without nuance, to the depths, to the point of pain, of sickness—his abundant *concealed* suffering is enraged against the noble taste that seems to *deny* suffering. Nor was skepticism concerning suffering, at bottom merely a pose of aristocratic morality, the least cause of the origin of the last great slave rebellion which began with the French Revolution.

47

Wherever on earth the religious neurosis has appeared we find it tied to three dangerous dietary demands: solitude, fasting, and sexual abstinence. But one cannot decide with certainty what is cause and what effect, and *whether* any relation of cause and effect is involved here. The final doubt seems justified because among its most regular symptoms, among both savage and tame peoples, we also find the most sudden, most extravagant voluptuousness which then, just as suddenly, changes into a penitential spasm and denial of the world and will—both perhaps to be interpreted as masked epilepsy? But nowhere should one resist interpretation more: no other type has yet been surrounded by such a lavish growth of nonsense and superstition, no other type seems to have interested men, even philosophers, more. The time has come for becoming a bit cold right here, to learn caution—better yet: to look away, *to go away*.

Even in the background of the most recent philosophy, that of Schopenhauer, we find, almost as the problem-in-itself, this gruesome question mark of the religious crisis and awakening. How is the denial of the will *possible*? how is the saint possible? This really seems to have been the question over which Schopenhauer became a philosopher and began. And so it was a genuinely Schopenhauerian conclusion when his most convinced adherent (perhaps also the last one, as far as Germany is concerned), namely, Richard Wagner, finished his life's work at precisely this point and in the end brought this horrible and eternal type on the stage as Kundry, *type vécu*,[6] in the flesh—at the very time when the psychiatrists of almost all the countries of Europe had occasion to study it at close quarters, wherever the religious neurosis—or what I call *"das religiöse Wesen"* [7]—had its latest epidemic outbreak and pageant in the "Salvation Army."

Let us ask what precisely about this whole phenomenon of the saint has seemed so enormously interesting to men of all types and ages, even to philosophers. Beyond any doubt, it was the air of the miraculous that goes with it—namely, the immediate *succession of opposites,* of states of the soul that are judged morally in opposite ways. It seemed palpable that a "bad man" was suddenly transformed into a "saint," a good man. The psychology we have had so far suffered shipwreck at this point: wasn't this chiefly because it had placed itself under the dominion of morals, because it, too, *believed* in opposite moral values and saw, read, *interpreted* these opposites into the text and the facts?

What? The "miracle" merely a mistake of interpretation? A lack of philology?

48

It seems that Catholicism is much more intimately related to the Latin races than all of Christianity in general is to us northerners—and unbelief therefore means something altogether different in Catholic and Protestant countries: among *them,* a kind of rebellion against the spirit of the race, while among us it is rather a return to the spirit (or anti-spirit) of the race. We northerners are undoubtedly descended from barbarian races, which also shows in

---

[6] A type that has lived.

[7] The title of this part of the book. See note 1 above.

our talent for religion: we have *little* talent for it. We may except the Celts, who therefore also furnished the best soil for the spread of the Christian infection to the north: in France the Christian ideal came to flourish as much as the pale sun of the north permitted it. How strangely pious for our taste are even the most recent French skeptics insofar as they have any Celtic blood! How Catholic, how un-German Auguste Comte's sociology smells to us with its Roman logic of the instincts! How Jesuitical that gracious and clever cicerone of Port-Royal, Sainte-Beuve, in spite of all his hostility against the Jesuits! And especially Ernest Renan: how inaccessible the language of such a Renan sounds to us northerners: at one instant after another some nothing of religious tension unbalances his soul, which is, in the more refined sense, voluptuous and inclined to stretch out comfortably. Let us speak after him these beautiful sentences—and how much malice and high spirits stir immediately in our probably less beautiful and harder, namely more German, soul as a response!

"*Disons donc hardiment que la religion est un produit de l'homme normal, que l'homme est le plus dans le vrai quand il est le plus religieux et le plus assuré d'une destinée infinie. . . . C'est quand il est bon qu'il veut que la vertu corresponde à un ordre éternel, c'est quand il contemple les choses d'une manière désintéressée qu'il trouve la morte révoltante et absurde. Comment ne pas supposer que c'est dans ces moments-là, que l'homme voit le mieux?*" [8]

These sentences are so utterly *antipodal* to my ears and habits that on finding them my first wrath wrote on the margin "*la niaiserie religieuse par excellence!*" But my subsequent wrath actually took a fancy to them—these sentences standing truth on her head! It is so neat, so distinguished to have one's own antipodes!

---

[8] "So let us make bold to say that religion is a product of the normal man, that man is closest to the truth when he is most religious and most certain of an infinite destiny. . . . It is when he is good that he wants virtue to correspond to an eternal order; it is when he contemplates things in a disinterested manner that he finds death revolting and absurd. How can we but suppose that it is in moments like this that man sees best?"

49

What is amazing about the religiosity of the ancient Greeks is the enormous abundance of gratitude it exudes: it is a very noble type of man that confronts nature and life in *this* way.[9]

Later, when the rabble gained the upper hand in Greece, *fear* became rampant in religion, too—and the ground was prepared for Christianity.—

50

The passion for God: there are peasant types, sincere and obtrusive, like Luther—the whole of Protestantism lacks southern *delicatezza*.[10] There is sometimes an Oriental ecstasy worthy of a slave who, without deserving it, has been pardoned and elevated— for example, in Augustine, who lacks in a truly offensive manner all nobility of gestures and desires. There is a womanly tenderness and lust that presses bashfully and ignorantly toward a *unio mystica et physica*[11]—as in Madame de Guyon.[12] In many cases it appears oddly enough as a disguise for the puberty of a girl or youth; here and there even as the hysteria of an old maid, also as her final ambition—and in several such instances the church has proclaimed the female a saint.

---

[9] In other words, that affirms life as a great boon, in spite of all its terrors: this shows great strength and a remarkable and noble freedom from resentment.

[10] Delicacy.

[11] Mystical and physical union.

[12] Madame Guyon (Jeanne-Marie Bouvier de la Motte-Guyon, 1648-1717), was a French mystic who is considered one of the chief advocates of Quietism, introduced before 1675 by Miguel Molinos (1640-96), a Spanish priest who was arrested by the Roman Inquisition in 1685 and sentenced to perpetual imprisonment in 1687. Madame Guyon was imprisoned from 1695 to 1703. The Quietist doctrine was condemned by Innocent XII in 1699. (These dates are taken from *The Oxford Companion to French Literature*, Oxford, Clarendon Press, 1959.)

51

So far the most powerful human beings have still bowed wor-
shipfully before the saint as the riddle of self-conquest and deliberate final renunciation. Why did they bow? In him—and as it were
behind the question mark of his fragile and miserable appearance
—they sensed the superior force that sought to test itself in such a
conquest, the strength of the will in which they recognized and
honored their own strength and delight in dominion: they honored
something in themselves when they honored the saint. Moreover,
the sight of the saint awakened a suspicion in them: such an enormity of denial, of anti-nature will not have been desired for nothing, they said to and asked themselves. There may be a reason for
it, some very great danger about which the ascetic, thanks to his secret comforters and visitors, might have inside information. In
short, the powerful of the world learned a new fear before him;
they sensed a new power, a strange, as yet unconquered enemy—
it was the "will to power" that made them stop before the saint.
They had to ask him——

52

In the Jewish "Old Testament," the book of divine justice,
there are human beings, things, and speeches in so grand a style
that Greek and Indian literature have nothing to compare with it.
With terror and reverence one stands before these tremendous
remnants of what man once was, and will have sad thoughts about
ancient Asia and its protruding little peninsula Europe, which wants
by all means to signify as against Asia the "progress of man." To be
sure, whoever is himself merely a meager, tame domestic animal
and knows only the needs of domestic animals (like our educated
people of today, including the Christians of "educated" Christianity) has no cause for amazement or sorrow among these ruins—
the taste for the Old Testament is a touchstone for "great" and

"small" [13]—perhaps he will find the *New* Testament, the book of grace, still rather more after his heart (it contains a lot of the real, tender, musty true-believer and small-soul smell). To have glued this New Testament, a kind of rococo of taste in every respect, to the Old Testament to make *one* book, as the "Bible," as "the book par excellence"—that is perhaps the greatest audacity and "sin against the spirit" that literary Europe has on its conscience.[14]

53

Why atheism today?—"The father" in God has been thoroughly refuted; ditto, "the judge," "the rewarder." Also his "free will": he does not hear—and if he heard he still would not know how to help. Worst of all: he seems incapable of clear communication: is he unclear?

This is what I found to be causes for the decline of European theism, on the basis of a great many conversations, asking and listening. It seems to me that the religious instinct is indeed in the process of growing powerfully—but the theistic satisfaction it refuses with deep suspicion.

54

What is the whole of modern philosophy doing at bottom? Since Descartes—actually more despite him than because of his precedent—all the philosophers seek to assassinate the old soul concept, under the guise of a critique of the subject-and-predicate concept—which means an attempt on the life of the basic presupposition of the Christian doctrine. Modern philosophy, being an epistemological skepticism, is, covertly or overtly, *anti-Christian*—although, to say this for the benefit of more refined ears, by no means anti-religious.

---

[13] Another suggestion for an "order of rank." Cf. section 39, note 19 above.
[14] Cf. *The Genealogy of Morals*, Third Essay, section 22.

For, formerly, one believed in "the soul" as one believed in grammar and the grammatical subject: one said, "I" is the condition, "think" is the predicate and conditioned—thinking is an activity to which thought *must* supply a subject as cause. Then one tried with admirable perseverance and cunning to get out of this net—and asked whether the opposite might not be the case: "think" the condition, "I" the conditioned; "I" in that case only a synthesis which is *made* by thinking. At bottom, *Kant* wanted to prove that, starting from the subject, the subject could not be proved—nor could the object: the possibility of a *merely apparent existence* of the subject, "the soul" in other words, may not always have remained strange to him—that thought which as Vedanta philosophy existed once before on this earth and exercised tremendous power.

55

There is a great ladder of religious cruelty, with many rungs; but three of these are the most important.

Once one sacrificed human beings to one's god, perhaps precisely those whom one loved most: the sacrifices of the first-born in all prehistoric religions belong here, as well as the sacrifice of the Emperor Tiberius in the Mithras grotto of the isle of Capri, that most gruesome of all Roman anachronisms.

Then, during the moral epoch of mankind, one sacrificed to one's god one's own strongest instincts, one's "nature": *this* festive joy lights up the cruel eyes of the ascetic, the "anti-natural" enthusiast.

Finally—what remained to be sacrificed? At long last, did one not have to sacrifice for once whatever is comforting, holy, healing; all hope, all faith in hidden harmony, in future blisses and justices? didn't one have to sacrifice God himself and, from cruelty against oneself, worship the stone, stupidity, gravity, fate, the nothing? To sacrifice God for the nothing—this paradoxical mystery of the final cruelty was reserved for the generation that is now coming up: all of us already know something of this.—

56

Whoever has endeavored with some enigmatic longing, as I have, to think pessimism through to its depths and to liberate it from the half-Christian, half-German narrowness and simplicity in which it has finally presented itself to our century, namely, in the form of Schopenhauer's philosophy; whoever has really, with an Asiatic and supra-Asiatic eye, looked into, down into the most world-denying of all possible ways of thinking—beyond good and evil and no longer, like the Buddha and Schopenhauer, under the spell and delusion of morality—may just thereby, without really meaning to do so, have opened his eyes to the opposite ideal: the ideal of the most high-spirited, alive, and world-affirming human being who has not only come to terms and learned to get along with whatever was and is, but who wants to have *what was and is* repeated into all eternity,[15] shouting insatiably *da capo*[16]—not only to himself but to the whole play and spectacle, and not only to a spectacle but at bottom to him who needs precisely this spectacle—and who makes it necessary because again and again he needs himself—and makes himself necessary——— What? And this wouldn't be—*circulus vitiosus deus?* [17]

57

With the strength of his spiritual eye and insight grows distance and, as it were, the space around man: his world becomes more profound; ever new stars, ever new riddles and images become visible for him. Perhaps everything on which the spirit's eye has exercised its acuteness and thoughtfulness was nothing but an

---

[15] An allusion to Nietzsche's doctrine of the eternal recurrence of all events. Cf. the penultimate chapter of *Thus Spoke Zarathustra,* especially sections 10 and 11 (*Portable Nietzsche,* pp. 435f.), and, for critical expositions, Kaufmann's *Nietzsche,* Chapter 11, section II, and A. Danto's *Nietzsche as Philosopher* (New York, Macmillan, 1965), Chapter 7.

[16] From the beginning: a musical direction.

[17] A vicious circle made god? or: God is a vicious circle? or, least likely: the circle is a vicious god?

occasion for this exercise, a playful matter, something for children and those who are childish. Perhaps the day will come when the most solemn concepts which have caused the most fights and suffering, the concepts "God" and "sin," will seem no more important to us than a child's toy and a child's pain seem to an old man—and perhaps "the old man" will then be in need of another toy and another pain—still child enough, an eternal child!

58

Has it ever been really noted to what extent a genuinely religious life (both its microscopic favorite occupation of self-examination and that tender composure which calls itself "prayer" and is a continual readiness for the "coming of God") requires a leisure class, or half-leisure—I mean leisure with a good conscience, from way back, by blood, to which the aristocratic feeling that work *disgraces* is not altogether alien—the feeling that it makes soul and body common. And that consequently our modern, noisy, time-consuming industriousness, proud of itself, stupidly proud, educates and prepares people, more than anything else does, precisely for "unbelief."

Among those, for example, who now live in Germany at a distance from religion I find people whose "free-thinking" is of diverse types and origins, but above all a majority of those in whom industriousness has, from generation unto generation, dissolved the religious instincts, so they no longer even know what religions are good for and merely register their presence in the world with a kind of dumb amazement. They feel abundantly committed, these good people, whether to their business or to their pleasures, not to speak of the "fatherland" and the newspapers and "family obligations": it seems that they simply have no time left for religion, the more so because it remains unclear to them whether it involves another business or another pleasure—for it is not possible, they say to themselves, that one goes to church merely to dampen one's good spirits. They are not enemies of religious customs; when participation in such customs is required in certain cases, by the state, for example, they do what is required, as one does so many things—with a patient and modest seriousness and without much curiosity and discomfort: they simply live too much apart and outside to feel any need for any pro and con in such matters.

Those indifferent in this way include today the great majority of German middle-class Protestants, especially in the great industrious centers of trade and traffic; also the great majority of industrious scholars and the other accessories of the universities (excepting the theologians, whose presence and possibility there pose ever increasing and ever subtler riddles for a psychologist). Pious or even merely churchly people rarely have the slightest idea *how much* good will—one might say caprice—is required of a German scholar today if he is to take the problem of religion seriously. On the basis of his whole trade (and, as noted, on the basis of the tradelike industriousness to which he is committed by his modern conscience) he is inclined toward a superior, almost good-natured amusement in the face of religion, occasionally mixed with a dash of disdain for the "uncleanliness" of the spirit which he assumes wherever a church is still acknowledged. The scholar succeeds only with the help of history (*not* on the basis of his own personal experience) to muster a reverent seriousness and a certain shy consideration in the face of religion. But even if he raises his feeling into real gratitude toward it,[18] he still has not personally approached, not even by a single step, what still exists now as church or piety; perhaps even the opposite. The practical indifference toward religious matters into which he has been born and brought up is generally sublimated in him into caution and cleanliness that shun contact with religious men and matters; and it may be precisely the depth of his tolerance and humanity that bids him dodge the subtle distress involved in tolerance.

Every age has its own divine type of naïveté for whose invention other ages may envy it—and how much naïveté, venerable, childlike, and boundlessly clumsy naïveté lies in the scholar's faith in his superiority, in the good conscience of his tolerance, in the un-

---

[18] In other words, even if he rises above all resentment and sees only the good done by religion.

suspecting simple certainty with which his instinct treats the religious man as an inferior and lower type that he has outgrown, leaving it behind, *beneath* him—him, that presumptuous little dwarf and rabble man, the assiduous and speedy head- and handiworker of "ideas," of "modern ideas"!

59

Anyone who has looked deeply into the world may guess how much wisdom lies in the superficiality of men. The instinct that preserves them teaches them to be flighty, light, and false. Here and there one encounters an impassioned and exaggerated worship of "pure forms," among both philosophers and artists: let nobody doubt that whoever stands that much in *need* of the cult of surfaces must at some time have reached *beneath* them with disastrous results.

Perhaps there even exists an order of rank among these burnt children, these born artists who can find the enjoyment of life only in the intention of *falsifying* its image (as it were, in a longwinded revenge on life): the degree to which life has been spoiled for them might be inferred from the degree to which they wish to see its image falsified, thinned down, transcendentalized, deified—the *homines religiosi* might be included among artists, as their highest rank.

It is the profound, suspicious fear of an incurable pessimism that forces whole millennia to bury their teeth in and cling to a religious interpretation of existence: the fear of that instinct which senses that one might get a hold of the truth *too soon,* before man has become strong enough, hard enough, artist enough.

Piety, the "life in God," seen in this way, would appear as the subtlest and final offspring of the *fear* of truth, as an artist's worship and intoxication before the most consistent of all falsifications, as the will to the inversion of truth, to untruth at any price. It may be that until now there has been no more potent means for beautifying man himself than piety: it can turn man into so much art, surface, play of colors, graciousness that his sight no longer makes one suffer.—

60

To love man *for God's sake*—that has so far been the noblest and most remote feeling attained among men. That the love of man is just one more stupidity and brutishness if there is no ulterior intent to sanctify it; that the inclination to such love of man must receive its measure, its subtlety, its grain of salt and dash of ambergris from some higher inclination—whoever the human being may have been who first felt and "experienced" this, however much his tongue may have stumbled [19] as it tried to express such *délicatesse,* let him remain holy and venerable for us for all time as the human being who has flown highest yet and gone astray most beautifully!

61

The philosopher as *we* understand him, we free spirits—as the man of the most comprehensive responsibility who has the conscience for the over-all development of man—this philosopher will make use of religions for his project of cultivation[20] and education, just as he will make use of whatever political and economic states are at hand. The selective and cultivating[21] influence, always destructive as well as creative and form-giving, which can be exerted with the help of religions, is always multiple and different according to the sort of human beings who are placed under its spell and protection. For the strong and independent who are prepared and predestined to command and in whom the reason and art of a governing race become incarnate, religion is one more means for overcoming resistances, for the ability to rule—as a bond that unites rulers and subjects and betrays and delivers the consciences of the latter, that which is most concealed and intimate and would like to elude obedience, to the former. And if a few individuals of such

---

[19] Probably an allusion to Exodus 4:10: the context requires us to think of Moses, in any case.

[20] *Seinem Züchtungs- und Erziehungswerke.*

[21] *Züchtende.*

noble descent are inclined through lofty spirituality to prefer a more withdrawn and contemplative life and reserve for themselves only the most subtle type of rule (over selected disciples or brothers in some order), then religion can even be used as a means for obtaining peace from the noise and exertion of *cruder* forms of government, and purity from the *necessary* dirt of all politics. That is how the Brahmins, for example, understood things: by means of a religious organization they gave themselves the power of nominating the kings of the people while they themselves kept and felt apart and outside, as men of higher and supra-royal tasks.

Meanwhile religion also gives to some of the ruled the instruction and opportunity to prepare themselves for future ruling and obeying: those slowly ascending classes—in which, thanks to fortunate marital customs, the strength and joy of the will, the will to self-control is ever growing—receive enough nudges and temptations from religion to walk the paths to higher spirituality, to test the feelings of great self-overcoming, of silence and solitude. Asceticism and puritanism are almost indispensable means for educating and ennobling a race that wishes to become master over its origins among the rabble and that works its way up toward future rule.

To ordinary human beings, finally—the vast majority who exist for service and the general advantage, and who *may* exist only for that—religion gives an inestimable contentment with their situation and type, manifold peace of the heart, an ennobling of obedience, one further happiness and sorrow with their peers and something transfiguring and beautifying, something of a justification for the whole everyday character, the whole lowliness, the whole half-brutish poverty of their souls. Religion and religious significance spread the splendor of the sun over such ever-toiling human beings and make their own sight tolerable to them. Religion has the same effect which an Epicurean philosophy has on sufferers of a higher rank: it is refreshing, refining, makes, as it were, the most of suffering, and in the end even sanctifies and justifies. Perhaps nothing in Christianity or Buddhism is as venerable as their art of teaching even the lowliest how to place themselves through piety in an illusory higher order of things and thus to maintain their contentment with the real order, in which their life is hard enough—and precisely this hardness is necessary.

62

In the end, to be sure—to present the other side of the account of these religions, too, and to expose their uncanny dangerousness—one always pays dearly and terribly when religions do *not* want to be a means of education and cultivation in the philosopher's hand but insist on having their own *sovereign* way, when they themselves want to be ultimate ends and not means among other means. There is among men as in every other animal species an excess of failures, of the sick, degenerating, infirm, who suffer necessarily; the successful cases are, among men too, always the exception—and in view of the fact that man is the *as yet undetermined animal,* the rare exception. But still worse: the higher the type of man that a man represents, the greater the improbability that he will turn out *well.* The accidental, the law of absurdity in the whole economy of mankind, manifests itself most horribly in its destructive effect on the higher men whose complicated conditions of life can only be calculated with great subtlety and difficulty.

What, then, is the attitude of the above-mentioned two greatest religions toward this *excess* of cases that did not turn out right? They seek to preserve, to preserve alive whatever can possibly be preserved; indeed, as a matter of principle, they side with these cases as religions for *sufferers;* they agree with all those who suffer life like a sickness and would like to make sure that every other feeling about life should be considered false and should become impossible. Even if the very highest credit is given to this considerate and preserving care, which, besides being directed toward all the others, was and is also directed toward the highest type of man, the type that so far has almost always suffered most; nevertheless, in a total accounting, the *sovereign* religions we have had so far are among the chief causes that have kept the type "man" on a lower rung—they have preserved too much of *what ought to perish.* What we have to thank them for is inestimable; and who could be rich enough in gratitude not to be impoverished in view of all that the "spiritual men" of Christianity, for example, have so far done for Europe! And yet, when they gave comfort to sufferers, courage to the oppressed and despairing, a staff and support to the dependent, and lured away from society into monasteries and penitentiaries for the soul those who had been destroyed inwardly and who had become savage: how much more did they have to do besides, in order to work with a good conscience and on principle, to preserve all that was sick and that suffered—which means, in fact and in truth, to *worsen the European race?* Stand all valuations *on their head—that* is what they had to do. And break the strong, sickly o'er[22] great hopes, cast suspicion on the joy in beauty, bend everything haughty, manly, conquering, domineering, all the instincts characteristic of the highest and best-turned-out type of "man," into unsureness, agony of conscience, self-destruction—indeed, invert all love of the earthly and of dominion over the earth into hatred of the earth and the earthly—*that* is the task the church posed for itself and had to pose, until in its estimation "becoming unworldly," "unsensual," and "higher men" were fused into a single feeling.

Suppose we could contemplate the oddly painful and equally crude and subtle comedy of European Christianity with the mocking and aloof eyes of an Epicurean god, I think our amazement and laughter would never end: doesn't it seem that a single will dominated Europe for eighteen centuries—to turn man into a *sublime miscarriage?* Anyone, however, who approached this almost deliberate degeneration and atrophy of man represented by the Christian European (Pascal, for example), feeling the opposite kind of desire, not in an Epicurean spirit but rather with some divine hammer in his hand, would surely have to cry out in wrath, in pity, in horror: "O you dolts, you presumptuous, pitying dolts, what have you done! Was that work for your hands? How have you bungled and botched my beautiful stone! What presumption!"

I meant to say: Christianity has been the most calamitous

---

22 An allusion to Hamlet's "sicklied o'er by the pale cast of thought."

kind of arrogance yet. Men, not high and hard enough to have any right to try to form *man* as artists; men, not strong and far-sighted enough to *let* the foreground law of thousandfold failure and ruin prevail, though it cost them sublime self-conquest; men, not noble enough to see the abysmally different order of rank, chasm of rank, between man and man—*such* men have so far held sway over the fate of Europe, with their "equal before God," until finally a smaller, almost ridiculous type, a herd animal, something eager to please, sickly, and mediocre has been bred, the European of today—

PART FOUR

---❖---

EPIGRAMS AND INTERLUDES

Part Four

63

Whoever is a teacher through and through takes all things seriously only in relation to his students—even himself.

64

"Knowledge for its own sake"—that is the last snare of morality: with that one becomes completely entangled in it once more.

65

The attraction of knowledge would be small if one did not have to overcome so much shame on the way.

65a[1]

One is most dishonest to one's god: he is not *allowed* to sin.

66

The inclination to depreciate himself, to let himself be robbed, lied to, and taken advantage of, could be the modesty[2] of a god among men.

67

Love of *one* is a barbarism; for it is exercised at the expense of all others. The love of God, too.

---

[1] In the original edition of 1886 and in the second edition of 1891 this section bears the same number (65) as that preceding it. In the third and fourth editions of 1893 and 1894, the editor introduced minor changes and renumbered all the sections from this point on. In the standard editions (the so-called Grossoktav and the Musarion editions) this section is distinguished from the one preceding it by the addition of an "a." Schlechta, whose edition of the works in three volumes is widely considered impeccable philologically. follows the standard editions although he purports to follow the edition of 1886. Similar instances will be noted in subsequent notes.

[2] *Scham:* in most other places (see sections 40 and 65 above) this word has been translated as "shame."

68

"I have done that," says my memory. "I cannot have done that," says my pride, and remains inexorable. Eventually—memory yields.[3]

69

One has watched life badly if one has not also seen the hand that considerately—kills.

70

If one has character one also has one's typical experience, which recurs repeatedly.

71

The sage as astronomer.— As long as you still experience the stars as something "above you" you lack the eye of knowledge.

72

Not the intensity but the duration of high feelings makes high men.

73

Whoever reaches his ideal transcends it *eo ipso*.

73a[4]

Many a peacock hides his peacock tail from all eyes—and calls that his pride.

74

A man with spirit is unbearable if he does not also have at least two other things: gratitude[5] and cleanliness.

---

[3] Freud's theory of repression *in nuce*—or *in ovo*. Other sections that put one in mind of Freud include 3 above and 75 below; but this list could easily be lengthened.

[4] See section 65a, note 1, above.

[5] Again, as in sections 49 and 58, gratitude is virtually an antonym of resentment.

75

The degree and kind of a man's sexuality reach up into the ultimate pinnacle of his spirit.

76

Under peaceful conditions a warlike man sets upon himself.

77

With one's principles one wants to bully one's habits, or justify, honor, scold, or conceal them: two men with the same principles probably aim with them at something basically different.

78

Whoever despises himself still respects himself as one who despises.

79

A soul that knows it is loved but does not itself love betrays its sediment: what is at the bottom comes up.

80

A matter that becomes clear ceases to concern us.— What was on the mind of that god who counseled: "Know thyself!" Did he mean: "Cease to concern yourself! Become objective!"— And Socrates?— And "scientific men"?—

81

It is terrible to die of thirst in the ocean. Do you have to salt your truth so heavily that it does not even—quench thirst any more?

82

"Pity for all"—would be hardness and tyranny toward *you*, my dear neighbor!—

83

Instinct.— When the house burns one forgets even lunch.— Yes, but one eats it later in the ashes.

84

Woman learns to hate to the extent to which her charms—decrease.

85

The same affects in man and woman are yet different in *tempo:* therefore man and woman do not cease to misunderstand each other.

86

Women themselves always still have in the background of all personal vanity an impersonal contempt—for "woman."—

87

Tethered heart, free spirit.— If one tethers one's heart severely and imprisons it, one can give one's spirit many liberties: I have said that once before. But one does not believe me, unless one already knows it—

88

One begins to mistrust very clever people when they become embarrassed.

89

Terrible experiences pose the riddle whether the person who has them is not terrible.

90

Heavy, heavy-spirited people become lighter precisely through what makes others heavier, through hatred and love, and for a time they surface.

91

So cold, so icy that one burns one's fingers on him! Every hand is startled when touching him.— And for that very reason some think he glows.

92

Who has not, for the sake of his good reputation—sacrificed himself once?—

93

Affability contains no hatred of men, but for that very reason too much contempt for men.

94

A man's maturity—consists in having found again the seriousness one had as a child, at play.

95

To be ashamed of one's immorality—that is a step on the staircase at whose end one is also ashamed of one's morality.

96

One should part from life as Odysseus parted from Nausicaa—blessing it rather than in love with it.

97

What? A great man? I always see only the actor of his own ideal.

98

If we train our conscience, it kisses us while it hurts us.

99

The voice of disappointment:[6] "I listened for an echo and heard nothing but praise—"

100

In front of ourselves we all pose as simpler than we are: thus we take a rest from our fellow men.

---

[6] Emphasized in most editions, but not in that of 1886 nor in Schlechta's.

101

Today the man of knowledge might well feel like God become animal.

102·

Discovering that one is loved in return really ought to disenchant the lover with the beloved. "What? this person is modest enough to love even you? Or stupid enough? Or—or—"

103

Danger in happiness.[7]— "Now everything redounds to my best, now I love every destiny—who feels like being my destiny?"

104

Not their love of men but the impotence of their love of men keeps the Christians of today from—burning us.[8]

105

The *pia fraus*[9] offends the taste (the "piety") of the free spirit, who has "the piety of the search for knowledge," even more than the *impia fraus*. Hence his profound lack of understanding for the church, a characteristic of the type "free spirit"—*his* unfreedom.

106

In music the passions enjoy themselves.

107

Once the decision has been made, close your ear even to the best counterargument: sign of a strong character. Thus an occasional will to stupidity.

---

[7] See note 6 above.

[8] If Christians were really passionately concerned for the salvation of their fellow men in the hereafter, they would still burn those whose heresies lead legions into eternal damnation.

[9] "Pious fraud" or holy lie; here juxtaposed with "impious fraud" or unholy lie. The former means deceiving men for the sake of their own salvation, as in Plato's *Republic*, 414C.

108

There are no moral phenomena at all, but only a moral interpretation of phenomena—

109

A criminal is frequently not equal to his deed: he makes it smaller and slanders it.[10]

110

The lawyers defending a criminal are rarely artists enough to turn the beautiful terribleness of his deed to his advantage.

111

Our vanity is hardest to wound when our pride has just been wounded.

112

Those who feel predestined to see and not to believe will find all believers too noisy and obtrusive: they fend them off.

113

"You want to prepossess him in your favor? Then pretend to be embarrassed in his presence—"

114

The enormous expectation in sexual love and the sense of shame in this expectation spoils all perspective for women from the start.

115

Where neither love nor hatred is in the game, a woman's game is mediocre.

---

[10] One of Sartre's leitmotifs; cf. Electra in *Les Mouches* (*The Flies*) and the problem of *Les Mains sales* (*Dirty Hands*).

116

The great epochs of our life come when we gain the courage to rechristen our evil as what is best in us.

117

The will to overcome an affect is ultimately only the will of another, or of several other, affects.

118

There is an innocence in admiration; it is found in those to whom it has never yet occurred that they, too, might be admired some day.

119

The disgust with dirt can be so great that it keeps us from cleaning ourselves—from "justifying" ourselves.

120

Sensuality often hastens the growth of love so much that the roots remain weak and are easily torn up.

121

It was subtle of God to learn Greek when he wished to become an author—and not to learn it better.

122

Enjoying praise is in some people merely a courtesy of the heart—and just the opposite of vanity of the spirit.

123

Even concubinage has been corrupted—by marriage.

124

Whoever rejoices on the very stake triumphs not over pain but at the absence of pain that he had expected. A parable.

125

When we have to change our mind about a person, we hold the inconvenience he causes us very much against him.

126

A people[11] is a detour of nature to get to six or seven great men.— Yes, and then to get around them.

127

Science offends the modesty of all real women. It makes them feel as if one wanted to peep under their skin—yet worse, under their dress and finery.

128

The more abstract the truth is that you would teach, the more you have to seduce the senses to it.

129

The devil has the broadest perspectives for God; therefore he keeps so far away from God—the devil being the most ancient friend of wisdom.

130

What a man *is* begins to betray itself when his talent decreases —when he stops showing what he *can do*. Talent, too, is finery; finery, too, is a hiding place.

131

The sexes deceive themselves about each other—because at bottom they honor and love only themselves (or their own ideal, to put it more pleasantly). Thus man likes woman peaceful—but woman is *essentially* unpeaceful, like a cat, however well she may have trained herself to seem peaceable.

---

[11] *Ein Volk:* the polemical and sarcastic thrust of this epigram depends on the heavy reliance of German nationalism—both in Nietzsche's time and in the twentieth century—on the mystique of the *Volk*.

132

One is best punished for one's virtues.

133

Whoever does not know how to find the way to *his* ideal lives more frivolously and impudently than the man without an ideal.

134

All credibility, all good conscience, all evidence of truth come only from the senses.

135

Pharisaism is not a degeneration in a good man: a good deal of it is rather the condition of all being good.

136

One seeks a midwife for his thoughts, another someone whom he can help: origin of a good conversation.

137

When associating with scholars and artists we easily miscalculate in opposite directions: behind a remarkable scholar one finds, not infrequently, a mediocre man, and behind a mediocre artist quite often—a very remarkable man.

138

When we are awake we also do what we do in our dreams: we invent and make up the person with whom we associate—and immediately forget it.

139

In revenge and in love woman is more barbarous than man.

140

Rule as a riddle.— "If the bond shan't burst—bite upon it first."

141

The abdomen is the reason why man does not easily take himself for a god.

142

The chastest words I have heard: *"Dans le véritable amour c'est l'âme, qui enveloppe le corps."* [12]

143

Our vanity desires that what we do best should be considered what is hardest for us. Concerning the origin of many a morality.

144

When a woman has scholarly inclinations there is usually something wrong with her sexually. Sterility itself disposes one toward a certain masculinity of taste; for man is, if I may say so, "the sterile animal."

145

Comparing man and woman on the whole, one may say: woman would not have the genius for finery if she did not have an instinct for a *secondary* role.

146

Whoever fights monsters should see to it that in the process he does not become a monster. And when you look long into an abyss, the abyss also looks into you.

147

From old Florentine novels; also—from life: *"Buona femmina e mala femmina vuol bastone."* [13] Sacchetti, Nov. 86.

148

Seducing one's neighbor to a good opinion and afterwards be-

---

[12] "In true love it is the soul that envelops the body."
[13] "Good and bad women want a stick."

lieving piously in this opinion—who could equal women in this art?—

149

What a time experiences as evil is usually an untimely echo of what was formerly experienced as good—the atavism of a more ancient ideal.

150

Around the hero everything turns into a tragedy; around the demi-god, into a satyr play; and around God—what? perhaps into "world"?—

151

Having a talent is not enough: one also requires your permission for it—right, my friends?

152

"Where the tree of knowledge stands, there is always Paradise": thus speak the oldest and the youngest serpents.

153

Whatever is done from love always occurs beyond good and evil.

154

Objections, digressions, gay mistrust, the delight in mockery are signs of health: everything unconditional belongs in pathology.

155

The sense of the tragic gains and wanes with sensuality.

156

Madness is rare in individuals—but in groups, parties, nations, and ages it is the rule.

157

The thought of suicide is a powerful comfort: it helps one through many a dreadful night.

158

To our strongest drive, the tyrant in us, not only our reason bows but also our conscience.

159

One *has* to repay good and ill—but why precisely to the person who has done us good or ill?

160

One no longer loves one's insight enough once one communicates it.

161

Poets treat their experiences shamelessly: they exploit them.

162

"Our neighbor[14]—is not our neighbor but *his* neighbor"—thus thinks every nation.

163

Love brings the high and concealed characteristics of the lover into the light—what is rare and exceptional in him: to that extent it easily deceives regarding his normality.

164

Jesus said to his Jews: "The law was for servants—love God as I love him, as his son! What are morals to us sons of God!"

165

Regarding all parties.— A shepherd always needs a bell-wether—or he himself must occasionally be a wether.

---

[14] In the religious sense.

166

Even when the mouth lies, the way it looks still tells the truth.

167

In men who are hard, intimacy involves shame—and is precious.

168

Christianity gave Eros poison to drink: he did not die of it but degenerated—into a vice.

169

Talking much about oneself can also be a means to conceal oneself.

170

Praise is more obtrusive than a reproach.

171

In a man devoted to knowledge, pity seems almost ridiculous, like delicate hands on a cyclops.

172

From love of man one occasionally embraces someone at random (because one cannot embrace all): but one must not tell him this—

173

One does not hate as long as one still despises, but only those whom one esteems equal or higher.

174

You utilitarians, you, too, love everything *useful* only as a *vehicle* for your inclinations; you, too, really find the noise of its wheels insufferable?

175

In the end one loves one's desire and not what is desired.

176

The vanity of others offends our taste only when it offends our vanity.

177

Perhaps nobody yet has been truthful enough about what "truthfulness" is.

178

One does not credit clever people with their follies: what a loss of human rights!

179

The consequences of our actions take hold of us, quite indifferent to our claim that meanwhile we have "improved."

180

There is an innocence in lying which is the sign of good faith in a cause.

181

It is inhuman to bless where one is cursed.

182

The familiarity of those who are superior embitters because it may not be returned.—

183

"Not that you lied to me, but that I no longer believe you, has shaken me"—

184

The high spirits of kindness may look like malice.

185

"I don't like him."— Why?— "I am not equal to him."—
Has any human being ever answered that way?

PART FIVE

---◈---

NATURAL HISTORY
OF MORALS

Part Five

186

The moral sentiment in Europe today is as refined, old, diverse, irritable, and subtle, as the "science of morals" that accompanies it is still young, raw, clumsy, and butterfingered—an attractive contrast that occasionally even becomes visible and incarnate in the person of a moralist. Even the term "science of morals" is much too arrogant considering what it designates, and offends *good* taste—which always prefers more modest terms.

One should own up in all strictness to what is still necessary here for a long time to come, to what alone is justified so far: to collect material, to conceptualize and arrange a vast realm of subtle feelings of value and differences of value which are alive, grow, beget, and perish—and perhaps attempts to present vividly some of the more frequent and recurring forms of such living crystallizations—all to prepare a *typology* of morals.

To be sure, so far one has not been so modest. With a stiff seriousness that inspires laughter, all our philosophers demanded something far more exalted, presumptuous, and solemn from themselves as soon as they approached the study of morality: they wanted to supply a *rational foundation* for morality—and every philosopher so far has believed that he has provided such a foundation. Morality itself, however, was accepted as "given." How remote from their clumsy pride was that task which they considered insignificant and left in dust and must—the task of description—although the subtlest fingers and senses can scarcely be subtle enough for it.

Just because our moral philosophers knew the facts of morality only very approximately in arbitrary extracts or in accidental epitomes—for example, as the morality of their environment, their class, their church, the spirit of their time, their climate and part of the world—just because they were poorly informed and not even very curious about different peoples, times, and past ages—they never laid eyes on the real problems of morality; for these emerge only when we compare *many* moralities. In all "science of morals" so far one thing was *lacking,* strange as it may sound: the problem of morality itself; what was lacking was any suspicion that there was something problematic here. What the philosophers called "a rational foundation for morality" and tried to supply was, seen in the right light, merely a scholarly variation of the common *faith* in the prevalent morality; a new means of *expression* for this faith; and thus just another fact within a particular morality; indeed, in the last analysis a kind of denial that this morality might ever be considered problematic—certainly the very opposite of an examination, analysis, questioning, and vivisection of this very faith.

Listen, for example, with what almost venerable innocence Schopenhauer still described his task, and then draw your conclusions about the scientific standing of a "science" whose ultimate masters still talk like children and little old women: "The principle," he says (p. 136 of *Grundprobleme der Moral*),[1] "the fundamental

---

[1] First edition of 1886 and second edition of 1891: "das Princip, sagt er (p. 136 der Grundprobleme der Moral), der Grundsatz . . ."

Musarion edition of the *Werke:* "das Princip, sagt er (p. 137 der Grundprobleme der Ethik), der Grundsatz . . ."

Schlechta's edition, which purports to follow the original edition, actually departs even a little further from it than the Musarionausgabe: "das Princip" sagt er (S. 137 der Grundprobleme der Ethik), "der Grundsatz . . ."

The correct title of Schopenhauer's book is *Die beiden Grundprobleme der Ethik* (the two fundamental problems of ethics), and in the original edition of 1841 the quoted passage is found on p. 138. Nietzsche neither placed the title in quotes nor italicized it, and his slight variation of the title is less odd than the fact that on Schopenhauer's own title page of 1841 the title of the second essay, which Nietzsche cites, is given as *"Ueber das Fundament der Moral, nicht gekrönt* von der K. Dänischen Societät der Wissenschaften, zu Kopenhagen, den 30. Januar 1840" ("On the Foundation of Morals, not awarded a prize by the Danish Royal Society . . ."). Turning the page, one finds the table of contents, in which the title of the second essay is given as follows: *"Preisschrift über die Grundlage der Moral"* (Prize essay on the basis of morals). (The heading on p. 101 agrees with the table of contents, not with Schopenhauer's title page.) If Schopenhauer could say in one instance *Fundament* and in the other *Grundlage,* Nietzsche might as well say *Moral* instead of *Ethik;* moreover, the word in the title that concerned Nietzsche was *Moral,* not *Ethik.*

The editors who changed the title and page reference given by Nietzsche failed to insert three dots in the quotation itself, to indicate a minor omis-

proposition on whose contents all moral philosophers are *really*[2] agreed—*neminem laede, immo omnes, quantum potes, juva*[3]— that is *really* the proposition for which all moralists endeavor to find the rational foundation . . . the *real* basis of ethics for which one has been looking for thousands of years as for the philosopher's stone."

The difficulty of providing a rational foundation for the principle cited may indeed be great—as is well known, Schopenhauer did not succeed either—and whoever has once felt deeply how insipidly false and sentimental this principle is in a world whose essence is will to power, may allow himself to be reminded that Schopenhauer, though a pessimist, *really*—played the flute. Every day, after dinner: one should read his biography on that. And incidentally: a pessimist, one who denies God and the world but *comes to a stop* before morality—who affirms morality and plays the flute—the *laede neminem* morality—what? is that really—a pessimist?

187

Even apart from the value of such claims as "there is a categorical imperative in us," one can still always ask: what does such a claim tell us about the man who makes it? There are moralities which are meant to justify their creator before others. Other moralities are meant to calm him and lead him to be satisfied with himself. With yet others he wants to crucify himself and humiliate himself. With others he wants to wreak revenge, with others conceal himself, with others transfigure himself and place himself way up, at a distance. This morality is used by its creator to forget, that one to have others forget him or something about him. Some moralists want to vent their power and creative whims on humanity; some others,

---

sion of two and a half lines between "agreed" and the Latin quotation. This omission does not change the sense and is in no way unfair to Schopenhauer.

[2] "Really" and "real": *eigentlich.* The emphasis is Nietzsche's, not Schopenhauer's.

[3] "Hurt no one; rather, help all as much as you can."

perhaps including Kant, suggest with their morality: "What deserves respect in me is that I can obey—and you *ought* not to be different from me."— In short, moralities are also merely a *sign language of the affects.*

188

Every morality is, as opposed to *laisser aller,*[4] a bit of tyranny against "nature"; also against "reason"; but this in itself is no objection, as long as we do not have some other morality which permits us to decree that every kind of tyranny and unreason is impermissible. What is essential and inestimable in every morality is that it constitutes a long compulsion: to understand Stoicism or Port-Royal or Puritanism, one should recall the compulsion under which every language so far has achieved strength and freedom— the metrical compulsion of rhyme and rhythm.

How much trouble the poets and orators of all peoples have taken—not excepting a few prose writers today in whose ear there dwells an inexorable conscience—"for the sake of some foolishness," as utilitarian dolts say, feeling smart—"submitting abjectly to capricious laws," as anarchists say, feeling "free," even "free-spirited." But the curious fact is that all there is or has been on earth of freedom, subtlety, boldness, dance, and masterly sureness, whether in thought itself or in government, or in rhetoric and persuasion, in the arts just as in ethics, has developed only owing to the "tyranny of such capricious laws"; and in all seriousness, the probability is by no means small that precisely this is "nature" and "natural"—and *not* that *laisser aller.*

Every artist knows how far from any feeling of letting himself go his "most natural" state is—the free ordering, placing, disposing, giving form in the moment of "inspiration"—and how strictly and subtly he obeys thousandfold laws precisely then, laws that precisely on account of their hardness and determination defy all formulation through concepts (even the firmest concept is, com-

---

[4] Letting go.

pared with them, not free of fluctuation, multiplicity, and ambiguity).

What is essential "in heaven and on earth" seems to be, to say it once more, that there should be *obedience* over a long period of time and in a *single* direction: given that, something always develops, and has developed, for whose sake it is worth while to live on earth; for example, virtue, art, music, dance, reason, spirituality—something transfiguring, subtle, mad, and divine. The long unfreedom of the spirit, the mistrustful constraint in the communicability of thoughts, the discipline thinkers imposed on themselves to think within the directions laid down by a church or court, or under Aristotelian presuppositions, the long spiritual will to interpret all events under a Christian schema and to rediscover and justify the Christian god in every accident—all this, however forced, capricious, hard, gruesome, and anti-rational, has shown itself to be the means through which the European spirit has been trained to strength, ruthless curiosity, and subtle mobility, though admittedly in the process an irreplaceable amount of strength and spirit had to be crushed, stifled, and ruined (for here, as everywhere, "nature" manifests herself as she is, in all her prodigal and indifferent magnificence which is outrageous but noble).

That for thousands of years European thinkers thought merely in order to prove something—today, conversely, we suspect every thinker who "wants to prove something"—that the conclusions that *ought* to be the result of their most rigorous reflection were always settled from the start, just as it used to be with Asiatic astrology, and still is today with the innocuous Christian-moral interpretation of our most intimate personal experiences "for the glory of God" and "for the salvation of the soul"—this tyranny, this caprice, this rigorous and grandiose stupidity has *educated* the spirit. Slavery is, as it seems, both in the cruder and in the more subtle sense, the indispensable means of spiritual discipline and cultivation,[5] too. Consider any morality with this in mind: what there is in it of "nature" teaches hatred of the *laisser aller,* of any all-too-great

---

[5] *Zucht und Züchtung.*

freedom, and implants the need for limited horizons and the nearest tasks—teaching the *narrowing of our perspective,* and thus in a certain sense stupidity, as a condition of life and growth.

"You shall obey—someone and for a long time: *else* you will perish and lose the last respect for yourself"—this appears to me to be the moral imperative of nature which, to be sure, is neither "categorical" as the old Kant would have it (hence the "else") nor addressed to the individual (what do individuals matter to her?), but to peoples, races, ages, classes—but above all to the whole human animal, to *man.*

189

Industrious races find it very troublesome to endure leisure: it was a masterpiece of *English* instinct to make the Sabbath so holy and so boring that the English begin unconsciously to lust again for their work- and week-day. It is a kind of cleverly invented, cleverly inserted *fast,* the like of which is also encountered frequently in the ancient world (although, in fairness to southern peoples, not exactly in regard to work). There have to be fasts of many kinds; and wherever powerful drives and habits prevail, legislators have to see to it that intercalary days are inserted on which such a drive is chained and learns again to hunger. Viewed from a higher vantage point, whole generations and ages that make their appearance, infected with some moral fanaticism, seem to be such times of constraint and fasting during which a drive learns to stoop and submit, but also to *purify* and *sharpen* itself. A few philosophical sects, too, permit such an interpretation (for example, the Stoa in the midst of Hellenistic culture with its lascivious atmosphere, overcharged with aphrodisiac odors).

This is also a hint for an explanation of the paradox: why it was precisely during the most Christian period of Europe and altogether only under the pressure of Christian value judgments that the sex drive sublimated [6] itself into love (*amour-passion*).

---

[6] Nietzsche was the first to use *sublimiren* in its specifically modern sense, which is widely associated with Freud. On the history of this interesting term see Kaufmann's *Nietzsche,* Chapter 7, section II.

190

There is something in the morality of Plato that does not really belong to Plato but is merely encountered in his philosophy—one might say, in spite of Plato: namely, the Socratism for which he was really too noble. "Nobody wants to do harm to himself, therefore all that is bad is done involuntarily. For the bad do harm to themselves: this they would not do if they knew that the bad is bad. Hence the bad are bad only because of an error; if one removes the error, one necessarily makes them—good."

This type of inference smells of the *rabble* that sees nothing in bad actions but the unpleasant consequences and really judges, "it is *stupid* to do what is bad," while "good" is taken without further ado to be identical with "useful and agreeable." In the case of every moral utilitarianism one may immediately infer the same origin and follow one's nose: one will rarely go astray.

Plato did everything he could in order to read something refined and noble into the proposition of his teacher—above all, himself. He was the most audacious of all interpreters and took the whole Socrates only the way one picks a popular tune and folk song from the streets in order to vary it into the infinite and impossible—namely, into all of his own masks and multiplicities. In a jest, Homeric at that: what is the Platonic Socrates after all if not *prosthe Platōn opithen te Platōn messē te Chimaira.*[7]

191

The ancient theological problem of "faith" and "knowledge" —or, more clearly, of instinct and reason—in other words, the question whether regarding the valuation of things instinct deserves more authority than rationality, which wants us to evaluate

---

[7] "Plato in front and Plato behind, in the middle Chimaera." Cf. *Iliad,* VI:181, where Chimaera is described: "Lion in front and serpent behind, in the middle a goat." For Nietzsche's complex and seemingly contradictory view of Socrates, see Kaufmann's *Nietzsche,* Chapter 13.

and act in accordance with reasons, with a "why?"—in other words, in accordance with expedience and utility—this is still the ancient moral problem that first emerged in the person of Socrates and divided thinking people long before Christianity. Socrates himself, to be sure, with the taste of his talent—that of a superior dialectician—had initially sided with reason; and in fact, what did he do his life long but laugh at the awkward incapacity of noble Athenians who, like all noble men, were men of instinct and never could give sufficient information about the reasons for their actions? In the end, however, privately and secretly, he laughed at himself, too: in himself he found, before his subtle conscience and self-examination, the same difficulty and incapacity. But is that any reason, he encouraged himself, for giving up the instincts? One has to see to it that they as well as reason receive their due—one must follow the instincts but persuade reason to assist them with good reasons. This was the real *falseness* of that great ironic, so rich in secrets; he got his conscience to be satisfied with a kind of self-trickery: at bottom, he had seen through the irrational element in moral judgments.

Plato, more innocent in such matters and lacking the craftiness of the plebeian, wanted to employ all his strength—the greatest strength any philosopher so far has had at his disposal—to prove to himself that reason and instinct of themselves tend toward one goal, the good, "God." And since Plato, all theologians and philosophers are on the same track—that is, in moral matters it has so far been instinct, or what the Christians call "faith," or "the herd," as I put it, that has triumphed. Perhaps Descartes should be excepted, as the father of rationalism (and hence the grandfather of the Revolution) who conceded authority to reason alone: but reason is merely an instrument, and Descartes was superficial.

192

Whoever has traced the history of an individual science finds a clue in its development for understanding the most ancient and common processes of all "knowledge and cognition." There as here it is the rash hypotheses, the fictions, the good dumb will to "believe," the lack of mistrust and patience that are developed first; our senses learn only late, and never learn entirely, to be subtle, faithful, and cautious organs of cognition. Our eye finds it more comfortable to respond to a given stimulus by reproducing once more an image that it has produced many times before, instead of registering what is different and new in an impression. The latter would require more strength, more "morality." Hearing something new is embarrassing and difficult for the ear; foreign music we do not hear well. When we hear another language we try involuntarily to form the sounds we hear into words that sound more familiar and more like home to us: thus the German, for example, transformed *arcubalista,* when he heard that, into *Armbrust.*[8] What is new finds our senses, too, hostile and reluctant; and even in the "simplest" processes of sensation the affects dominate, such as fear, love, hatred, including the passive affects of laziness.

Just as little as a reader today reads all of the individual words (let alone syllables) on a page—rather he picks about five words at random out of twenty and "guesses" at the meaning that probably belongs to these five words—just as little do we see a tree exactly and completely with reference to leaves, twigs, color, and form; it is so very much easier for us simply to improvise some approximation of a tree. Even in the midst of the strangest experiences we still do the same: we make up the major part of the experience and can scarcely be forced *not* to contemplate some event as its "inventors." All this means: basically and from time immemorial we are—*accustomed to lying.* Or to put it more virtuously and hypocritically, in short, more pleasantly: one is much more of an artist than one knows.

In an animated conversation I often see the face of the person with whom I am talking so clearly and so subtly determined in accordance with the thought he expresses, or that I believe has been produced in him, that this degree of clarity far surpasses my powers of vision: so the subtle shades of the play of the muscles and the expression of the eyes *must* have been made up by me. Probably the person made an altogether different face, or none at all.

---

[8] Literally, arm-breast; both words mean crossbow.

193

Quidquid luce fuit, tenebris agit:[9] but the other way around, too. What we experience in dreams—assuming that we experience it often—belongs in the end just as much to the over-all economy of our soul as anything experienced "actually": we are richer or poorer on account of it, have one need more or less, and finally are led a little by the habits of our dreams even in broad daylight and in the most cheerful moments of our wide-awake spirit.

Suppose someone has flown often in his dreams and finally, as soon as he dreams, he is conscious of his power and art of flight as if it were his privilege, also his characteristic and enviable happiness. He believes himself capable of realizing every kind of arc and angle simply with the lightest impulse; he knows the feeling of a certain divine frivolity, an "upward" without tension and constraint, a "downward" without condescension and humiliation—without *gravity!* How could a human being who had had such dream experiences and dream habits fail to find that the word "happiness" had a different color and definition in his waking life, too? How could he fail to—desire happiness differently? "Rising" as described by poets must seem to him, compared with this "flying," too earthbound, muscle-bound, forced, too "grave."

194

The difference among men becomes manifest not only in the difference between their tablets of goods—in the fact that they consider different goods worth striving for and also disagree about what is more and less valuable, about the order of rank of the goods they recognize in common—it becomes manifest even more in what they take for really *having* and *possessing* something good.

Regarding a woman, for example, those men who are more modest consider the mere use of the body and sexual gratification a sufficient and satisfying sign of "having," of possession. Another

---

9 "What occurred in the light, goes on in the dark."

type, with a more suspicious and demanding thirst for possession, sees the "question mark," the illusory quality of such "having" and wants subtler tests, above all in order to know whether the woman does not only give herself to him but also gives up for his sake what she has or would like to have: only then does she seem to him "possessed." A third type, however, does not reach the end of his mistrust and desire for having even so: he asks himself whether the woman, when she gives up everything for him, does not possibly do this for a phantom of him. He wants to be known deep down, abysmally deep down, before he is capable of being loved at all; he dares to let himself be fathomed. He feels that his beloved is fully in his possession only when she no longer deceives herself about him, when she loves him just as much for his devilry and hidden insatiability as for his graciousness, patience, and spirituality.

One type wants to possess a people—and all the higher arts of a Cagliostro and Catiline suit him to that purpose. Someone else, with a more subtle thirst for possession, says to himself: "One may not deceive where one wants to possess." The idea that a mask of him might command the heart of the people[10] irritates him and makes him impatient: "So I must *let* myself be known, and first must know myself."

Among helpful and charitable people one almost regularly encounters that clumsy ruse which first doctors the person to be helped—as if, for example, he "deserved" help, required just *their* help, and would prove to be profoundly grateful for all help, faithful and submissive. With these fancies they dispose of the needy as of possessions, being charitable and helpful people from a desire for possessions. One finds them jealous if one crosses or anticipates them when they want to help.

Involuntarily, parents turn children into something similar to themselves—they call that "education." Deep in her heart, no mother doubts that the child she has borne is her property; no father contests his own right to subject it to *his* concepts and valuations. Indeed, formerly it seemed fair for fathers (among the ancient Germans, for example) to decide on the life or death of the new-

---

[10] This, of course, was what happened to Nietzsche himself after his death.

born as they saw fit. And like the father, teachers, classes, priests, and princes still see, even today, in every new human being an unproblematic opportunity for another possession. So it follows——

195

The Jews—a people "born for slavery," as Tacitus and the whole ancient world say; "the chosen people among the peoples," as they themselves say and believe—the Jews have brought off that miraculous feat of an inversion of values, thanks to which life on earth has acquired a novel and dangerous attraction for a couple of millennia: their prophets have fused "rich," "godless," "evil," "violent," and "sensual" into one and were the first to use the word "world" as an opprobrium. This inversion of values (which includes using the word "poor" as synonymous with "holy" and "friend") constitutes the significance of the Jewish people: they mark the beginning of the slave rebellion in morals.[11]

196

Countless dark bodies are to be *inferred* beside the sun—and we shall never see them. Among ourselves, this is a parable; and a psychologist of morals reads the whole writing of the stars only as a parable- and sign-language which can be used to bury much in silence.

197

We misunderstand the beast of prey and the man of prey (for example, Cesare Borgia)[12] thoroughly, we misunderstand "na-

---

[11] But compare section 52 above; also *Human, All-Too-Human,* section 475, and *The Dawn,* section 205 (*Portable Nietzsche,* pp. 61ff.; 86f.); and, above all, sections 248 and 250 below. For a discussion of Nietzsche's image of the Jews and the many pertinent passages in his writings, see Kaufmann, *Nietzsche,* Chapter 10.

[12] It has often been alleged that Cesare Borgia was Nietzsche's ideal, but an examination of all of Nietzsche's references to him shows that this is plainly false (Kaufmann, *Nietzsche,* Chapter 7, section III). One can consider a type healthy without admiring it or urging others to emulate it.

ture," as long as we still look for something "pathological" at the bottom of these healthiest of all tropical monsters and growths, or even for some "hell" that is supposed to be innate in them; yet this is what almost all moralists so far have done. Could it be that moralists harbor a hatred of the primeval forest and the tropics? And that the "tropical man" must be discredited at any price, whether as sickness and degeneration of man or as his own hell and self-torture? Why? In favor of the "temperate zones"? In favor of temperate men? Of those who are "moral"? Who are mediocre?— This for the chapter "Morality as Timidity."

198

All these moralities that address themselves to the individual, for the sake of his "happiness," as one says—what are they but counsels for behavior in relation to the degree of *dangerousness* in which the individual lives with himself; recipes against his passions, his good and bad inclinations insofar as they have the will to power and want to play the master; little and great prudences and artifices that exude the nook odor of old nostrums and of the wisdom of old women; all of them baroque and unreasonable in form —because they address themselves to "all," because they generalize where one must not generalize. All of them speak unconditionally, take themselves for unconditional, all of them flavored with more than one grain of salt and tolerable only—at times even seductive—when they begin to smell over-spiced and dangerous, especially "of the other world." All of it is, measured intellectually, worth very little and not by a long shot "science," much less "wisdom," but rather, to say it once more, three times more, prudence, prudence, prudence, mixed with stupidity, stupidity, stupidity—whether it be that indifference and statue coldness against the hot-headed folly of the affects which the Stoics advised and administered; or that laughing-no-more and weeping-no-more of Spinoza, his so naïvely advocated destruction of the affects through their analysis and vivisection; or that tuning down of the affects to a harmless mean according to which they may be satisfied, the Aristotelianism of morals; even morality as enjoyment of the affects in a deliberate thinness and spiritualization by means of the symbolism of art, say, as music, or as love of God and of man for God's sake—for in religion the passions enjoy the rights of citizens again, assuming that——; finally even that accommodating and playful surrender to the affects, as Hafiz and Goethe taught it, that bold dropping of the reins, that spiritual-physical *licentia morum*[13] in the exceptional case of wise old owls and sots[14] for whom it "no longer holds much danger." This, too, for the chapter "Morality as Timidity."

199

Inasmuch as at all times, as long as there have been human beings, there have also been herds of men (clans, communities, tribes, peoples, states, churches) and always a great many people who obeyed, compared with the small number of those commanding—considering, then, that nothing has been exercised and cultivated better and longer among men so far than obedience—it may fairly be assumed that the need for it is now innate in the average man, as a kind of *formal conscience* that commands: "thou shalt unconditionally do something, unconditionally not do something else," in short, "thou shalt." This need seeks to satisfy itself and to fill its form with some content. According to its strength, impatience, and tension, it seizes upon things as a rude appetite, rather indiscriminately, and accepts whatever is shouted into its ears by someone who issues commands—parents, teachers, laws, class prejudices, public opinions.

The strange limits of human development, the way it hesitates, takes so long, often turns back, and moves in circles, is due to the fact that the herd instinct of obedience is inherited best, and at the expense of the art of commanding. If we imagine this instinct progressing for once to its ultimate excesses, then those who command

---

13 Moral license.

14 The association of Goethe and Hafiz is suggested by Goethe's great collection of poems, *West-Östlicher Divan* (West-Eastern Divan, 1819), in which he identifies himself with the Persian poet. But the old Goethe, unlike Hafiz, was certainly no sot.

and are independent would eventually be lacking altogether; or they would secretly suffer from a bad conscience and would find it necessary to deceive themselves before they could command—as if they, too, merely obeyed. This state is actually encountered in Europe today: I call it the moral hypocrisy of those commanding. They know no other way to protect themselves against their bad conscience than to pose as the executors of more ancient or higher commands (of ancestors, the constitution, of right, the laws, or even of God). Or they even borrow herd maxims from the herd's way of thinking, such as "first servants of their people" or "instruments of the common weal."

On the other side, the herd man in Europe today gives himself the appearance of being the only permissible kind of man, and glorifies his attributes, which make him tame, easy to get along with, and useful to the herd, as if they were the truly human virtues: namely, public spirit, benevolence, consideration, industriousness, moderation, modesty, indulgence, and pity. In those cases, however, where one considers leaders and bellwethers indispensable, people today make one attempt after another to add together clever herd men by way of replacing commanders: all parliamentary constitutions, for example, have this origin. Nevertheless, the appearance of one who commands unconditionally strikes these herd-animal Europeans as an immense comfort and salvation from a gradually intolerable pressure, as was last attested in a major way by the effect of Napoleon's appearance. The history of Napoleon's reception is almost the history of the higher happiness attained by this whole century in its most valuable human beings and moments.

200

In an age of disintegration that mixes races indiscriminately, human beings have in their bodies the heritage of multiple origins, that is, opposite, and often not merely opposite, drives and value standards that fight each other and rarely permit each other any rest. Such human beings of late cultures and refracted lights will on the average be weaker human beings: their most profound desire is that the war they *are* should come to an end. Happiness appears to them, in agreement with a tranquilizing (for example, Epicurean or Christian) medicine and way of thought, pre-eminently as the happiness of resting, of not being disturbed, of satiety, of finally attained unity, as a "sabbath of sabbaths," to speak with the holy rhetorician Augustine who was himself such a human being.

But when the opposition and war in such a nature have the effect of one more charm and incentive of life—and if, moreover, in addition to his powerful and irreconcilable drives, a real mastery and subtlety in waging war against oneself, in other words, self-control, self-outwitting, has been inherited or cultivated, too—then those magical, incomprehensible, and unfathomable ones arise, those enigmatic men predestined for victory and seduction, whose most beautiful expression is found in Alcibiades and Caesar (to whose company I should like to add that *first* European after my taste, the Hohenstaufen Frederick II),[15] and among artists perhaps Leonardo da Vinci. They appear in precisely the same ages when that weaker type with its desire for rest comes to the fore: both types belong together and owe their origin to the same causes.

201

As long as the utility reigning in moral value judgments is solely the utility of the herd, as long as one considers only the preservation of the community, and immorality is sought exactly and exclusively in what seems dangerous to the survival of the community—there can be no morality of "neighbor love." Supposing that even then there was a constant little exercise of consideration, pity, fairness, mildness, reciprocity of assistance; supposing that even in that state of society all those drives are active that later receive the honorary designation of "virtues" and eventually almost

---

[15] Medieval German emperor, 1215-50. The members of the Stefan George Circle cultivated "monumentalistic" historiography, in the sense of Nietzsche's second "Untimely Meditation," and penned portraits of great men partly aimed to show the qualities that constitute human greatness. Two of their most celebrated studies are Friedrich Gundolf's *Caesar* (1924) and Ernst Kantorowicz's *Kaiser Friedrich II* (1927). Another such study is Ernst Bertram's *Nietzsche* (1918), whose faults are summed up in the subtitle: "Attempt at a Mythology."

coincide with the concept of "morality"—in that period they do not yet at all belong in the realm of moral valuations; they are still *extra-moral*. An act of pity, for example, was not considered either good or bad, moral or immoral, in the best period of the Romans; and even when it was praised, such praise was perfectly compatible with a kind of disgruntled disdain as soon as it was juxtaposed with an action that served the welfare of the whole, of the *res publica*.[16]

In the last analysis, "love of the neighbor" is always something secondary, partly conventional and arbitrary-illusory in relation to *fear of the neighbor*. After the structure of society is fixed on the whole and seems secure against external dangers, it is this fear of the neighbor that again creates new perspectives of moral valuation. Certain strong and dangerous drives, like an enterprising spirit, foolhardiness, vengefulness, craftiness, rapacity, and the lust to rule, which had so far not merely been honored insofar as they were socially useful—under different names, to be sure, from those chosen here—but had to be trained and cultivated to make them great (because one constantly needed them in view of the dangers to the whole community, against the enemies of the community), are now experienced as doubly dangerous, since the channels to divert them are lacking, and, step upon step, they are branded as immoral and abandoned to slander.

Now the opposite drives and inclinations receive moral honors; step upon step, the herd instinct draws its conclusions. How much or how little is dangerous to the community, dangerous to equality, in an opinion, in a state or affect, in a will, in a talent—that now constitutes the moral perspective: here, too, fear is again the mother of morals.

The highest and strongest drives, when they break out passionately and drive the individual far above the average and the flats of the herd conscience, wreck the self-confidence of the community, its faith in itself, and it is as if its spine snapped. Hence just these drives are branded and slandered most. High and independent spirituality, the will to stand alone, even a powerful reason are

---

[16] Commonwealth.

experienced as dangers; everything that elevates an individual above the herd and intimidates the neighbor is henceforth called *evil;* and the fair, modest, submissive, conforming mentality, the *mediocrity* of desires attains moral designations and honors. Eventually, under very peaceful conditions, the opportunity and necessity for educating one's feelings to severity and hardness is lacking more and more; and every severity, even in justice, begins to disturb the conscience; any high and hard nobility and self-reliance is almost felt to be an insult and arouses mistrust; the "lamb," even more the "sheep," gains in respect.

There is a point in the history of society when it becomes so pathologically soft and tender that among other things it sides even with those who harm it, criminals, and does this quite seriously and honestly. Punishing somehow seems unfair to it, and it is certain that imagining "punishment" and "being supposed to punish" hurts it, arouses fear in it. "Is it not enough to render him *undangerous?* Why still punish? Punishing itself is terrible." With this question, herd morality, the morality of timidity, draws its ultimate consequence. Supposing that one could altogether abolish danger, the reason for fear, this morality would be abolished, too, *eo ipso:* it would no longer be needed, it would no longer *consider itself* necessary.

Whoever examines the conscience of the European today will have to pull the same imperative out of a thousand moral folds and hideouts—the imperative of herd timidity: "we want that some day there should be *nothing any more to be afraid of!*" Some day—throughout Europe, the will and way to this day is now called "progress." [17]

---

[17] Cf. F. D. Roosevelt's celebrated demand for "freedom from fear." The idea that much of man's conduct and culture can be explained in terms of fear was first explored extensively by Nietzsche in *The Dawn* (1881). For some discussion and pertinent quotations, see Kaufmann's *Nietzsche,* Chapter 6, section II; for Nietzsche's own opposition to punishment and resentment, *ibid.,* Chapter 12, section V. Nietzsche's critique of one type of opposition to punishment, above, should be compared with *Twilight of the Idols,* section 37 (*Portable Nietzsche,* pp. 538ff.), and Rilke's *Sonnets to Orpheus,* II.9 (original and translation in *Twenty German Poets,* ed. and trans. W. Kaufmann, New York, Modern Library, 1963, pp. 234f.).

202

Let us immediately say once more what we have already said a hundred times, for today's ears resist such truths—*our* truths. We know well enough how insulting it sounds when anybody counts man, unadorned and without metaphor, among the animals; but it will be charged against us as almost a *guilt* that precisely for the men of "modern ideas" we constantly employ such expressions as "herd," "herd instincts," and so forth. What can be done about it? We cannot do anything else; for here exactly lies our novel insight. We have found that in all major moral judgments Europe is now of one mind, including even the countries dominated by the influence of Europe: plainly, one now *knows* in Europe what Socrates thought he did not know and what that famous old serpent once promised to teach—today one "knows" what is good and evil.[18]

Now it must sound harsh and cannot be heard easily when we keep insisting: that which here believes it knows, that which here glorifies itself with its praises and reproaches, calling itself good, that is the instinct of the herd animal, man, which has scored a breakthrough and attained prevalence and predominance over other instincts—and this development is continuing in accordance with the growing physiological approximation and assimilation of which it is the symptom. *Morality in Europe today is herd animal morality*—in other words, as we understand it, merely *one* type of human morality beside which, before which, and after which many other types, above all *higher* moralities, are, or ought to be, possible. But this morality resists such a "possibility," such an "ought"

---

[18] Cf. *Zarathustra*, "On Old and New Tablets," section 2 (*Portable Nietzsche*, p. 308): "When I came to men I found them sitting on an old conceit: the conceit that they have long known what is good and evil for man . . . whoever wanted to sleep well still talked of good and evil before going to sleep."

And in Shaw's *Major Barbara* (Act III) Undershaft says: "What! no capacity for business, no knowledge of law, no sympathy with art, no pretension to philosophy; only a simple knowledge of the secret that has puzzled all the philosophers, baffled all the lawyers . . . : the secret of right and wrong. Why, man, you are a genius, a master of masters, a god! At twenty-four, too!"

with all its power: it says stubbornly and inexorably, "I am moral-ity itself, and nothing besides is morality." Indeed, with the help of a religion which indulged and flattered the most sublime herd-animal desires, we have reached the point where we find even in political and social institutions an ever more visible expression of this morality: the *democratic* movement is the heir of the Christian movement.

But there are indications that its tempo is still much too slow and sleepy for the more impatient, for the sick, the sufferers of the instinct mentioned: witness the ever madder howling of the anarchist dogs who are baring their fangs more and more obviously and roam through the alleys of European culture. They seem op-posites of the peacefully industrious democrats and ideologists of revolution, and even more so of the doltish philosophasters and brotherhood enthusiasts who call themselves socialists and want a "free society"; but in fact they are at one with the lot in their thor-ough and instinctive hostility to every other form of society except that of the *autonomous* herd (even to the point of repudiating the very concepts of "master" and "servant"—*ni dieu ni maître*[19] runs a socialist formula). They are at one in their tough resistance to every special claim, every special right and privilege (which means in the last analysis, *every* right: for once all are equal nobody needs "rights" any more). They are at one in their mistrust of punitive justice (as if it were a violation of those who are weaker, a wrong against the *necessary* consequence of all previous society). But they are also at one in the religion of pity, in feeling with all who feel, live, and suffer (down to the animal, up to "God"—the ex-cess of a "pity with God" belongs in a democratic age). They are at one, the lot of them, in the cry and the impatience of pity, in their deadly hatred of suffering generally, in their almost feminine ina-bility to remain spectators, to *let* someone suffer. They are at one in their involuntary plunge into gloom and unmanly tenderness under whose spell Europe seems threatened by a new Buddhism. They are at one in their faith in the morality of *shared* pity, as if that were

---

[19] "Neither god nor master"; cf. section 22 above.

morality in itself, being the height, the *attained* height of man, the sole hope of the future, the consolation of present man, the great absolution from all former guilt. They are at one, the lot of them, in their faith in the community as the *savior,* in short, in the herd, in "themselves"—

203

We have a different faith; to us the democratic movement is not only a form of the decay of political organization but a form of the decay, namely the diminution, of man, making him mediocre and lowering his value. Where, then, must *we* reach with our hopes?

Toward *new philosophers;* there is no choice; toward spirits strong and original enough to provide the stimuli for opposite valuations and to revalue and invert "eternal values"; toward forerunners, toward men of the future who in the present tie the knot and constraint that forces the will of millennia upon *new* tracks. To teach man the future of man as his *will,* as dependent on a human will, and to prepare great ventures and over-all attempts of discipline and cultivation by way of putting an end to that gruesome dominion of nonsense and accident that has so far been called "history"—the nonsense of the "greatest number" is merely its ultimate form: at some time new types of philosophers and commanders will be necessary for that, and whatever has existed on earth of concealed, terrible, and benevolent spirits, will look pale and dwarfed by comparison. It is the image of such leaders that *we* envisage: may I say this out loud, you free spirits? The conditions that one would have partly to create and partly to exploit for their genesis; the probable ways and tests that would enable a soul to grow to such a height and force that it would feel the *compulsion* for such tasks; a revaluation of values under whose new pressure and hammer a conscience would be steeled, a heart turned to bronze, in order to endure the weight of such responsibility; on the other hand, the necessity of such leaders, the frightening danger that they might fail to appear or that they might turn out badly or degenerate—these are *our* real worries and gloom—do you know that, you free spirits?—these are the heavy distant thoughts and storms that pass over the sky of *our* life.

There are few pains as sore as once having seen, guessed, felt how an extraordinary human being strayed from his path and degenerated.[20] But anyone who has the rare eye for the over-all danger that "man" himself *degenerates;* anyone who, like us, has recognized the monstrous fortuity that has so far had its way and play regarding the future of man—a game in which no hand, and not even a finger, of God took part as a player; anyone who fathoms the calamity that lies concealed in the absurd guilelessness and blind confidence of "modern ideas" and even more in the whole Christian-European morality—suffers from an anxiety that is past all comparisons. With a single glance he sees what, given a favorable accumulation and increase of forces and tasks, might yet *be made of man;* he knows with all the knowledge of his conscience how man is still unexhausted for the greatest possibilities and how often the type "man" has already confronted enigmatic decisions and new paths—he knows still better from his most painful memories what wretched things have so far usually broken a being of the highest rank that was in the process of becoming. so that it broke, sank, and became contemptible.

The *over-all degeneration of man* down to what today appears to the socialist dolts and flatheads as their "man of the future"— as their ideal—this degeneration and diminution of man into the perfect herd animal (or, as they say, to the man of the "free society"), this animalization of man into the dwarf animal of equal rights and claims, is *possible,* there is no doubt of it. Anyone who has once thought through this possibility to the end, no longer knows any other nausea than other men[21]—but perhaps also a new *task!*—

---

20 Perhaps an allusion to Richard Wagner.
21 Compare Sartre's famous epigram, in *Huis Clos* (*No Exit*): "Hell is— other men."

PART SIX

———◆———

WE SCHOLARS [1]

---

[1] *Wir Gelehrten.* This can only mean "Scholars," not "Intellectuals" (Cowan translation).

Part Six

204

At the risk that moralizing will here, too, turn out to be what it has always been—namely, according to Balzac, an intrepid *montrer ses plaies*[2]—I venture to speak out against an unseemly and harmful shift in the respective ranks of science[3] and philosophy, which is now threatening to become established, quite unnoticed and as if it were accompanied by a perfectly good conscience. I am of the opinion that only *experience*—experience always seems to mean bad experience?—can entitle us to participate in the discussion of such higher questions of rank, lest we talk like blind men about colors—*against* science the way women and artists do ("Oh, this dreadful science!" sigh their instinct and embarrassment; "it always gets to the *bottom* of things!").

The scholar's[4] declaration of independence, his emancipation from philosophy, is one of the more refined effects of the democratic order—and disorder: the self-glorification and self-exaltation of scholars[5] now stand in full bloom, in their finest spring, everywhere—which is not meant to imply that in this case self-praise smells pleasant.[6] "Freedom from all masters!" that is what the instinct of the rabble wants in this case, too; and after science has most happily rid itself of theology whose "handmaid" it was too long, it now aims with an excess of high spirits and a lack of understanding to lay down laws for philosophy and to play the "master" herself—what am I saying? the *philosopher*.

My memory—the memory of a scientific man, if you'll for-

---

2 "Showing one's wounds."

3 *Wissenschaft* might just as well be rendered as "scholarship" in this section —and in much German literature: the term does not have primary reference to the natural sciences as it does in twentieth-century English.

4 *Des wissenschaftlichen Menschen.*

5 *Des Gelehrten.*

6 An allusion the German proverb: "Self-praise stinks."

give me—is bulging with naïvetés of overbearing that I have heard about philosophy and philosophers from the lips of young natural scientists and old physicians (not to speak of the most learned [7] and conceited [8] of all scholars, the philologists and schoolmen, who are both by profession). Sometimes it was the specialist and nook dweller who instinctively resisted any kind of synthetic enterprise and talent; sometimes the industrious worker who had got a whiff of *otium*[9] and the noble riches in the psychic economy of the philosopher which had made him feel defensive and small. Sometimes it was that color blindness of the utility man who sees nothing in philosophy but a series of *refuted* systems and a prodigal effort that "does nobody any good." Sometimes the fear of masked mysticism and a correction of the limits of knowledge leaped forward; sometimes lack of respect for individual philosophers that had involuntarily generalized itself into lack of respect for philosophy.

Most frequently, finally, I found among young scholars that what lay behind the arrogant contempt for philosophy was the bad aftereffect of—a philosopher to whom they now denied allegiance on the whole without, however, having broken the spell of his cutting evaluation of other philosophers—with the result of an over-all irritation with all philosophy. (Schopenhauer's aftereffect on our most modern Germany, for example, seems to me to be of this kind: with his unintelligent wrath against Hegel [10] he has succeeded in wrenching the whole last generation of Germans out of the context of German culture—a culture that was, considering everything, an elevation and divinatory subtlety of the *historical sense*. But precisely at this point Schopenhauer was poor, unreceptive, and un-German to the point of genius.)

Altogether, taking a large view, it may have been above all what was human, all too human, in short, the wretchedness of the most recent philosophy itself that most thoroughly damaged re-

---

[7] *Gebildet.*
[8] *Eingebildet.*
[9] Leisure.
[10] Cf. section 252 below.

spect for philosophy and opened the gates to the instinct of the rabble. Let us confess how utterly our modern world lacks the whole type[11] of a Heraclitus, Plato, Empedocles, and whatever other names these royal and magnificent hermits of the spirit had; and how it is with considerable justification that, confronted with such representatives of philosophy as are today, thanks to fashion, as much on top as they are really at the bottom—in Germany, for example, the two lions of Berlin, the anarchist Eugen Dühring and the amalgamist Eduard von Hartmann[12]—a solid man of science *may* feel that he is of a better type and descent. It is especially the sight of those hodgepodge philosophers who call themselves "philosophers of reality" or "positivists" that is capable of injecting a dangerous mistrust into the soul of an ambitious young scholar: these are at best scholars and specialists themselves—that is palpable—they are all losers who have been *brought back* under the hegemony of science, after having desired *more* of themselves at some time without having had the right to this "more" and its responsibilities—and who now represent, in word and deed, honorably, resentfully, and vengefully, the *unbelief* in the masterly task and masterfulness of philosophy.

Finally: how could it really be otherwise? Science is flourishing today and her good conscience is written all over her face, while the level to which all modern philosophy has gradually sunk, this rest of philosophy today, invites mistrust and displeasure, if not mockery and pity. Philosophy reduced to "theory of knowledge," in fact no more than a timid epochism and doctrine of abstinence—a philosophy that never gets beyond the threshold and takes pains to *deny* itself the right to enter—that is philosophy in its last throes, an end, an agony, something inspiring pity. How could such a philosophy—*dominate!*

---

[11] The German word *Art* in this context could mean manner, but the same word near the end of the sentence plainly means type.

[12] Eugen Dühring (1833-1921) and Eduard von Hartmann (1842-1906) were highly regarded at the time. Dühring was a virulent anti-Semite; Hartmann attempted to amalgamate Schopenhauer's philosophy with Hegel's.

205

The dangers for a philosopher's development are indeed so
manifold today that one may doubt whether this fruit can still
ripen at all. The scope and the tower-building of the sciences has
grown to be enormous, and with this also the probability that the
philosopher grows weary while still learning or allows himself to be
detained somewhere to become a "specialist"—so he never attains
his proper level, the height for a comprehensive look, for looking
around, for looking *down*. Or he attains it too late. when his best
time and strength are spent—or impaired, coarsened, degenerated, so his view, his over-all value judgment does not mean much
any more. It may be precisely the sensitivity of his intellectual conscience that leads him to delay somewhere along the way and to be
late: he is afraid of the seduction to become a dilettante, a milli-
pede, an insect with a thousand antennae; he knows too well that
whoever has lost his self-respect cannot command or *lead* in the
realm of knowledge—unless he would like to become a great actor, a philosophical Cagliostro and pied piper, in short, a seducer.
This is in the end a question of taste, even if it were not a question of conscience.

Add to this, by way of once more doubling the difficulties for
a philosopher, that he demands of himself a judgment, a Yes or
No, not about the sciences but about life and the value of life—
that he is reluctant to come to believe that he has a right, or even a
duty, to such a judgment, and must seek his way to this right and
faith only from the most comprehensive—perhaps most disturbing
and destructive[13]—experiences, and frequently hesitates, doubts,
and lapses into silence.

Indeed, the crowd has for a long time misjudged and mistaken the philosopher, whether for a scientific man and ideal
scholar or for a religiously elevated, desensualized,[14] "desecular-

---

[13] *Störendsten, zerstörendsten.*
[14] *Entsinnlichten.* Cowan mistakenly translates this word as "demoralized."

ized" enthusiast and sot of God.[15] And if a man is praised today for living "wisely" or "as a philosopher," it hardly means more than "prudently and apart." Wisdom—seems to the rabble a kind of escape, a means and trick for getting well out of a wicked game. But the genuine philosopher—as it seems to *us,* my friends?—lives "unphilosophically" and "unwisely," above all *imprudently,* and feels the burden and the duty of a hundred attempts and temptations of life—he risks *himself* constantly, he plays the wicked game—

206

Compared to a genius—that is, to one who either *begets* or *gives birth,* taking both terms in their most elevated sense—the scholar, the scientific average man, always rather resembles an old maid: like her he is not conversant with the two most valuable functions of man. Indeed, one even concedes to both, to the scholars and to old maids, as it were by way of a compensation, that they are respectable—one stresses their respectability—and yet feels annoyed all over at having to make this concession.

Let us look more closely: what is the scientific man? To begin with, a type of man that is not noble, with the virtues of a type of man that is not noble, which is to say, a type that does not dominate and is neither authoritative nor self-sufficient: he has industriousness, patient acceptance of his place in rank and file, evenness and moderation in his abilities and needs, an instinct for his equals and for what they need; for example, that bit of independence and green pasture without which there is no quiet work, that claim to honor and recognition (which first of all presupposes literal recognition and recognizability), that sunshine of a good name, that constant attestation of his value and utility which is needed to overcome again and again the internal *mistrust* which is the sediment in the hearts of all dependent men and herd animals.

---

[15] An allusion to the conception of Spinoza as "God-intoxicated." Cowan: "divine alcoholic."

The scholar also has, as is only fair, the diseases and bad manners of a type that is not noble: he is rich in petty envy and has lynx eyes for what is base in natures to whose heights he cannot attain. He is familiar, but only like those who let themselves go, not *flow;* and just before those who flow like great currents he freezes and becomes doubly reserved: his eye becomes like a smooth and reluctant lake with not a ripple of delight or sympathy. The worst and most dangerous thing of which scholars are capable comes from their sense of the mediocrity of their own type—from that Jesuitism of mediocrity which instinctively works at the annihilation of the uncommon man and tries to break every bent bow or, preferably, to unbend it. Unbending—considerately, of course, with a solicitous hand—*unbending* with familiar pity, that is the characteristic art of Jesuitism which has always known how to introduce itself as a religion of pity.—

207

However gratefully we may welcome an *objective* spirit—and is there anyone who has never been mortally sick of everything subjective and of his accursed ipsissimosity? [16]—in the end we also have to learn caution against our gratitude and put a halt to the exaggerated manner in which the "unselfing" and depersonalization of the spirit is being celebrated nowadays as if it were the goal itself and redemption and transfiguration. This is particularly characteristic of the pessimist's school, which also has good reasons for according the highest honors to "disinterested knowledge."

The objective person who no longer curses and scolds like the pessimist, the *ideal* scholar in whom the scientific instinct, after thousands of total and semi-failures, for once blossoms and blooms to the end, is certainly one of the most precious instruments there are; but he belongs in the hand of one more powerful. He is only an instrument; let us say, he is a *mirror*—he is no "end in himself." The objective man is indeed a mirror: he is accustomed to sub-

---

[16] Coinage, formed from *ipsissima* (very own).

mit before whatever wants to be known, without any other pleasure than that found in knowing and "mirroring"; he waits until something comes, and then spreads himself out tenderly lest light footsteps and the quick passage of spiritlike beings should be lost on his plane and skin.

Whatever still remains in him of a "person" strikes him as accidental, often arbitrary, still more often disturbing: to such an extent has he become a passageway and reflection of strange forms and events even to himself. He recollects "himself" only with an effort and often mistakenly; he easily confuses himself with others, he errs about his own needs and is in this respect alone unsubtle and slovenly. Perhaps his health torments him, or the pettiness and cramped atmosphere of wife and friend, or the lack of companions and company—yes, he forces himself to reflect on his torments—in vain. Already his thoughts roam—to a *more general* case, and tomorrow he knows no more than he did yesterday how he might be helped. He has lost any seriousness for himself, also time: he is cheerful, *not* for lack of distress, but for lack of fingers and handles for *his* need. His habit of meeting every thing and experience halfway, the sunny and impartial hospitality with which he accepts everything that comes his way, his type of unscrupulous benevolence, of dangerous unconcern about Yes and No—alas, there are cases enough in which he has to pay for these virtues! And as a human being he becomes all too easily the *caput mortuum*[17] of these virtues.

If love and hatred are wanted from him—I mean love and hatred as God, woman, and animal understand them—he will do what he can and give what he can. But one should not be surprised if it is not much—if just here he proves inauthentic, fragile, questionable, and worm-eaten. His love is forced, his hatred artificial and rather *un tour de force,* a little vanity and exaggeration. After all, he is genuine only insofar as he may be objective: only in his cheerful "totalism" he is still "nature" and "natural." His mirror soul, eternally smoothing itself out, no longer knows how to af-

---

[17] Dross.

firm or negate; he does not command, neither does he destroy. *"Je ne méprise presque rien,"* [18] he says with Leibniz: one should not overlook and underestimate that *presque*.[19]

Neither is he a model man; he does not go before anyone, nor behind; altogether he places himself too far apart to have any reason to take sides for good or evil. When confusing him for so long with the *philosopher,* with the Caesarian cultivator and cultural dynamo,[20] one accorded him far too high honors and overlooked his most essential characteristics: he is an instrument, something of a slave though certainly the most sublime type of slave, but in himself nothing—*presque rien!* The objective man is an instrument, a precious, easily injured and clouded instrument for measuring and, as an arrangement of mirrors, an artistic triumph that deserves care and honor; but he is no goal, no conclusion and sunrise,[21] no complementary man in whom the *rest* of existence is justified, no termination—and still less a beginning, a begetting and first cause, nothing tough, powerful, self-reliant that wants to be master —rather only a delicate, carefully dusted, fine, mobile pot for forms that still has to wait for some content and substance in order to "shape" itself accordingly—for the most part, a man without substance and content, a "selfless" man. Consequently, also nothing for women, *in parenthesi.*—

208

When a philosopher suggests these days that he is not a skeptic—I hope this is clear from the description just given of the objective spirit—everybody is annoyed. One begins to look at him apprehensively, one would like to ask, to ask so much—— Indeed, among timid listeners, of whom there are legions now, he is henceforth considered dangerous. It is as if at his rejection of skepticism they heard some evil, menacing rumbling in the distance, as if a new explosive were being tried somewhere, a dynamite of the

---

[18] "I despise almost nothing."

[19] Almost.

[20] *Dem cäsarischen Züchter und Gewaltmenschen der Cultur.*

[21] *Ausgang und Aufgang;* literally, going out and going up.

spirit, perhaps a newly discovered Russian *nihiline*,[22] a pessimism *bonae voluntatis*[23] that does not merely say No, want No, but—horrible thought!—*does* No.

Against this type of "good will"—a will to the actual, active denial of life—there is today, according to common consent, no better soporific and sedative than skepticism, the gentle, fair, lulling poppy of skepticism; and even *Hamlet* is now prescribed by the doctors of the day against the "spirit" [24] and its underground rumblings. "Aren't our ears filled with wicked noises as it is?" asks the skeptic as a friend of quiet, and almost as a kind of security police; "this subterranean No is terrible! Be still at last, you pessimistic moles!"

For the skeptic, being a delicate creature, is frightened all too easily; his conscience is trained to quiver at every No, indeed even at a Yes that is decisive and hard, and to feel as if it had been bitten.[25] Yes and No—that goes against his morality; conversely, he likes to treat his virtue to a feast of noble abstinence, say, by repeating Montaigne's "What do I know?" or Socrates' "I know that I know nothing." Or: "Here I don't trust myself, here no door is open to me." Or: "Even if one were open, why enter right away?" Or: "What use are all rash hypotheses? Entertaining no hypotheses at all might well be part of good taste. Must you insist on immediately straightening what is crooked? on filling up every hole with oakum? Isn't there time? Doesn't time have time? O you devilish brood, are you incapable of *waiting?* The uncertain has its charms,

---

[22] Coinage, modeled on "nicotine"; cf. *Antichrist,* section 2 (*Portable Nietzsche,* p. 570).

[23] Of good will.

[24] The Cowan translation has, instead of "against the 'spirit'" [*gegen den "Geist"*], "to cure mind," which misses the point of the remark about *Hamlet.*

Nietzsche had argued in one of the most brilliant passages of his first book, *The Birth of Tragedy,* that Hamlet is no skeptic: "Action requires the veils of illusion: that is the doctrine of Hamlet, not that cheap wisdom of Jack the Dreamer who reflects too much . . . Not reflection, no—true knowledge, an insight into the horrible truth, outweighs any motive for action" (section 7).

[25] In German, conscience bites. Cf. the medieval "agenbite of inwit" of which James Joyce makes much in *Ulysses.*

too; the sphinx, too, is a Circe; Circe, too, was a philosopher."

Thus a skeptic consoles himself; and it is true that he stands in need of some consolation. For skepticism is the most spiritual expression of a certain complex physiological condition that in ordinary language is called nervous exhaustion and sickliness; it always develops when races or classes that have long been separated are crossed suddenly and decisively. In the new generation that, as it were, has inherited in its blood diverse standards and values, everything is unrest, disturbance, doubt, attempt; the best forces have an inhibiting effect, the very virtues do not allow each other to grow and become strong; balance, a center of gravity, and perpendicular poise are lacking in body and soul. But what becomes sickest and degenerates most in such hybrids is the *will:* they no longer know independence of decisions and the intrepid sense of pleasure in willing—they doubt the "freedom of the will" even in their dreams.

Our Europe of today, being the arena of an absurdly sudden attempt at a radical mixture of classes, and *hence* races, is therefore skeptical in all its heights and depths—sometimes with that mobile skepticism which leaps impatiently and lasciviously from branch to branch, sometimes dismal like a cloud overcharged with question marks—and often mortally sick of its will. Paralysis of the will: where today does one not find this cripple sitting? And often in such finery! How seductive the finery looks! This disease enjoys the most beautiful pomp- and lie-costumes; and most of what today displays itself in the showcases, for example, as "objectivity," "being scientific," *"l'art pour l'art,"* "pure knowledge, free of will," is merely dressed-up skepticism and paralysis of the will: for this diagnosis of the European sickness I vouch.

The sickness of the will is spread unevenly over Europe: it appears strongest and most manifold where culture has been at home longest; it disappears to the extent to which the "barbarian" still—or again—claims his rights under the loose garments of Western culture. In France today the will is accordingly most seriously sick, which is as easy to infer as it is palpable. And France, having always possessed a masterly skill at converting even the most calamitous turns of its spirit into something attractive and seductive, now really shows its cultural superiority over Europe by being the school and display of all the charms of skepticism.

The strength to will, and to will something for a long time, is a little greater in Germany, and more so in the German north than in the center of Germany; but much stronger yet in England, Spain, and Corsica, here in association with indolence, there with hard heads—not to speak of Italy, which is too young to know what it wants and still has to prove whether it is able to will—but it is strongest and most amazing by far in that enormous empire in between, where Europe, as it were, flows back into Asia, in Russia. There the strength to will has long been accumulated and stored up, there the will—uncertain whether as a will to negate or a will to affirm—is waiting menacingly to be discharged, to borrow a pet phrase of our physicists today. It may well take more than Indian wars and complications in Asia to rid Europe of its greatest danger: internal upheavals would be needed, too, the shattering of the empire into small units, and above all the introduction of the parliamentary nonsense, including the obligation for everybody to read his newspaper with his breakfast.

I do not say this because I want it to happen: the opposite would be rather more after my heart—I mean such an increase in the menace of Russia that Europe would have to resolve to become menacing, too, namely, *to acquire one will* by means of a new caste that would rule Europe, a long, terrible will of its own that would be able to cast its goals millennia hence—so the long-drawn-out comedy of its many splinter states as well as its dynastic and democratic splinter wills would come to an end. The time for petty politics is over: the very next century will bring the fight for the dominion of the earth—the *compulsion* to large-scale politics.

209

To what extent the new warlike age into which we Europeans have evidently entered may also favor the development of another and stronger type of skepticism, on that I want to comment for the present only in the form of a parable which those who like German history should understand readily. That unscrupulous enthusiast for handsome and very tall grenadiers who, as King of Prussia,[26] brought into being a military and skeptical genius—and thus, when you come right down to it, that new type of German which has just now come to the top triumphantly—the questionable, mad father of Frederick the Great himself had the knack and lucky claw of genius, though only at one point: he knew what was missing in Germany at that time, and what lack was a hundred times more critical and urgent than, say, the lack of education and social graces—his antipathy against the young Frederick came from the fear of a deep instinct. *Men were missing;* and he suspected with the most bitter dismay that his own son was not man enough. In this he was deceived: but who, in his place, wouldn't have deceived himself about that? He saw his son surrender to atheism, to *esprit,* to the hedonistic frivolity of clever Frenchmen: in the background he saw that great vampire, the spider of skepticism; he suspected the incurable misery of a heart that is no longer hard enough for evil or good, of a broken will that no longer commands, no longer is capable of commanding. Meanwhile there grew up in his son that more dangerous and harder new type of skepticism— who knows *how much* it owed precisely to the hatred of the father and the icy melancholy of a will condemned to solitude?—the skepticism of audacious manliness which is most closely related to the genius for war and conquest and first entered Germany in the shape of the great Frederick.

This skepticism despises and nevertheless seizes; it undermines and takes possession; it does not believe but does not lose itself in the process; it gives the spirit dangerous freedom, but it is severe on the heart; it is the *German* form of skepticism which, in the form of a continued Frederickianism that had been sublimated spiritually, brought Europe for a long time under the hegemony of the German spirit and its critical and historical mistrust. Thanks to the unconquerably strong and tough virility of the great German philologists and critical historians (viewed properly, all of them were also artists of destruction and dissolution), a *new* concept of the German spirit crystallized gradually in spite of all romanticism

---

[26] Frederick William I, reigned 1713-40.

in music and philosophy, and the inclination to virile skepticism became a decisive trait, now, for example, as an intrepid eye, now as the courage and hardness of analysis, as the tough will to undertake dangerous journeys of exploration and spiritualized North Pole expeditions under desolate and dangerous skies.[27]

There may be good reasons why warmblooded and superficial humanitarians cross themselves just when they behold this spirit— *cet esprit fataliste, ironique, méphistophélique,*[28] Michelet calls it, not without a shudder. But if we want to really feel what a distinction such fear of the "man" in the German spirit confers—a spirit through which Europe was after all awakened from her "dogmatic slumber" [29]—we have to remember the former conception which was replaced by this one: it was not so long ago that a masculinized woman could dare with unbridled presumption to commend the Germans to the sympathy of Europe as being gentle, goodhearted, weak-willed, and poetic dolts.[30] At long last we ought to understand deeply enough Napoleon's surprise when he came to see Goethe: it shows what people had associated with the "German spirit" for centuries. *"Voilà un homme!"*—that meant: "But this is a *man!* And I had merely expected a German." [31]—

---

[27] It is essential for understanding Nietzsche to realize that he is not "for" or "against" skepticism, but that he analyzes one type of skepticism with disdain (section 208) before describing another with which he clearly identifies himself. It is equally characteristic that when he joins his countrymen in admiration of Frederick the Great, he pays tribute to him not for his exploits and conquests but rather for his skepticism, and that his praise of "tough virility" is aimed at the sublimated, spiritual version found, for example, in philologists and historians. For Nietzsche's anti-romanticism cf., e.g., *The Gay Science* (1887), section 370, cited at length and discussed in Kaufmann's *Nietzsche*, Chapter 12, section V.

[28] "That fatalistic, ironical, Mephistophelic spirit." "Mephistophelic" obviously refers to Goethe's Mephistopheles, not to Marlowe's. For Goethe's conception see *Goethe's Faust: The Original German and a New Translation and Introduction* by Walter Kaufmann (Garden City, Anchor Books, 1962), pp. 22-25.

[29] Allusion to Kant's famous dictum, in the Preface to his *Prolegomena* (1783), that it was Hume who had first interrupted his "dogmatic slumber."

[30] Allusion to Madame de Staël's *De l'Allemagne* (Paris, 1810).

[31] For Nietzsche's conception of Goethe see, e.g., *Twilight of the Idols*, sections 49-51 (*Portable Nietzsche*, pp. 553-55.). Cf. also the title of one of Nietzsche's last works, *Ecce Homo* (written in 1888).

210

Suppose then that some trait in the image of the philosophers of the future poses the riddle whether they would not perhaps have to be skeptics in the sense suggested last, this would still designate only one feature and *not* them as a whole. With just as much right one could call them critics: and certainly they will be men of experiments.[32] With the name in which I dared to baptize them I have already stressed expressly their attempts and delight in attempts: was this done because as critics in body and soul they like to employ experiments in a new, perhaps wider, perhaps more dangerous sense? Does their passion for knowledge force them to go further with audacious and painful experiments than the softhearted and effeminate taste of a democratic century could approve?

No doubt, these coming philosophers will be least able to dispense with those serious and by no means unproblematic qualities which distinguish the critic from the skeptic; I mean the certainty of value standards, the deliberate employment of a unity of method, a shrewd courage, the ability to stand alone and give an account of themselves. Indeed, they admit to a pleasure in saying No and in taking things apart, and to a certain levelheaded cruelty that knows how to handle a knife surely and subtly, even when the heart bleeds. They will be *harder* (and perhaps not always only against themselves) than humane people might wish; they will not dally with "Truth" to be "pleased" or "elevated" or "inspired" by her. On the contrary, they will have little faith that *truth* of all things should be accompanied by such amusements for our feelings.

They will smile, these severe spirits, if somebody should say in front of them: "This thought elevates me; how could it fail to be true?" Or: "This work delights me; how could it fail to be beautiful?" Or: "This artist makes me greater; how could he fail to be great?" Perhaps they do not merely have a smile but feel a gen-

---

[32] *Experimente*. In the following, as earlier, *Versuch* is rendered as "attempt." Cf. section 42 above.

uine nausea over everything that is enthusiastic, idealistic, feminine, hermaphroditic in this vein. And whoever knew how to follow them into the most secret chambers of their hearts would scarcely find any intention there to reconcile "Christian feelings" with "classical taste" and possibly even with "modern parliamentarism" (though such conciliatory attempts are said to occur even among philosophers in our very unsure and consequently very conciliatory century).

Critical discipline and every habit that is conducive to cleanliness and severity in matters of the spirit will be demanded by these philosophers not only of themselves: they could display them as their kind of jewels—nevertheless they still do not want to be called critics on that account. They consider it no small disgrace for philosophy when people decree, as is popular nowadays: "Philosophy itself is criticism and critical science—and nothing whatever besides." This evaluation of philosophy may elicit applause from all the positivists of France and Germany (and it might even have pleased the heart and taste of *Kant*—one should remember the titles of his major works); our new philosophers will say nevertheless: critics are instruments of the philosopher and for that very reason, being instruments, a long ways from being philosophers themselves. Even the great Chinese of Königsberg[33] was merely a great critic.—

211

I insist that people should finally stop confounding philosophical laborers, and scientific men generally, with philosophers; precisely at this point we should be strict about giving "each his due," and not far too much to those and far too little to these.

It may be necessary for the education of a genuine philosopher that he himself has also once stood on all these steps on which his servants, the scientific laborers of philosophy, remain standing —*have to* remain standing. Perhaps he himself must have been

---

[33] Kant. Cf. *Antichrist*, section 11 (*Portable Nietzsche*, p. 577).

critic and skeptic and dogmatist and historian and also poet and collector and traveler and solver of riddles and moralist and seer and "free spirit" and almost everything in order to pass through the whole range of human values and value feelings and to be *able* to see with many different eyes and consciences, from a height and into every distance, from the depths into every height, from a nook into every expanse. But all these are merely preconditions of his task: this task itself demands something different—it demands that he *create values.*

Those philosophical laborers after the noble model of Kant and Hegel have to determine and press into formulas, whether in the realm of *logic* or *political* (moral) thought or *art,* some great data of valuations—that is, former *positings* of values, creations of value which have become dominant and are for a time called "truths." It is for these investigators to make everything that has happened and been esteemed so far easy to look over, easy to think over, intelligible and manageable, to abbreviate everything long, even "time," and to *overcome* the entire past—an enormous and wonderful task in whose service every subtle pride, every tough will can certainly find satisfaction. *Genuine philosophers, however, are commanders and legislators:* they say, *"thus* it *shall* be!" They first determine the Whither and For What of man, and in so doing have at their disposal the preliminary labor of all philosophical laborers, all who have overcome the past. With a creative hand they reach for the future, and all that is and has been becomes a means for them, an instrument, a hammer. Their "knowing" is *creating,* their creating is a legislation, their will to truth is—*will to power.*

Are there such philosophers today? Have there been such philosophers yet? *Must* there not be such philosophers? [34]—

---

[34] The dichotomy proposed in this section is highly questionable: we find both analyses and normative suggestions in the works of the major moral philosophers from Plato and Aristotle to Spinoza and Kant; and normative thinkers or legislators who are not also analysts are not philosophers. Yet Nietzsche's point that something vital is lacking in the work of those who are merely "laborers" is certainly worth pondering, and the immediately following section offers a far superior suggestion about the ethos of the "true" philosopher.

212

More and more it seems to me that the philosopher, being *of necessity* a man of tomorrow and the day after tomorrow, has always found himself, and *had* to find himself, in contradiction to his today: his enemy was ever the ideal of today. So far all these extraordinary furtherers of man whom one calls philosophers, though they themselves have rarely felt like friends of wisdom but rather like disagreeable fools and dangerous question marks, have found their task, their hard, unwanted, inescapable task, but eventually also the greatness of their task, in being the bad conscience of their time.

By applying the knife vivisectionally to the chest of the very *virtues of their time,* they betrayed what was their own secret: to know of a *new* greatness of man, of a new untrodden way to his enhancement. Every time they exposed how much hypocrisy, comfortableness, letting oneself go and letting oneself drop, how many lies lay hidden under the best honored type of their contemporary morality, how much virtue was *outlived*. Every time they said: "We must get there, that way, where *you* today are least at home."

Facing a world of "modern ideas" that would banish everybody into a corner and "specialty," a philosopher—if today there could be philosophers—would be compelled to find the greatness of man, the concept of "greatness," precisely in his range and multiplicity, in his wholeness in manifoldness. He would even determine value and rank in accordance with how much and how many things one could bear and take upon himself, how *far* one could extend his responsibility.

Today the taste of the time and the virtue of the time weakens and thins down the will; nothing is as timely as weakness of the will. In the philosopher's ideal, therefore, precisely strength of the will, hardness, and the capacity for long-range decisions must belong to the concept of "greatness"—with as much justification as the opposite doctrine and the ideal of a dumb, renunciatory, humble, selfless humanity was suitable for an opposite age, one that suffered, like the sixteenth century, from its accumulated energy of will and from the most savage floods and tidal waves of selfishness.

In the age of Socrates, among men of fatigued instincts, among the conservatives of ancient Athens who let themselves go—"toward happiness," as they said; toward pleasure, as they acted—and who all the while still mouthed the ancient pompous words to which their lives no longer gave them any right, *irony* may have been required for greatness of soul,[35] that Socratic sarcastic assurance of the old physician and plebeian who cut ruthlessly into his own flesh, as he did into the flesh and heart of the "noble," with a look that said clearly enough: "Don't dissemble in front of me! Here—we are equal."

Today, conversely, when only the herd animal receives and dispenses honors in Europe, when "equality of rights" could all too

---

[35] Aristotle's discussion of greatness of soul (*megalopsychia*) is worth quoting here, at least in part, because it evidently influenced Nietzsche. The valuations that find expression in Aristotle's account are exceedingly remote from those of the New Testament and help us understand Nietzsche's contrast of master morality and slave morality, introduced below (section 260). Moreover, in his long discussion of "what is noble," Nietzsche emulates Aristotle's descriptive mode.

"A person is thought to be great-souled if he claims much and deserves much [as Socrates did in the *Apology* when he said he deserved the greatest honor Athens could bestow]. . . . He that claims less than he deserves is small-souled. . . . The great-souled man is justified in despising other people—his estimates are correct; but most proud men have no good ground for their pride. . . . He is fond of conferring benefits. but ashamed to receive them, because the former is a mark of superiority and the latter of inferiority. . . . It is also characteristic of the great-souled men never to ask help from others, or only with reluctance, but to render aid willingly; and to be haughty towards men of position and fortune, but courteous towards those of moderate station. . . . He must be open both in love and in hate, since concealment shows timidity; and care more for the truth than for what people will think; . . . he is outspoken and frank, except when speaking with ironical self-depreciation, as he does to common people. . . . He does not bear a grudge, for it is not a mark of greatness of soul to recall things against people, especially the wrongs they have done you, but rather to overlook them. He is . . . not given to speaking evil himself, even of his enemies, except when he deliberately intends to give offence. . . . Such then being the great-souled man, the corresponding character on the side of deficiency is the small-souled man, and on that of excess the vain man" (*Nicomachean Ethics* IV.3, Rackham translation Cambridge, Mass., Harvard University Press, 1947).

The whole passage is relevant and extremely interesting.

easily be changed into equality in violating rights—I mean, into a common war on all that is rare, strange, privileged, the higher man, the higher soul, the higher duty, the higher responsibility, and the abundance of creative power and masterfulness—today the concept of greatness entails being noble, wanting to be by oneself, being able to be different, standing alone and having to live independently. And the philosopher will betray something of his own ideal when he posits: "He shall be greatest who can be loneliest, the most concealed, the most deviant, the human being beyond good and evil, the master of his virtues, he that is overrich in will. Precisely this shall be called *greatness:* being capable of being as manifold as whole, as ample as full." And to ask it once more: today—is greatness *possible?*

213

What a philosopher is, that is hard to learn because it cannot be taught: one must "know" it, from experience—or one should have the pride *not* to know it. But nowadays all the world talks of things of which it *cannot* have any experience, and this is most true, and in the worst way, concerning philosophers and philosophical states: exceedingly few know them, may know them, and all popular opinions about them are false.

That genuinely philosophical combination, for example, of a bold and exuberant spirituality that runs *presto* and a dialectical severity and necessity that takes no false step is unknown to most thinkers and scholars from their own experience, and therefore would seem incredible to them if somebody should speak of it in their presence. They picture every necessity as a kind of need, as a painstaking having-to-follow and being-compelled. And thinking itself they consider something slow and hesitant, almost as toil, and often enough as "worthy of the *sweat* of the noble"—but not in the least as something light, divine, closely related to dancing and high spirits. "Thinking" and taking a matter "seriously," considering it "grave"—for them all this belongs together: that is the only way they have "experienced" it.

Artists seem to have more sensitive noses in these matters,

knowing only too well that precisely when they no longer do anything "voluntarily" but do everything of necessity, their feeling of
freedom, subtlety, full power, of creative placing, disposing, and
forming reaches its peak—in short, that necessity and "freedom of
the will" then become one in them.

Ultimately, there is an order of rank among states of the soul,
and the order of rank of problems accords with this. The highest
problems repulse everyone mercilessly who dares approach them
without being predestined for their solution by the height and
power of his spirituality. What does it avail when nimble smarties
or clumsy solid mechanics and empiricists push near them, as is
common today, trying with their plebeian ambition to enter the
"court of courts." Upon such carpets coarse feet may never step:
the primeval law of things takes care of that; the doors remain
closed to such obtrusiveness, even if they crash and crush their
heads against them.

For every high world one must be born; or to speak more
clearly, one must be *cultivated* for it: a right to philosophy—taking
that word in its great sense—one has only by virtue of one's origins; one's ancestors, one's "blood" [36] decide here, too. Many generations must have labored to prepare the origin of the philosopher;
every one of his virtues must have been acquired, nurtured, inherited, and digested singly, and not only the bold, light, delicate gait
and course of his thoughts but above all the readiness for great responsibilities, the loftiness of glances that dominate and look down,
feeling separated from the crowd and its duties and virtues, the af-
fable protection and defense of whatever is misunderstood and
slandered, whether it be god or devil, the pleasure and exercise of
the great justice, the art of command, the width of the will, the slow
eye that rarely admires, rarely looks up, rarely loves[37]—

---

[36] *"Geblüt."* Nietzsche's conception of "blood" is discussed, and other relevant passages are quoted, in Kaufmann's *Nietzsche,* at the end of Chapter 10.

[37] The element of snobbery and the infatuation with "dominating" and
"looking down" are perhaps more obvious than Nietzsche's perpetual sublimation and spiritualization of these and other similar qualities. It may be
interesting to compare Nietzsche's view with Dr. Thomas Stockmann's in
Act IV of Ibsen's *An Enemy of the People:*

"What a difference there is between a cultivated and an uncultivated animal family! Just look at a common barnyard hen. . . . But now take a cultivated Spanish or Japanese hen, or take a noble pheasant or a turkey; indeed, you'll see the difference. And then I refer you to dogs, which are so amazingly closely related to us men. Consider first a common plebeian dog—I mean, a disgusting, shaggy, moblike cur that merely runs down the streets and fouls the houses. And then compare the cur with a poodle that for several generations is descended from a noble house where it received good food and has had occasion to hear harmonious voices and music. Don't you suppose that the poodle's brain has developed in a way quite different from the cur's? You can count on it. It is such cultivated young poodles that jugglers can train to do the most astonishing tricks. A common peasant cur could never learn anything of the kind, even if stood on its head."

Not only do Nietzsche and Ibsen's Dr. Stockmann share Lamarck's belief in the heredity of acquired characteristics; both are concerned with spiritual nobility and realize that—to put it plainly—of two brothers one may have it and the other not. Thus Stockmann says a little later: "But that's how it always goes when plebeian descent is still in one's limbs and one has not worked one's way up to spiritual nobility. . . . That kind of rabble of which I am speaking isn't to be found only in the lower strata. . . . My brother Peter—he is also a plebeian straight out of the book."

PART SEVEN

OUR VIRTUES

Part Seven

214

Our virtues?—It is probable that we, too, still have our virtues, although in all fairness they will not be the simpleminded and foursquare virtues for which we hold our grandfathers in honor—and at arm's length. We Europeans of the day after tomorrow, we firstborn of the twentieth century—with all our dangerous curiosity, our multiplicity and art of disguises, our mellow and, as it were, sweetened cruelty in spirit and senses—*if* we should have virtues we shall presumably have only virtues which have learned to get along best with our most secret and cordial inclinations, with our most ardent needs. Well then, let us look for them in our labyrinths —where, as is well known, all sorts of things lose themselves, all sorts of things are lost for good. And is there anything more beautiful than *looking for* one's own virtues? Doesn't this almost mean: *believing* in one's own virtue? But this "believing in one's virtue"—isn't this at bottom the same thing that was formerly called one's "good conscience," that venerable long pigtail of a concept which our grandfathers fastened to the backs of their heads, and often enough also to the backside of their understanding? So it seems that however little we may seem old-fashioned and grandfatherly-honorable to ourselves in other matters, in one respect we are nevertheless the worthy grandsons of these grandfathers, we last Europeans with a good conscience: we, too, still wear their pigtail.— Alas, if you knew how soon, very soon—all will be different!—

215

As in the realm of stars the orbit of a planet is in some cases determined by two suns; as in certain cases suns of different colors shine near a single planet, sometimes with red light, sometimes with green light, and then occasionally illuminating the planet at the same time and flooding it with colors—so we modern men are determined, thanks to the complicated mechanics of our "starry sky," by *different* moralities; our actions shine alternately in different colors, they are rarely univocal—and there are cases enough in which we perform actions *of many colors*.

216

Love one's enemies? I think this has been learned well: it is done thousands of times today, in small ways and big ways. Indeed, at times something higher and more sublime is done: we learn to *despise* when we love, and precisely when we love best—but all of this unconsciously, without noise, without pomp, with that modesty and concealed goodness which forbids the mouth solemn words and virtue formulas. Morality as a pose—offends our taste today. That, too, is progress—just as it was progress when religion as a pose finally offended our fathers' taste, including hostility and Voltairian bitterness against religion (and everything that formerly belonged to the gestures of free-thinkers). It is the music in our conscience, the dance in our spirit, with which the sound of all puritan litanies, all moral homilies and old-fashioned respectability won't go.

217

Beware of those who attach great value to being credited with moral tact and subtlety in making moral distinctions. They never forgive us once they have made a mistake *in front of* us (or, worse, *against* us): inevitably they become our instinctive slanderers and detractors, even if they should still remain our "friends."

Blessed are the forgetful: for they get over their stupidities, too.

218

The psychologists of France—and where else are any psychologists left today?—still have not exhausted their bitter and manifold delight in the *bêtise bourgeoise*,[1] just as if——enough, this betrays something. Flaubert, for example, that solid citizen of Rouen, in the end no longer saw, heard, or tasted anything else any more: this was his kind of self-torture and subtler cruelty. Now, for a change—since this is becoming boring—I propose another source of amusement: the unconscious craftiness with which all good, fat, solid, mediocre spirits react to higher spirits and their tasks—that subtle, involved, Jesuitical craftiness which is a thousand times more subtle than not only the understanding and taste of this middle class is at its best moments, but even the understanding of its victims—which proves once again that "instinct" is of all the kinds of intelligence that have been discovered so far —the most intelligent. In short, my dear psychologists, study the philosophy of the "norm" in its fight against the "exception": there you have a spectacle that is good enough for gods and godlike malice! Or, still more clearly: vivisect the "good man," the *"homo bonae voluntatis"* [2]—*yourselves!*

219

Moral judgments and condemnations constitute the favorite revenge of the spiritually limited against those less limited—also a sort of compensation for having been ill-favored by nature—finally an opportunity for acquiring spirit and *becoming* refined—malice spiritualized. It pleases them deep down in their hearts that there are standards before which those overflowing with the wealth and privileges of the spirit are their equals: they fight for the "equality of all men before God" and almost *need* faith in God just for that. They include the most vigorous foes of atheism. Anyone who said to them, "high spirituality is incomparable with any kind of solidity and respectability of a merely moral man" would enrage them— and I shall beware of doing this. Rather I want to flatter them with my proposition, that high spirituality itself exists only as the ulti-

---

[1] Bourgeois stupidity.

[2] "Man of good will."

mate product of moral qualities; that it is a synthesis of all those states which are attributed to "merely moral" men, after they have been acquired singly through long discipline and exercise, perhaps through whole chains of generations; that high spirituality is the spiritualization of justice and of that gracious severity which knows that it is its mission to maintain the *order of rank* in the world, among things themselves—and not only among men.

220

In view of the modern popularity of praise of the "disinterested," we should bring to consciousness, perhaps not without some danger, what it is that elicits the people's interest, and what are the things about which the common man is deeply and profoundly concerned—including the educated, even the scholars, and unless all appearances deceive, perhaps even the philosophers. Then the fact emerges that the vast majority of the things that interest and attract choosier and more refined tastes and every higher nature seem to the average man totally "uninteresting"; and when he nevertheless notices a devotion to such matters he calls it *"désintéressé"* and wonders how it is possible to act "without interest." There have been philosophers who have known how to lend to this popular wonder a seductive and mystical-transcendental expression[3] (—perhaps because they did not know the higher nature from experience?)—instead of positing the naked truth, which is surely not hard to come by, that the "disinterested" action is an *exceedingly* interesting and interested action, assuming——

"And love?"— What? Even an action done from love is supposed to be "unegoistic"? But you dolts! "And the praise of sacrifices?"— But anyone who has really made sacrifices knows that he wanted and got something in return—perhaps something of himself in return for something of himself—that he gave up here in order to have more there, perhaps in order to *be* more or at least to feel that he was "more." But this a realm of questions and answers in which a choosier spirit does not like to dwell: even now truth finds

---

[3] Notably Kant.

it necessary to stifle her yawns when she is expected to give answers. In the end she is a woman: she should not be violated.

221

It does happen, said a moralistic pedant and dealer in trifles, that I honor and exalt a man free of self-interest—not because he is free of self-interest but because he seems to me to be entitled to profit another human being at his own expense. Enough; the question is always who *he* is, and who the *other* person is. In a person, for example, who is called and made to command, self-denial and modest self-effacement would not be a virtue but the waste of a virtue: thus it seems to me. Every unegoistic morality that takes itself for unconditional and addresses itself to all does not only sin against taste: it is a provocation to sins of omission, one *more* seduction under the mask of philanthropy—and precisely a seduction and injury for the higher, rarer, privileged. Moralities must be forced to bow first of all before the *order of rank;* their presumption must be brought home to their conscience—until they finally reach agreement that it is *immoral* to say: "what is right for one is fair for the other."

Thus my moralistic pedant and *bonhomme:*[4] does he deserve to be laughed at for thus admonishing moralities to become moral? But one should not be too right if one wants to have those who laugh on one's own side; a grain of wrong actually belongs to good taste.

222

Where pity is preached today—and, if you listen closely, this is the only religion preached now—psychologists should keep their

---

[4] What the "moralistic pedant" says, especially after the "Enough" (several lines above), seems very close, to put it mildly, to Nietzsche's own position. Yet Nietzsche here dissociates himself from these remarks and ascribes them to a "pedant"—not because they are wrong but because he considers it pedantic and self-righteous to be so unhumorously and completely right. See sections 30 and 40 above. With the final sentence of section 221 compare *Ecce Homo,* Chapter 1, end of section 5.

ears open: through all the vanity, through all the noise that characterizes these preachers (like all preachers) they will hear a hoarse, groaning, genuine sound of *self-contempt*. This belongs to that darkening and uglification of Europe which has been growing for a century now (and whose first symptoms were registered in a thoughtful letter Galiani wrote to Madame d'Épinay)[5]—*unless it is the cause of this process*. The man of "modern ideas," this proud ape, is immeasurably dissatisfied with himself: that is certain. He suffers—and his vanity wants him to suffer only with others, to feel pity.—

223

The hybrid European—all in all, a tolerably ugly plebeian—simply needs a costume: he requires history as a storage room for costumes. To be sure, he soon notices that not one fits him very well; so he keeps changing. Let anyone look at the nineteenth century with an eye for these quick preferences and changes of the style masquerade; also for the moments of despair over the fact that "nothing is becoming." It is no use to parade as romantic or classical, Christian or Florentine, baroque or "national," *in moribus et artibus:* it "does not look good." But the "spirit," especially the "historical spirit," finds its advantage even in this despair: again and again a new piece of prehistory or a foreign country is tried on, put on, taken off, packed away, and above all *studied:* we are the first age that has truly studied "costumes"—I mean those of moralities, articles of faith, tastes in the arts, and religions—prepared like no previous age for a carnival in the grand style, for the laughter and high spirits of the most spiritual revelry, for the transcendental heights of the highest nonsense and Aristophanean derision of the world. Perhaps this is where we shall still discover the realm of our *invention,* that realm in which we, too, can still be original, say, as parodists of world history and God's buffoons—perhaps, even if nothing else today has any future, our *laughter* may yet have a future.

---

[5] See note for section 26 above.

224

The *historical sense* (or the capacity for quickly guessing the order of rank of the valuations according to which a people, a society, a human being has lived; the "divinatory instinct" for the relations of these valuations, for the relation of the authority of values to the authority of active forces)—this historical sense to which we Europeans lay claim as our specialty has come to us in the wake of that enchanting and mad *semi-barbarism* into which Europe had been plunged by the democratic mingling of classes and races: only the nineteenth century knows this sense, as its sixth sense. The past of every form and way of life, of cultures that formerly lay right next to each other or one on top of the other, now flows into us "modern souls," thanks to this mixture; our instincts now run back everywhere; we ourselves are a kind of chaos. Finally, as already mentioned, "the spirit" sees its advantage in this.

Through our semi-barbarism in body and desires we have secret access in all directions, as no noble age ever did; above all, access to the labyrinths of unfinished cultures and to every semi-barbarism that ever existed on earth. And insofar as the most considerable part of human culture so far was semi-barbarism, "historical sense" almost means the sense and instinct for everything, the taste and tongue for everything—which immediately proves it to be an *ignoble* sense. We enjoy Homer again, for example: perhaps it is our most fortunate advantage that we know how to relish Homer whom the men of a noble culture (say, the French of the seventeenth century, like Saint-Évremond, who reproached him for his *esprit vaste*,[6] and even their afterglow, Voltaire) cannot and could not assimilate so easily—whom to enjoy they scarcely permitted themselves. The very definite Yes and No of their palate, their easy nausea, their hesitant reserve toward everything foreign, their horror of the poor taste even of a lively curiosity, and altogether the reluctance of every noble and self-sufficient culture to own a new desire, a dissatisfaction with what is one's own, and ad-

---

[6] Vast or comprehensive spirit.

miration for what is foreign—all this inclines and disposes them unfavorably even against the best things in the world which are not theirs or *could* not become their prey. No sense is more incomprehensible for such people than the historical sense and its submissive plebeian curiosity.

It is no different with Shakespeare, that amazing Spanish-Moorish-Saxon synthesis of tastes that would have all but killed an ancient Athenian of Aeschylus' circle with laughter or irritation. But we—accept precisely this wild abundance of colors, this medley of what is most delicate, coarsest, and most artificial, with a secret familiarity and cordiality; we enjoy him as a superb subtlety of art saved up especially for us; and the disgusting odors and the proximity of the English rabble in which Shakespeare's art and taste live we do not allow to disturb us any more than on the Chiaja of Naples, where we go our way with all our senses awake, enchanted and willing, though the sewer smells of the plebeian quarters fill the air.

As men of the "historical sense" we also have our virtues; that cannot be denied: we are unpretentious, selfless, modest, courageous, full of self-overcoming, full of devotion, very grateful, very patient, very accommodating; but for all that we are perhaps not paragons of good taste. Let us finally own it to ourselves: what we men of the "historical sense" find most difficult to grasp, to feel, to taste once more, to love once more, what at bottom finds us prejudiced and almost hostile, is precisely the perfection and ultimate maturity of every culture and art,[7] that which is really noble in a work or human being, the moment when their sea is smooth and they have found halcyon self-sufficiency, the golden and cold aspect of all things that have consummated themselves.

Perhaps our great virtue of the historical sense is necessarily opposed to *good* taste, at least to the very best taste; and precisely the highest little strokes of luck and transfigurations of human life that briefly light up here and there we can recapture only poorly,

---

[7] When Nietzsche wrote this, the taste for archaic and primitive art was not yet widespread and classical art was still considered the norm: Praxiteles and Raphael were supposed to be the ultimate in beauty. Nietzsche thus foresees developments of the twentieth century.

hesitantly, by forcing ourselves—those moments and marvels when great power voluntarily stopped this side of the immeasurable and boundless, when an excess of subtle delight in sudden restraint and petrification, in standing firm and taking one's measure, was enjoyed on still trembling ground. *Measure* is alien to us; let us own it; our thrill is the thrill of the infinite, the unmeasured. Like a rider on a steed that flies forward, we drop the reins before the infinite, we modern men, like semi-barbarians—and reach *our* bliss only where we are most—*in danger*.

225

Whether it is hedonism or pessimism, utilitarianism or eudaemonism—all these ways of thinking that measure the value of things in accordance with *pleasure* and *pain*, which are mere epiphenomena and wholly secondary, are ways of thinking that stay in the foreground and naïvetés on which everyone conscious of *creative* powers and an artistic conscience will look down not without derision, nor without pity. Pity with *you*—that, of course, is not pity in your sense: it is not pity with social "distress," with "society" and its sick and unfortunate members, with those addicted to vice and maimed from the start, though the ground around us is littered with them; it is even less pity with grumbling, sorely pressed, rebellious slave strata who long for dominion, calling it "freedom." *Our* pity is a higher and more farsighted pity: we see how *man* makes himself smaller, how *you* make him smaller—and there are moments when we behold *your* very pity with indescribable anxiety, when we resist this pity—when we find your seriousness more dangerous than any frivolity. You want, if possible—and there is no more insane "if possible"—*to abolish suffering*. And we? It really seems that *we* would rather have it higher and worse than ever. Well-being as you understand it—that is no goal, that seems to us an *end*, a state that soon makes man ridiculous and contemptible—that makes his destruction[8] *desirable*.

---

[8] *Untergang*. Compare with this whole passage the Prologue of *Zarathustra*, especially sections 3-6, where Nietzsche plays with the words *Untergang*, *Übermensch* (overman), and *überwinden* (overcome) and contrasts the

The discipline of suffering, of *great* suffering—do you not know that only *this* discipline has created all enhancements of man so far? That tension of the soul in unhappiness which cultivates its strength, its shudders face to face with great ruin, its inventiveness and courage in enduring, persevering, interpreting, and exploiting suffering, and whatever has been granted to it of profundity, secret, mask, spirit, cunning, greatness—was it not granted to it through suffering, through the discipline of great suffering? In man *creature* and *creator* are united: in man there is material, fragment, excess, clay, dirt, nonsense, chaos; but in man there is also creator, form-giver, hammer hardness, spectator divinity, and seventh day: do you understand this contrast? And that *your* pity is for the "crea-ture in man," for what must be formed, broken, forged, torn, burnt, made incandescent, and purified—that which *necessarily* must and *should* suffer? And *our* pity—do you not comprehend for whom our *converse* pity is when it resists your pity as the worst of all pam-perings and weaknesses?

Thus it is pity *versus* pity.

But to say it once more: there are higher problems than all problems of pleasure, pain, and pity; and every philosophy that stops with them is a naïveté.—

226

We immoralists!— This world that concerns *us,* in which *we* fear and love, this almost invisible and inaudible world of subtle commanding and subtle obeying, in every way a world of the "al-most," involved, captious, peaked, and tender—indeed, it is de-fended well against clumsy spectators and familiar curiosity. We have been spun into a severe yarn and shirt of duties and *cannot* get out of that—and in this we are "men of duty," we, too. Occa-sionally, that is true, we dance in our "chains" and between our "swords"; more often, that is no less true, we gnash our teeth and feel impatient with all the secret hardness of our destiny. But we

overman with "the last man" who has "invented happiness" and is con-temptible.

can do what we like—the dolts and appearances speaks against us, saying: "These are men *without* duty." We always have the dolts and appearances against us.

227

Honesty,[9] supposing that this is our virtue from which we cannot get away, we free spirits—well, let us work on it with all our malice and love and not weary of "perfecting" ourselves in *our* virtue, the only one left us. May its splendor remain spread out one day like a gilded blue mocking evening light over this aging culture and its musty and gloomy seriousness! And if our honesty should nevertheless grow weary one day and sigh and stretch its limbs and find us too hard, and would like to have things better, easier, tenderer, like an agreeable vice—let us remain *hard*, we last Stoics! And let us dispatch to her assistance whatever we have in us of devilry: our disgust with what is clumsy and approximate, our *"nitimur in vetitum,"* [10] our adventurous courage, our seasoned and choosy curiosity, our subtlest, most disguised, most spiritual will to power and overcoming of the world that flies and flutters covetously around all the realms of the future—let us come to the assistance of our "god" with all our "devils"!

It is probable that we shall be misunderstood and mistaken for others on this account: what matter?[11] And even if they were right!

---

[9] *Redlichkeit.*

[10] "We strive for the forbidden." The quotation is from Ovid's *Amores,* III, 4, 17.

[11] Cf. *Schopenhauer as Educator* (1874), section 4: ". . . He will be mistaken for another and long be considered an ally of powers which he abominates. . . ." There, too, this is pictured as a consequence of honesty and courage. But when Nietzsche wrote *Ecce Homo,* in 1888, he no longer felt: "what matter?" Thus the first section of the Preface ends: "Under these circumstances there is a duty against which my custom, and even more the pride of my instincts, revolts at bottom; namely, to say: *Listen to me! For I am not this one or that! Above all, do not mistake me for someone else!*" There is also a note of the period 1885-88, published posthumously: "One generally mistakes me for someone else: I confess it; also that I should be done a great service if someone else were to defend and define me against these mistakes [*Verwechselungen*]" (*Werke,* Musarion edition, vol. XIV, 318f.).

Have not all gods so far been such devils who have become holy and been rebaptized? And what ultimately do we know of ourselves? And how the spirit that leads us would like to be *called*? (It is a matter of names.) And how many spirits we harbor?

Our honesty, we free spirits—let us see to it that it does not become our vanity, our finery and pomp, our limit, our stupidity. Every virtue inclines toward stupidity; every stupidity, toward virtue. "Stupid to the point of holiness," they say in Russia; let us see to it that out of honesty we do not finally become saints and bores. Is not life a hundred times too short—for boredom? One really would have to believe in eternal life to——

228

May I be forgiven the discovery that all moral philosophy so far has been boring and was a soporific and that "virtue" has been impaired more for me by its *boring* advocates than by anything else, though I am not denying their general utility. It is important that as few people as possible should think about morality; hence it is *very* important that morality should not one day become interesting. But there is no reason for worry. Things still stand today as they have always stood: I see nobody in Europe who has (let alone, *promotes*) any awareness that thinking about morality could become dangerous, captious, seductive—that there might be any *calamity* involved.

Consider, for example, the indefatigable, inevitable British utilitarians, how they walk clumsily and honorably in Bentham's footsteps, walking along (a Homeric simile says it more plainly), even as he himself had already walked in the footsteps of the honorable Helvetius[12] (no, he was no dangerous person, this Helvétius, *ce sénateur Pococurante*,[13] to speak with Galiani). Not a new idea, no trace of a subtler version or twist of an old idea, not even a real

---

[12] Claude Adrien Helvétius (1715-71) was a French philosopher whose ancestors had borne the name of Schweitzer. He was a materialist and utilitarian.

[13] *Poco:* little; *curante:* careful, caring; *pococurante:* easygoing.

history of what had been thought before: altogether an *impossible* literature, unless one knows how to flavor it with some malice.

For into these moralists, too (one simply has to read them with ulterior thoughts, if one *has* to read them), that old English vice has crept which is called *cant* and consists in *moral Tartuffery;* only this time it hides in a new, scientific, form. A secret fight against a bad conscience is not lacking either, as it is only fair that a race of former Puritans will have a bad conscience whenever it tries to deal with morality scientifically. (Isn't a moral philosopher the opposite of a Puritan? Namely, insofar as he is a thinker who considers morality questionable, as calling for question marks, in short as a problem? Should moralizing not be—immoral?)

Ultimately they all want *English* morality to be proved right— because this serves humanity best, or "the general utility," or "the happiness of the greatest number"—no, the happiness of *England.* With all their powers they want to prove to themselves that the striving for *English* happiness—I mean for comfort and fashion[14] (and at best a seat in Parliament)—is at the same time also the right way to virtue; indeed that whatever virtue has existed in the world so far must have consisted in such striving.

None of these ponderous herd animals with their unquiet consciences (who undertake to advocate the cause of egoism as the cause of the general welfare) wants to know or even sense that "the general welfare" is no ideal, no goal, no remotely intelligible concept, but only an emetic—that what is fair for one *cannot* by any means for that reason alone also be fair for others; that the demand of one morality for all is detrimental for the higher men; in short, that there is an order of rank between man and man, hence also between morality and morality. They are a modest and thoroughly mediocre type of man, these utilitarian Englishmen, and, as said above, insofar as they are boring one cannot think highly enough of their utility. They should even be *encouraged:* the following rhymes represent an effort in this direction.

> Hail, dear drudge and patient fretter!
> "More drawn out is always better,"

---

[14] Nietzsche uses the English words "comfort" and "fashion."

Stiffness grows in head and knee,
No enthusiast and no joker,
Indestructibly mediocre,
Sans génie et sans esprit! [15]

229

In late ages that may be proud of their humanity, so much fear remains, so much *superstitious* fear of the "savage cruel beast" whose conquest is the very pride of these more humane ages, that even palpable truths remain unspoken for centuries, as if by some agreement, because they look as if they might reanimate that savage beast one has finally "mortified." Perhaps I dare something when I let one of these truths slip out: let others catch it again and give it "milk of the pious ways of thinking" [16] to drink until it lies still and forgotten in its old corner.

We should reconsider cruelty and open our eyes. We should at long last learn impatience lest such immodest fat errors keep on strutting about virtuously and saucily, as have been fostered about tragedy, for example, by philosophers both ancient and modern. Almost everything we call "higher culture" is based on the spiritualization of *cruelty*, on its becoming more profound: this is my proposition. That "savage animal" has not really been "mortified"; it lives and flourishes, it has merely become—divine.

What constitutes the painful voluptuousness of tragedy is cruelty; what seems agreeable in so-called tragic pity, and at bottom in everything sublime, up to the highest and most delicate shudders of metaphysics, receives its sweetness solely from the admixture of

---

[15] *Heil euch, brave Karrenschieber,*
   Stets "je länger desto lieber,"
   Steifer stets an Kopf und Knie,
   Unbegeistert, ungespässig,
   Unverwüstlich-mittelmässig,
   Sans génie et sans esprit!
The phrase in quotes is a German cliché.

[16] Quoted from Tell's famous monologue in Schiller's *Wilhelm Tell*, Act IV, Scene 3. Schiller had earlier translated *Macbeth* into German and was, no doubt, influenced by "the milk of human kindness."

cruelty. What the Roman in the arena, the Christian in the ecstasies of the cross, the Spaniard at an auto-da-fe or bullfight, the Japanese of today when he flocks to tragedies, the laborer in a Parisian suburb who feels a nostalgia for bloody revolutions, the Wagnerienne who "submits to" *Tristan and Isolde,* her will suspended—what all of them enjoy and seek to drink in with mysterious ardor are the spicy potions of the great Circe, "cruelty."

To see this we must, of course, chase away the clumsy psychology of bygone times which had nothing to teach about cruelty except that it came into being at the sight of the sufferings of *others*. There is also an abundant, over-abundant enjoyment at one's own suffering, at making oneself suffer—and wherever man allows himself to be persuaded to self-denial in the *religious* sense, or to self-mutilation, as among Phoenicians and ascetics, or altogether to desensualization, decarnalization, contrition, Puritanical spasms of penitence, vivisection of the conscience, and *sacrifizio dell'intelletto*[17] à la Pascal, he is secretly lured and pushed forward by his cruelty, by those dangerous thrills of cruelty turned *against oneself*.

Finally consider that even the seeker after knowledge forces his spirit to recognize things against the inclination of the spirit, and often enough also against the wishes of his heart—by way of saying No where he would like to say Yes, love, and adore—and thus acts as an artist and transfigurer of cruelty. Indeed, any insistence on profundity and thoroughness is a violation, a desire to hurt the basic will of the spirit which unceasingly strives for the apparent and superficial—in all desire to know there is a drop of cruelty.

230

What I have just said of a "basic will of the spirit" may not be readily understood: permit me an explanation.

That commanding something which the people call "the spirit" wants to be master in and around its own house and wants to feel that it is master; it has the will from multiplicity to simplicity, a will that ties up, tames, and is domineering and truly masterful. Its

---

[17] Sacrifice of the intellect.

needs and capacities are so far the same as those which physiologists posit for everything that lives, grows, and multiplies. The
spirit's power to appropriate the foreign stands revealed in its inclination to assimilate the new to the old, to simplify the manifold,
and to overlook or repulse whatever is totally contradictory—just
as it involuntarily emphasizes certain features and lines in what is
foreign, in every piece of the "external world," retouching and falsifying the whole to suit itself. Its intent in all this is to incorporate
new "experiences," to file new things in old files—growth, in a
word—or, more precisely, the *feeling* of growth, the feeling of increased power.

An apparently opposite drive serves this same will: a suddenly erupting decision in favor of ignorance, of deliberate exclusion, a shutting of one's windows, an internal No to this or that
thing, a refusal to let things approach, a kind of state of defense
against much that is knowable, a satisfaction with the dark, with the
limiting horizon, a Yea and Amen to ignorance—all of which is
necessary in proportion to a spirit's power to appropriate, its "digestive capacity," to speak metaphorically—and actually "the
spirit" is relatively most similar to a stomach.

Here belongs also the occasional will of the spirit to let itself
be deceived, perhaps with a capricious intimation of the fact that
such and such is *not* the case, that one merely accepts such and such
a delight in all uncertainty and ambiguity, a jubilant self-enjoyment
in the arbitrary narrowness and secrecy of some nook, in the all
too near, in the foreground, in what is enlarged, diminished, dis-
placed, beautified, a self-enjoyment in the caprice of all these expressions of power.

Here belongs also, finally, that by no means unproblematic
readiness of the spirit to deceive other spirits and to dissimulate in
front of them, that continual urge and surge of a creative, form-
giving, changeable force: in this the spirit enjoys the multiplicity
and craftiness of its masks, it also enjoys the feeling of its security
behind them: after all, it is surely its Protean arts that defend and
conceal it best.

This will to mere appearance, to simplification, to masks, to
cloaks, in short, to the surface—for every surface is a cloak—is

countered by that sublime inclination of the seeker after knowledge who insists on profundity, multiplicity, and thoroughness, with a *will* which is a kind of cruelty of the intellectual conscience and taste. Every courageous thinker will recognize this in himself, assuming only that, as fit, he has hardened and sharpened his eye for himself long enough and that he is used to severe discipline, as well as severe words. He will say: "there is something cruel in the inclination of my spirit"; let the virtuous and kindly try to talk him out of that!

Indeed, it would sound nicer if we were said, whispered, reputed[18] to be distinguished not by cruelty but by "extravagant honesty," we free, *very* free spirits—and perhaps *that* will actually be our—posthumous reputation.[19] Meanwhile—for there is plenty of time until then—we ourselves are probably least inclined to put on the garish finery of such moral word tinsels: our whole work so far makes us sick of this taste and its cheerful luxury. These are beautiful, glittering, jingling, festive words: honesty, love of truth, love of wisdom, sacrifice for knowledge, heroism of the truthful— they have something that swells one's pride. But we hermits and marmots have long persuaded ourselves in the full secrecy of a hermit's conscience that this worthy verbal pomp, too, belongs to the old mendacious pomp, junk, and gold dust of unconscious human vanity, and that under such flattering colors and make-up as well, the basic text of *homo natura* must again be recognized.

To translate man back into nature; to become master over the many vain and overly enthusiastic interpretations and connotations that have so far been scrawled and painted over that eternal basic text of *homo natura;* to see to it that man henceforth stands before man as even today, hardened in the discipline of science, he stands before the *rest* of nature, with intrepid Oedipus eyes and sealed Odysseus ears, deaf to the siren songs of old metaphysical bird catchers who have been piping at him all too long, "you are more, you are higher, you are of a different origin!"—that may be a

---

[18] *Nachsagte, nachraunte, nachrühmte:* literally, "said after, whispered after, praised after us an extravagant honesty."

[19] *Nachruhm:* literally, after-fame.

strange and insane task, but it is a *task*—who would deny that? Why did we choose this insane task? Or, putting it differently: "why have knowledge at all?"

Everybody will ask us that. And we, pressed this way, we who have put the same question to ourselves a hundred times, we have found and find no better answer—

231

Learning changes us; it does what all nourishment does which also does not merely "preserve"—as physiologists know. But at the bottom of us, really "deep down," there is, of course, something unteachable, some granite of spiritual *fatum*,[20] of predetermined decision and answer to predetermined selected questions. Whenever a cardinal problem is at stake, there speaks an unchangeable "this is I"; about man and woman, for example, a thinker cannot relearn but only finish learning—only discover ultimately how this is "settled in him." At times we find certain solutions of problems that inspire strong faith in *us;* some call them henceforth *their* "convictions." Later—we see them only as steps to self-knowledge, signposts to the problem we *are*—rather, to the great stupidity we are, to our spiritual *fatum,* to what is *unteachable* very "deep down." [21]

After this abundant civility that I have just evidenced in relation to myself I shall perhaps be permitted more readily to state a few truths about "woman as such"—assuming that it is now known from the outset how very much these are after all only—*my* truths.

232

Woman wants to become self-reliant—and for that reason she is beginning to enlighten men about "woman as such": *this* is one of the worst developments of the general *uglification* of Europe. For what must these clumsy attempts of women at scientific self-

---

[20] Fate.
[21] Cf. Freud.

exposure bring to light! Woman has much reason for shame; so much pedantry, superficiality, schoolmarmishness, petty presumption, petty licentiousness and immodesty lies concealed in woman —one only needs to study her behavior with children!—and so far all this was at bottom best repressed and kept under control by *fear* of man. Woe when "the eternally boring in woman" [22]—she is rich in that!—is permitted to venture forth! When she begins to unlearn thoroughly and on principle her prudence and art—of grace, of play, of chasing away worries, of lightening burdens and taking things lightly—and her subtle aptitude for agreeable desires!

Even now female voices are heard which—holy Aristophanes! —are frightening: they threaten with medical explicitness what woman *wants* from man, first and last. Is it not in the worst taste when woman sets about becoming scientific that way? So far enlightenment of this sort was fortunately man's affair, man's lot—we remained "among ourselves" in this; and whatever women write about "woman," we may in the end reserve a healthy suspicion whether woman really *wants* enlightenment about herself— whether she *can* will it—

Unless a woman seeks a new adornment for herself that way —I do think adorning herself is part of the Eternal-Feminine? —she surely wants to inspire fear of herself—perhaps she seeks mastery. But she does not *want* truth: what is truth to woman? From the beginning, nothing has been more alien, repugnant, and hostile to woman than truth—her great art is the lie, her highest concern is mere appearance and beauty. Let us men confess it: we honor and love precisely *this* art and *this* instinct in woman—we who have a hard time and for our relief like to associate with beings under whose hands, eyes, and tender follies our seriousness, our gravity and profundity[23] almost appear to us like folly.

Finally I pose the question: has ever a woman conceded pro-

---

[22] Allusion to "the Eternal-Feminine" in the penultimate line of Goethe's *Faust*.

[23] The embarrassing contrast with Nietzsche's own remarks in section 230, toward the end of the paragraph to which notes 18 and 19 refer, speaks for itself. If anything redeems section 232, and much of the remainder of Part VII, it is surely the disclaimer in 231.

fundity to a woman's head, or justice to a woman's heart? And is it not true that on the whole "woman" has so far been despised most by woman herself—and by no means by us?

We men wish that woman should not go on compromising herself through enlightenment—just as it was man's thoughtfulness and consideration for woman that found expression in the church decree: *mulier taceat in ecclesia!* [24] It was for woman's good when Napoleon gave the all too eloquent Madame de Staël to understand: *mulier taceat in politicis!* [25] And I think it is a real friend of women that counsels them today: *mulier taceat de muliere!* [26]

233

It betrays a corruption of the instincts—quite apart from the fact that it betrays bad taste—when a woman adduces Madame Roland or Madame de Staël or Monsieur George Sand, of all people, as if they proved anything in *favor* of "woman as such." Among men these three are the three *comical* women as such— nothing more!—and precisely the best involuntary *counterarguments* against emancipation and feminine vainglory.

234

Stupidity in the kitchen; woman as cook: the gruesome thoughtlessness to which the feeding of the family and of the master of the house is abandoned! Woman does not understand what food *means*—and wants to be cook. If woman were a thinking creature, she, as cook for millennia, would surely have had to discover the greatest physiological facts, and she would have had to gain possession of the art of healing. Bad cooks—and the utter lack of reason in the kitchen—have delayed human development longest and impaired it most: nor have things improved much even today. A lecture for finishing-school girls.

---

[24] Woman should be silent in church.
[25] Woman should be silent when it comes to politics.
[26] Woman should be silent about woman.

235

There are expressions and bull's-eyes of the spirit, there are epigrams, a little handful of words, in which a whole culture, a whole society is suddenly crystallized. Among these belongs the occasional remark of Madame de Lambert to her son: *"mon ami, ne vous permettez jamais que de folies, qui vous feront grand plaisir"* [27]—incidentally the most motherly and prudent word ever directed to a son.

236

What Dante and Goethe believed about woman—the former when he sang, *"ella guardava suso, ed io in lei,"* [28] and the latter when he translated this, "the Eternal-Feminine attracts us *higher"* —I do not doubt that every nobler woman will resist this faith, for she believes the same thing about the Eternal-Masculine—

237

SEVEN EPIGRAMS ON WOMAN

※

How the longest boredom flees,   when a man comes on his knees!

※

Science and old age at length   give weak virtue, too, some strength.

※

Black dress and a silent part   make every woman appear—smart.

---

[27] "My friend, permit yourself nothing but follies—that will give you great pleasure."
[28] "She looked up, and I at her."

☸

Whom I thank for my success?   God!—and my dear tailoress.

☸

Young: flower-covered den.   Old: a dragon denizen.

☸

Noble name, the legs are fine,   man as well: that he were mine!

☸

Ample meaning, speech concise[29]*—she-ass, watch for slippery ice!*

☸

237a[30]

Men have so far treated women like birds who had strayed to
them from some height: as something more refined and vulnerable,
wilder, stranger, sweeter, and more soulful—but as something one
has to lock up lest it fly away.

238

To go wrong on the fundamental problem of "man and
woman," to deny the most abysmal antagonism between them and
the necessity of an eternally hostile tension, to dream perhaps of
equal rights, equal education, equal claims and obligations—that is
a *typical* sign of shallowness, and a thinker who has proved shallow
in this dangerous place—shallow in his instinct—may be consid-

---

29 *Kurze Rede, langer Sinn* inverts *der langen Rede kurzer Sinn* (the brief
meaning of the long speech), a familiar German quotation from Schiller's
Die Piccolomini, Act I, Scene 2. Cf. *Twilight of the Idols,* section 51, and the
succeeding section 1 of the last chapter of *Twilight* (*Portable Nietzsche,* pp.
555-57).

30 In the first two editions a new section begins at this point, but it is numbered 237, repeating the preceding number. In the standard editions, including Schlechta's (which falsely claims to follow the original edition), the
second 237 is omitted, and the verse and prose are offered as a single section.

ered altogether suspicious, even more—betrayed, exposed: probably he will be too "short" for all fundamental problems of life, of the life yet to come, too, and incapable of attaining *any* depth.[31] A man, on the other hand, who has depth, in his spirit as well as in his desires, including that depth of benevolence which is capable of severity and hardness and easily mistaken for them, must always think about woman as *Orientals* do: he must conceive of woman as a possession, as property that can be locked, as something predestined for service and achieving her perfection in that. Here he must base himself on the tremendous reason of Asia, on Asia's superiority in the instincts, as the Greeks did formerly, who were Asia's best heirs and students: as is well known, from Homer's time to the age of Pericles, as their culture *increased* along with the range of their powers, they also gradually became *more severe,* in brief, more Oriental, against woman. *How* necessary, *how* logical, *how* humanely desirable even, this was—is worth pondering.

239

In no age has the weaker sex been treated with as much respect by men as in ours: that belongs to the democratic inclination and basic taste, just like disrespectfulness for old age. No wonder that this respect is immediately abused. One wants more, one learns to demand, finally one almost finds this tribute of respect insulting, one would prefer competition for rights, indeed even a genuine fight: enough, woman loses her modesty. Let us immediately add that she also loses taste. She unlearns her *fear* of man: but the woman who "unlearns fear" surrenders her most womanly instincts.

---

[31] Fortunately for Nietzsche, this is surely wrong. But it is worth asking which, if any, of his other ideas are of a piece with his secondhand wisdom about "woman": probably his embarrassingly frequent invocation of "severity" and "hardness" and other such terms—the almost ritual repetition of the words, not necessarily, if at all, the spiritualized conceptions he develops with their aid—and perhaps also the tenor of his remarks about democracy and parliaments. Goethe said: "The greatest human beings are always connected with their century by means of some weakness" (*Elective Affinities*). At these points Nietzsche's deliberate "untimeliness" now seems time-bound, dated, and as shallow as what he attacked.

That woman ventures forth when the aspect of man that inspires fear—let us say more precisely, when the *man* in man is no longer desired and cultivated—that is fair enough, also comprehensible enough. What is harder to comprehend is that, by the same token—woman degenerates. This is what is happening today: let us not deceive ourselves about that.

Wherever the industrial spirit has triumphed over the military and aristocratic spirit, woman now aspires to the economic and legal self-reliance of a clerk: [32] "woman as clerk" is inscribed on the gate to the modern society that is taking shape now. As she thus takes possession of new rights, aspires to become "master" [33] and writes the "progress" of woman upon her standards and banners, the opposite development is taking place with terrible clarity: *woman is retrogressing*.

Since the French Revolution, woman's influence in Europe has *decreased* proportionally as her rights and claims have increased; and the "emancipation of woman," insofar as that is demanded and promoted by women themselves (and not merely by shallow males) is thus seen to be an odd symptom of the increasing weakening and dulling of the most feminine instincts. There is *stupidity* in this movement, an almost masculine stupidity of which a woman who had turned out well—and such women are always prudent—would have to be thoroughly ashamed.

To lose the sense for the ground on which one is most certain of victory; to neglect practice with one's proper weapons; to let oneself go before men, perhaps even "to the point of writing a book," when formerly one disciplined oneself to subtle and cunning humility; to work with virtuous audacity against men's faith in a basically different ideal that he takes to be *concealed* in woman, something Eternally-and-Necessarily-Feminine—to talk men emphatically and loquaciously out of their notion that woman must be maintained, taken care of, protected, and indulged like a more delicate, strangely wild, and often pleasant domestic animal; the awkward and indignant search for everything slavelike and serflike

---

[32] *Commis.*
[33] *"Herr."*

that has characterized woman's position in the order of society so far, and still does (as if slavery were a counterargument and not instead a condition of every higher culture, every enhancement of culture)—what is the meaning of all this if not a crumbling of feminine instincts, a defeminization?

To be sure, there are enough imbecilic friends and corrupters of woman among the scholarly asses of the male sex who advise woman to defeminize herself in this way and to imitate all the stupidities with which "man" in Europe, European "manliness," is sick: they would like to reduce woman to the level of "general education," probably even of reading the newspapers and talking about politics. Here and there they even want to turn women into freethinkers and scribblers—as if a woman without piety would not seem utterly obnoxious and ridiculous to a profound and godless man.

Almost everywhere one ruins her nerves with the most pathological and dangerous kind of music (our most recent German music) and makes her more hysterical by the day and more incapable of her first and last profession—to give birth to strong children. Altogether one wants to make her more "cultivated" and, as is said, make the weaker sex *strong* through culture—as if history did not teach us as impressively as possible that making men "cultivated" and making them weak—weakening, splintering, and sicklying over the *force of the will*—have always kept pace, and that the most powerful and influential women of the world (most recently Napoleon's mother) owed their power and ascendancy over men to the force of their will—and not to schoolmasters!

What inspires respect for woman, and often enough even fear, is her *nature,* which is more "natural" than man's, the genuine, cunning suppleness of a beast of prey, the tiger's claw under the glove, the naïveté of her egoism, her uneducability and inner wildness, the incomprehensibility, scope, and movement of her desires and virtues—

What, in spite of all fear, elicits pity for this dangerous and beautiful cat "woman" is that she appears to suffer more, to be more vulnerable, more in need of love, and more condemned to disappointment than any other animal. Fear and pity: with these feelings man has so far confronted woman, always with one foot in tragedy[34] which tears to pieces as it enchants.[35]

What? And this should be the end? And the breaking of woman's magic spell is at work? The "borification" of woman is slowly dawning? O Europe! Europe! We know the horned animal you always found most attractive; it still threatens you! Your old fable could yet become "history"—once more an immense stupidity might become master over you and carry you off. And this time no god would hide in it; no, only an "idea," a "modern idea"!——

---

[34] Ever since Aristotle's *Poetics* (1449b), pity and fear have been associated with tragedy. Cf. also 1452a, 1453b.

[35] Allusion to Schiller's famous line about fate in classical tragedy (in "Shakespeare's Shadow"): "which elevates man when it crushes man."

PART EIGHT

─────◆─────

PEOPLES AND FATHERLANDS

Part Eight

240

I heard once again for the first time—Richard Wagner's overture to the *Meistersinger:* [1] it is magnificent, overcharged, heavy, late art that has the pride of presupposing two centuries of music as still living, if it is to be understood: it is to the credit of the Germans that such pride did not miscalculate. What flavors and forces, what seasons and climes are not mixed here! It strikes us now as archaic, now as strange, tart, and too young, it is just as capricious as it is pompous-traditional, it is not infrequently saucy, still more often coarse and rude—it has fire and courage and at the same time the loose dun skin of fruit that ripens too late. It flows broad and full— and suddenly a moment of inexplicable hesitation, like a gap opening up between cause and effect, a pressure triggering dreams, almost nightmares—but already the old width and breadth are regained by the current of well-being, the most manifold well-being, of old and new happiness, very much including the artist's happiness with himself which he has no wish to hide, his amazed, happy sharing of the knowledge that the means he has employed here are masterly—new artistic devices, newly acquired, not yet tested, as he seems to let us know.

Altogether, no beauty, no south, nothing of southern and subtle brightness of the sky, nothing of gracefulness, no dance, scarcely any will to logic; even a certain clumsiness that is actually stressed, as if the artist wished to say to us, "that is part of my intention"; cumbersome drapery, something capricious, barbarian, and solemn, a flurry of erudite preciousness and lace; something German in the best and worst senses of the word, something manifold, formless, and inexhaustible in a German way; a certain German powerfulness and overfulness of the soul which is not afraid of hiding behind the refinements of decay—which perhaps really feels most at

[1] Nietzsche discusses Wagner at greater length in *The Birth of Tragedy, The Case of Wagner,* and *Nietzsche contra Wagner.*

home there; a truly genuine token of the German soul which is at the same time young and superannuated, overly mellow and still overrich in future. This kind of music expresses best what I think of the Germans: they belong to the day before yesterday and the day after tomorrow—*as yet they have no today.*

241

We "good Europeans"—we, too, know hours when we permit ourselves some hearty fatherlandishness, a plop and relapse into old loves and narrownesses—I have just given a sample of that— hours of national agitations, patriotic palpitations, and various other sorts of archaizing sentimental inundations. More ponderous spirits than we are may require more time to get over what with us takes only hours and in a few hours has run its course: some require half a year, others half a life, depending on the speed and power of their digestion and metabolism. Indeed, I could imagine dull[2] and sluggish races who would require half a century even in our rapidly moving Europe to overcome such atavistic attacks of fatherlandishness and soil addiction and to return to reason, meaning "good Europeanism."

As I am digressing to this possibility, it so happens that I become an ear-witness of a conversation between two old "patriots": apparently both were hard of hearing and therefore spoke that much louder.

"*He* thinks and knows as much of philosophy as a peasant or a fraternity student," said one; "he is still innocent. But what does it matter today? This is the age of the masses: they grovel on their bellies before anything massive. In *politicis,* too. A statesman who piles up for them another tower of Babel, a monster of empire and power, they call 'great'; what does it matter that we, more cautious

---

2 *Dumpf* has no perfect equivalent in English. It can mean hollow or muted when applied to a sound, heavy and musty applied to air, dull applied to wits, and is a cousin of the English words, dumb and damp. Goethe still used it with a positive connotation when he wrote poetry about inarticulate feelings; Nietzsche uses the word often—with a strongly negative, anti-romantic connotation.

and reserved, do not yet abandon the old faith that only a great thought can give a deed or cause greatness. Suppose a statesman put his people in a position requiring them to go in for 'great politics' from now on, though they were ill-disposed for that by nature and ill prepared as well, so that they would find it necessary to sacrifice their old and secure virtues for the sake of a novel and dubious mediocrity—suppose a statesman actually condemned his people to 'politicking' although so far they had had better things to do and think about, and deep down in their souls they had not got rid of a cautious disgust with the restlessness, emptiness, and noisy quarrelsomeness of peoples that really go in for politicking—suppose such a statesman goaded the slumbering passions and lusts of his people, turning their diffidence and delight in standing aside into a blot, their cosmopolitanism and secret infinity into a serious wrong, devaluating their most cordial inclinations, inverting their conscience, making their spirit narrow, their taste 'national'— what! a statesman who did all this, for whom his people would have to atone for all future time, if they have any future, such a statesman should be *great?*"

"Without a doubt!" the other patriot replied vehemently; "otherwise he would not have been *able* to do it. Perhaps it was insane to want such a thing? But perhaps everything great was merely insane when it started."

"An abuse of words!" his partner shouted back; "strong! strong! strong and insane! *Not* great!"

The old men had obviously become heated as they thus flung their truths into each other's faces; but I, in my happiness and beyond, considered how soon one stronger will become master over the strong; also that for the spiritual flattening[3] of a people there is a compensation, namely the deepening of another people.

---

[3] *Verflachung* (becoming shallower) contrasted with *Vertiefung* (becoming more profound). The first people is, without a doubt, Germany; the statesman, Bismarck; and the second people probably France. Of course, the points made are also meant to apply more generally, but this evaluation of Bismarck at the zenith of his success and power certainly shows an amazing independence of spirit, and without grasping the full weight of the final sentence one cannot begin to understand Nietzsche's conceptions of the will to power or of "beyond good and evil."

242

Call that in which the distinction of the European is sought
"civilization" or "humanization" or "progress," or call it simply—
without praise or blame—using a political formula, Europe's *democratic* movement: behind all the moral and political foregrounds
to which such formulas point, a tremendous *physiological* process is
taking place and gaining momentum. The Europeans are becoming more similar to each other; they become more and more detached from the conditions under which races originate that are
tied to some climate or class; they become increasingly independent of any *determinate* milieu that would like to inscribe itself for
centuries in body and soul with the same demands. Thus an essentially supra-national and nomadic type of man is gradually coming up, a type that possesses, physiologically speaking, a maximum
of the art and power of adaptation as its typical distinction.

The tempo of this process of the *"evolving European"* may be
retarded by great relapses, but perhaps it will gain in vehemence
and profundity and grow just on their account: the still raging
storm and stress of "national feeling" belongs here, also that
anarchism which is just now coming up. But this process will probably lead to results which would seem to be least expected by those
who naïvely promote and praise it, the apostles of "modern ideas."
The very same new conditions that will on the average lead to the
leveling and mediocritization of man—to a useful, industrious,
handy, multi-purpose herd animal—are likely in the highest degree to give birth to exceptional human beings of the most dangerous and attractive quality.

To be sure, that power of adaptation which keeps trying out
changing conditions and begins some new work with every generation, almost with every decade, does not make possible the *powerfulness* of the type, and the over-all impression of such future
Europeans will probably be that of manifold garrulous workers
who will be poor in will, extremely employable, and as much in
need of a master and commander as of their daily bread. But
while the democratization of Europe leads to the production of a

type that is prepared for *slavery* in the subtlest sense, in single, exceptional cases the *strong* human being will have to turn out stronger and richer than perhaps ever before—thanks to the absence of prejudice from his training, thanks to the tremendous manifoldness of practice, art, and mask. I meant to say: the democratization of Europe is at the same time an involuntary arrangement for the cultivation of *tyrants*—taking that word in every sense, including the most spiritual.

243

I hear with pleasure that our sun is swiftly moving toward the constellation of *Hercules*—and I hope that man on this earth will in this respect follow the sun's example? And we first of all, we good Europeans!—

244

There was a time when it was customary to attribute "profundity" to the Germans, as a distinction. Now that the most successful type of the new Germanism lusts after utterly different honors and perhaps misses "pluck" in everything profound, some doubt may almost be timely and patriotic as to whether that former praise was not based on self-deception—in short, whether German profundity is not at bottom something different and worse, and something that, thank God, one is about to shake off successfully. Let us make the attempt to relearn about German profundity: nothing more is needed for this than a little vivisection of the German soul.

The German soul is above all manifold, of diverse origins, more put together and superimposed than actually built: that is due to where it comes from. A German who would make bold to say, "two souls, alas, are dwelling in my breast," [4] would violate the truth rather grossly or, more precisely, would fall short of the truth by a good many souls. As a people of the most monstrous mixture

---

[4] Goethe's *Faust,* line 1112.

and medley of races, perhaps even with a preponderance of the pre-Aryan element, as "people of the middle" in every sense, the Germans are more incomprehensible, comprehensive, contradictory, unknown, incalculable, surprising, even frightening than other people are to themselves: they elude *definition* and would be on that account alone the despair of the French.

It is characteristic of the Germans that the question, "what is German?" never dies out among them. Kotzebue surely knew his Germans well enough: "we have been recognized!" they jubilated —but *Sand*, too, thought he knew them.[5] Jean Paul[6] knew what he was doing when he declared himself wrathfully against Fichte's mendacious but patriotic flatteries and exaggerations—but it is probable that Goethe did not think about the Germans as Jean Paul did, although he considered him right about Fichte. What did Goethe really think about the Germans?

But there were many things around him about which he never spoke clearly, and his life long he was a master of subtle silence— he probably had good reasons for that. What is certain is that it was not "the Wars of Liberation" [7] that made him look up more cheerfully, any more than the French Revolution; the event on whose account he *rethought* his *Faust,* indeed the whole problem of man, was the appearance of Napoleon. There are words of Goethe in which he deprecates with impatient hardness, as if he belonged to a foreign country, what the Germans take pride in: the celebrated German *Gemüt*[8] he once defined as "indulgence toward the weaknesses of others as well as one's own." Was he wrong in that? It is characteristic of the Germans that one is rarely completely wrong about them.

---

[5] August Friedrich Ferdinand von Kotzebue (1761-1819), a popular German writer in his time who had his differences with Goethe and also published attacks on Napoleon, was assassinated by Karl Ludwig Sand (1795-1820), a theology student who took the poet for a Russian spy. Sand was executed.

[6] Pen name of Johann Paul Friedrich Richter (1763-1825), one of the most renowned German writers of the romantic period.

[7] Against Napoleon.

[8] A word without any exact equivalent in English. It is variously rendered as feeling, soul, heart, while *gemütlich* might be translated as comfortable or cozy.

The German soul has its passageways and inter-passageways; there are caves, hideouts, and dungeons in it; its disorder has a good deal of the attraction of the mysterious; the German is an expert on secret paths to chaos. And just as everything loves its simile, the German loves clouds and everything that is unclear, becoming, twilit, damp, and overcast: whatever is in any way uncertain, unformed, blurred, growing, he feels to be "profound." The German himself *is* not, he *becomes,* he "develops." "Development" is therefore the truly German find and hit in the great realm of philosophical formulas—a governing concept that, united with German beer and German music, is at work trying to Germanize the whole of Europe.

Foreigners stand amazed and fascinated before the riddles posed for them by the contradictory nature at the bottom of the German soul (brought into a system by Hegel and finally set to music by Richard Wagner). "Good-natured and vicious"—such a conjunction, preposterous in relation to any other people, is unfortunately justified all too often in Germany: let anyone live for a while among Swabians! The ponderousness of the German scholar, his social bad taste, gets along alarmingly well with an inner rope-dancing and easy boldness which has taught all the gods what fear is. Whoever wants a demonstration of the "German soul" *ad oculos*[9] should merely look into German taste, into German arts and customs: What boorish indifference to "taste"! How the noblest stands right next to the meanest! How disorderly and rich this whole psychic household is! The German *drags* his soul along: whatever he experiences he drags. He digests his events badly, he never gets "done" with them; German profundity is often merely a hard and sluggish "digestion." And just as all chronic invalids, all dyspeptics, love comfort, Germans love "openness" and *"Biederkeit":* how *comfortable* it is to be open and *"bieder"!* [10]

Perhaps the German of today knows no more dangerous and successful disguise than this confiding, accommodating, cards-on-

---

[9] For the eyes.

[10] The word has no exact English equivalent but might be rendered "four-square."

the-table manner of German *honesty:* this is his true Mephistopheles-art; with that he can "still go far." The German lets himself go while making faithful blue, empty, German eyes—and immediately foreigners confound him with his dressing gown.

I meant to say: whatever "German profundity" may be—when we are entirely among ourselves, perhaps we permit ourselves to laugh at it?—we shall do well to hold its semblance and good name in honor in the future, too, and not to trade our old reputation as a people of profundity too cheaply for Prussian "pluck" and Berlin wit and sand.[11] It is clever for a people to make and let itself be considered profound, awkward, good-natured, honest, and not clever: it might even be—profound. Finally, one should live up to one's name: it is not for nothing that one is called the *"tiusche" Volk,* the *Täusche-Volk,* deceiver people.[12]—

245

The "good old time" is gone, in Mozart we hear its swan song. How fortunate *we* are that his rococo still speaks to us, that his "good company," his tender enthusiasms, his childlike delight in curlicues and Chinese touches, his courtesy of the heart, his longing for the graceful, those in love, those dancing, those easily moved to tears, his faith in the south, may still appeal to some *residue* in us. Alas, some day all this will be gone—but who may doubt that the understanding and taste for Beethoven will go long before that! Beethoven was after all merely the final chord of transition in style, a style break, and not, like Mozart, the last chord of a centuries-old great European taste.

Beethoven is the interlude of a mellow old soul that constantly breaks and an over-young future soul that constantly *comes;* on his music lies that twilight of eternal losing and eternal extravagant hoping—the same light in which Europe was bathed when it

---

11 The area around Berlin was at one time called "the sandbox of the Holy Roman Empire."

12 This is by no means the accepted German etymology of *deutsch.*

dreamed with Rousseau, danced around the freedom tree of the Revolution, and finally almost worshiped before Napoleon. But how quickly *this* feeling pales now; how difficult is mere *knowledge* of this feeling even today—how strange to our ears sounds the language of Rousseau, Schiller, Shelley, Byron, in whom, taken *together,* the same fate of Europe found its way into words that in Beethoven knew how to sing!

Whatever German music came after that belongs to romanticism, a movement that was, viewed historically, still briefer, still more fleeting, still more superficial than that great *entr'acte,* that transition of Europe from Rousseau to Napoleon and to the rise of democracy. Weber: but what are *Freischütz* and *Oberon* to us today! Or Marschner's *Hans Heiling* and *Vampyr!* Or even Wagner's *Tannhäuser.* That is music that has died away though it is not yet forgotten. All this music of romanticism, moreover, was not noble enough to remain valid anywhere except in the theater and before crowds; it was from the start second-rate music that was not considered seriously by genuine musicians.

It is different with Felix Mendelssohn, that halcyon master who, on account of his lighter, purer, more enchanted soul, was honored quickly and just as quickly forgotten: as the beautiful *intermezzo* of German music. But as for Robert Schumann, who was very serious and also was taken seriously from the start—he was the last to found a school—is it not considered a good fortune among us today, a relief, a liberation, that this Schumann romanticism has been overcome?

Schumann, fleeing into the "Saxon Switzerland" [13] of his soul, half like Werther, half like Jean Paul, certainly not like Beethoven, certainly not like Byron—his Manfred music is a mistake and misunderstanding to the point of an injustice—Schumann with his taste which was basically a *small* taste (namely, a dangerous propensity, doubly dangerous among Germans, for quiet lyricism and sottishness of feeling), constantly walking off to withdraw shyly

---

[13] A very rugged and picturesque mountain range about fifteen miles southeast of Dresden, not comparable in height, extent, or magnificence to the Swiss Alps.

and retire, a noble tender-heart who wallowed in all sorts of anony-
mous bliss and woe, a kind of girl and *noli me tangere*[14] from the
start: this Schumann was already a merely *German* event in music,
no longer a European one, as Beethoven was and, to a still greater
extent, Mozart. With him German music was threatened by its
greatest danger: losing *the voice for the soul of Europe* and descending to mere fatherlandishness.

246

What torture books written in German are for anyone who
has a *third* ear! How vexed one stands before the slowly revolving
swamp of sounds that do not sound like anything and rhythms that
do not dance, called a "book" among Germans! Yet worse is the
German who *reads* books! How lazily, how reluctantly, how badly
he reads! How many Germans know, and demand of themselves
that they should know, that there is *art* in every good sentence—art
that must be figured out if the sentence is to be understood! A misunderstanding about its tempo, for example—and the sentence itself is misunderstood.

That one must not be in doubt about the rhythmically decisive syllables, that one experiences the break with any excessively
severe symmetry as deliberate and attractive, that one lends a subtle and patient ear to every *staccato*[15] and every *rubato*,[16] that one
figures out the meaning in the sequence of vowels and diphthongs
and how delicately and richly they can be colored and change
colors as they follow each other—who among book-reading Germans has enough good will to acknowledge such duties and demands and to listen to that much art and purpose in language? In
the end one simply does not have "the ear for that"; and thus the
strongest contrasts of style go unheard, and the subtlest artistry is
wasted as on the deaf.

---

14 "Touch me not!" John 20:17.

15 A musical term, meaning detached, disconnected, with breaks between
successive notes.

16 *Tempo rubato*, literally robbed time, is a tempo in which some notes are
shortened in order that others may be lengthened.

These were my thoughts when I noticed how clumsily and un-discerningly two masters in the art of prose were confounded—one whose words drop hesitantly and coldly, as from the ceiling of a damp cave—he counts on their dull sound and resonance—and another who handles his language like a flexible rapier, feeling from his arm down to his toes the dangerous delight of the quivering, over-sharp blade that desires to bite, hiss, cut.[17]—

247[18]

How little German style has to do with sound and the ears is shown by the fact that precisely our good musicians write badly. The German does not read aloud, not for the ear but only with the eye: meanwhile his ears are put away in a drawer. In antiquity men read—when they did read, which happened rarely enough—to themselves, aloud, with a resounding voice; one was surprised when anyone read quietly, and secretly asked oneself for the reasons. With a resounding voice: that means, with all the crescendos, inflections, and reversals of tone and changes in tempo in which the ancient *public* world took delight.

The laws of written style were then the same as those for spoken style; and these laws depended partly on the amazing development and the refined requirements of ear and larynx, partly on the strength, perseverance, and power of ancient lungs. A period in the classical sense is above all a physiological unit, insofar as it is held together by a single breath. Such periods as are found in Demosthenes and Cicero, swelling twice and coming down twice, all within a single breath, are delights for the men of *antiquity* who, from their own training, knew how to esteem their virtue and how rare and difficult was the delivery of such a period. *We* really have no right to the *great* period, we who are modern and in every sense short of breath.[19]

---

[17] The second master is surely Nietzsche, and the whole passage may give some idea of the difficulty of translating him.

[18] In the first two editions this appears as 247a, although there is no section 247.

[19] But *Beyond Good and Evil* is full of examples, most of which have been

All of these ancients were after all themselves dilettantes in rhetoric, hence connoisseurs, hence critics and thus drove their rhetoricians to extremes; just as in the last century, when all Italians and Italiennes knew how to sing, virtuosity in singing (and with that also the art of melody) reached its climax among them. In Germany, however, there really was (until quite recently, when a kind of platform eloquence began shyly and clumsily enough to flap its young wings) only a single species of public and *roughly* artful rhetoric: that from the pulpit.

In Germany the preacher alone knew what a syllable weighs, or a word, and how a sentence strikes, leaps, plunges, runs, runs out; he alone had a conscience in his ears, often enough a bad conscience; for there is no lack of reasons why Germans rarely attain proficiency in rhetoric, and almost always too late. The masterpiece of German prose is therefore, fairly enough, the masterpiece of its greatest preacher: the *Bible* has so far been the best German book. Compared with Luther's Bible, almost everything else is mere "literature"—something that did not grow in Germany and therefore also did not grow and does not grow into German hearts—as the Bible did.

248

There are two types of genius: one which above all begets and wants to beget, and another which prefers being fertilized and giving birth. Just so, there are among peoples of genius those to whom the woman's problem of pregnancy and the secret task of forming, maturing, and perfecting has been allotted—the Greeks, for example, were a people of this type; also the French—and others who must fertilize and become the causes of new orders of life—like the Jews,[20] the Romans, and, asking this in all modesty, the Germans?

---

preserved in translation, though a few have been broken up into shorter sentences. Plainly it is part of the aim of these sections to tell the reader how the present book wants to be read.

[20] Nietzsche inverts the anti-Semitic cliché that the Jews are uncreative parasites who excel, if at all, only as performers and interpreters. (Cf. also, e.g., section 52 above and his praise of Mendelssohn in section 245.) The image of the Jews "lusting after foreign races" *was* a cliché of German anti-Semi-

Peoples, tormented and enchanted by unknown fevers and irre-sistibly pressed beyond themselves, in love and lusting after for-eign races (after those who like "being fertilized"), and at the same time domineering like all that knows itself to be full of creative powers and hence "by the grace of God." These two types of gen-ius seek each other, like man and woman; but they also misunder-stand each other—like man and woman.

249

Every people has its own Tartuffery and calls it its virtues.—What is best in us we do not know—we cannot know.

250

What Europe owes to the Jews? Many things, good and bad, and above all one thing that is both of the best and of the worst: the grand style in morality, the terribleness and majesty of infinite demands, infinite meanings, the whole romanticism and sublimity of moral questionabilities—and hence precisely the most attrac-tive, captious, and choicest part of those plays of color and seduc-tions to life in whose afterglow the sky of our European culture, its evening sky, is burning now—perhaps burning itself out. We artists among the spectators and philosophers are—grateful for this to the Jews.[21]

---

tism, but it is entirely characteristic of Nietzsche's style of thinking and writing that the phrase is "spiritualized" (to use his own term) and more-over used in a context which makes plain—for those who read and do not merely browse—that Nietzsche's meaning is utterly opposed to that previ-ously associated with the words. His famous "revaluation" begins with *words* that receive new values.

Nietzsche's conception of the Greeks and Romans also inverts the usual view. In his frequent insistence on the debt of the Greeks to earlier civiliza-tions he was at least half a century ahead of his time.

[21] Cf. section 195 above. In the light of these two sections it seems probable that the reference to the Germans ("in all modesty") in section 248 alludes to Nietzsche's own ambitions. He is hoping to initiate a "revaluation" com-parable to that ascribed to the Jews in section 195: they are his model. Of course, he does not agree with the values he ascribes to them; but the whole book represents an effort to rise "beyond" simpleminded agreement and

251

It must be taken into the bargain if all sorts of clouds and disturbances—in brief, little attacks of hebetation—pass over the spirit of a people that is suffering, and *wants* to suffer, of nationalistic nerve fever and political ambition. Examples among the Germans today include now the anti-French stupidity, now the anti-Jewish, now the anti-Polish, now the Christian-romantic, now the Wagnerian, now the Teutonic, now the Prussian (just look at the wretched historians, these Sybels and Treitschkes[22] and their

---

disagreement, beyond the vulgar faith in antithetic values, "beyond good and evil." The point of that title is *not* that the author considers himself beyond good and evil in the crudest sense, but it is in part that he is beyond saying such silly things as "the Jews are good" or "the Jews are evil"; or "free spirits" or "scholars" or "virtues" or "honesty" or "humaneness" are "good" or "evil." Everywhere he introduces distinctions, etching first one type and then another—both generally confounded under a single label. He asks us to shift perspectives, or to perceive hues and gradations instead of simple black and white. This has led superficial readers to suppose that he contradicts himself or that he never embraces any meaningful conclusions (Karl Jaspers); but this book abounds in conclusions. Only one can never be sure what they are as long as one tears sentences and half-sentences out of context (the method of Bertram and Jaspers)—or even whole aphorisms: section 240 is meant to be read before section 241, not in isolation.

[22] Heinrich von Sybel (1817-95) and Heinrich von Treitschke (1834-96) were among the leading German historians of their time. Sybel was for many years a member of the Prussian parliament. At one time a critic of Bismarck, he strongly supported many of Bismarck's policies, beginning in 1866. In 1875 Bismarck appointed him director of the Prussian archives. His major works include *Die deutsche Nation und das Kaiserreich* (the German nation and the Empire; 1862) and *Die Begründung des deutschen Reiches durch Wilhelm I* (1889-94; English version, *The Founding of the German Empire by William I*, trans. Marshall Livingston, 1890-98).

Treitschke, born at Dresden, was a Liberal as a young man. By 1866, when Prussia went to war against Austria, "his sympathies with Prussia were so strong that he went to Berlin [from Freiburg, where he had been a professor], became a Prussian subject, and was appointed editor of the *Preussische Jahrbücher*" (*Encyclopaedia Britannica*, 11th ed.). In 1871 he became a member of the new imperial parliament, and in 1874 a professor of history at Berlin. He became "the chief panegyrist of the house of Hohenzollern. He did more than anyone to mould the minds of the rising generation, and he carried them with him even in his violent attacks on all opinions and all parties which appeared in any way to be injurious to the rising power of Germany. He supported the government in its attempts to subdue by legisla-

thickly bandaged heads!) and whatever other names these little mistifications[23] of the German spirit and conscience may have. Forgive me, for during a brief daring sojourn in very infected territory I, too, did not altogether escape this disease and began like everyone else to develop notions about matters that are none of my business: the first sign of the political infection. For example about the Jews: only listen!

I have not met a German yet who was well disposed toward the Jews; and however unconditionally all the cautious and politically-minded repudiated real anti-Semitism,[24] even this caution and policy are not directed against the species of this feeling itself but only against its dangerous immoderation, especially against the insipid and shameful expression of this immoderate feeling—about this, one should not deceive oneself. That Germany has amply *enough* Jews, that the German stomach, the German blood has trouble (and will still have trouble for a long time) digesting even this quantum of "Jew"—as the Italians, French, and English have done, having a stronger digestive system—that is the clear testimony and language of a general instinct to which one must listen, in accordance with which one must act. "Admit no more new Jews! And especially close the doors to the east (also to Austria)!" thus commands the instinct of a people whose type is still weak and indefinite, so it could easily be blurred or extinguished by a stronger race. The Jews, however, are beyond any doubt the strongest, toughest, and purest race now living in Europe; they know how to prevail even under the worst conditions (even better than under favorable conditions), by means of virtues that today one would like to mark as vices—thanks above all to a resolute faith that

---

tion the Socialists, Poles, and Catholics; and he was one of the few men of eminence who gave the sanction of his name to the attacks on the Jews which began in 1878. As a strong advocate of colonial expansion, he was also a bitter enemy of Great Britain, and he was to a large extent responsible for the anti-British feeling of German Chauvinism during the last years of the 19th century" (*ibid.*).

Although all of Nietzsche's references to Treitschke are vitriolic (there are three in *Ecce Homo*), uninformed writers have occasionally linked Nietzsche and Treitschke as if both had been German nationalists.

[23] *Benebelungen.* Could also be translated "befoggings."

[24] *Antisemiterei* is more derogatory than *Antisemitismus*.

need not be ashamed before "modern ideas"; they change, *when* they change, always only as the Russian Empire makes its conquests—being an empire that has time and is not of yesterday—namely, according to the principle, "as slowly as possible."

A thinker who has the development of Europe on his conscience will, in all his projects for this future, take into account the Jews as well as the Russians as the provisionally surest and most probable factors in the great play and fight of forces. What is called a "nation" in Europe today, and is really rather a *res facta* than a *res nata* (and occasionally can hardly be told from a *res ficta et picta*)[25] is in any case something evolving, young, and easily changed, not yet a race, let alone such an *aere perennius*[26] as the Jewish type: these "nations" really should carefully avoid every hotheaded rivalry and hostility! That the Jews, if they wanted it—or if they were forced into it, which seems to be what the anti-Semites want—*could* even now have preponderance, indeed quite literally mastery over Europe, that is certain; that they are *not* working and planning for that is equally certain.

Meanwhile they want and wish rather, even with some importunity, to be absorbed and assimilated by Europe; they long to be fixed, permitted, respected somewhere at long last, putting an end to the nomads' life, to the "Wandering Jew"; and this bent and impulse (which may even express an attenuation of the Jewish instincts) should be noted well and *accommodated:* to that end it might be useful and fair to expel the anti-Semitic screamers from the country.[27] Accommodated with all caution, with selection; ap-

---

[25] Something made; something born; something fictitious and unreal.

[26] More enduring than bronze: quotation from Horace's *Odes,* III, 30.1.

[27] None of this prevented Richard Oehler from quoting a passage from this section, out of context, in one of the first Nazi books on Nietzsche, after saying: "To wish to give proof regarding Nietzsche's thoughts in order to establish that they agree with the race views and strivings of the National Socialist movement would be carrying coals to Newcastle" (*Friedrich Nietzsche und die deutsche Zukunft,* Leipzig [Friedrich Nietzsche and the German future], 1935, p. 86). Oehler knew better: he had been one of the editors of the collected works and had even then compiled elaborate indices for two editions—one of these indices comprised two and a half large volumes—and later he compiled a third one for yet another edition. But the Nazis' occa-

proximately as the English nobility does. It is obvious that the stronger and already more clearly defined types of the new Germanism can enter into relations with them with the least hesitation; for example, officers of the nobility from the March Brandenburg:[28] it would be interesting in many ways to see whether the hereditary art of commanding and obeying—in both of these, the land just named is classical today—could not be enriched with[29] the genius of money and patience (and above all a little spirituality, which is utterly lacking among these officers). But here it is proper to break off my cheerful Germanomania and holiday oratory; for I am beginning to touch on what is *serious* for me, the "European problem" as I understand it, the cultivation of a new caste that will rule Europe.

252

They are no philosophical race, these Englishmen: Bacon signifies an *attack* on the philosophical spirit; Hobbes, Hume, and Locke a debasement and lowering of the value of the concept of "philosophy" for more than a century. It was *against* Hume that Kant arose, and rose; it was Locke of whom Schelling said, *understandably, "je méprise Locke"*;[30] in their fight against the English-mechanistic doltification of the world, Hegel and Schopenhauer were of one mind (with Goethe)—these two hostile brother geniuses in philosophy who strove apart toward opposite poles of the German spirit and in the process wronged each other as only brothers wrong each other.[31]

---

sional use and perversion of Nietzsche was completely devoid of the most elementary scruples. For other examples see Kaufmann's *Nietzsche,* Chapter 10.

[28] The region around Berlin. In 1701 the Elector of Brandenburg was crowned the first King of Prussia, and in 1871 the kings of Prussia, his descendants, became German Emperors.

[29] *Hinzutun, hinzuzüchten.*

[30] "I despise Locke."

[31] In fact, Hegel, who was then very famous and influential, never wronged Schopenhauer, who was young, unknown, and deliberately provocative; but

What was lacking in England, and always has been lacking there, was known well enough to that semi-actor and rhetorician, the insipid muddlehead Carlyle, who tried to conceal behind passionate grimaces what he knew of himself—namely, what was *lacking* in Carlyle: real *power* of spirituality, real *profundity* of spiritual perception; in brief, philosophy.

It is characteristic of such an unphilosophical race that it clings firmly to Christianity: they *need* its discipline to become "moralized" and somewhat humanized. The English, being gloomier, more sensual, stronger in will, and more brutal than the Germans, are precisely for that reason more vulgar, also more pious than the Germans: they stand more in *need* of Christianity. For more sensitive nostrils even this English Christianity still has a typically English odor of *spleen* and alcoholic dissipation against which it is needed for good reasons as a remedy—the subtler poison against the coarser: a subtler poisoning is indeed for clumsy peoples some progress, a step toward spiritualization. English clumsiness and peasant seriousness is still disguised most tolerably —or rather elucidated and reinterpreted—by the language of Christian gestures and by prayers and singing of psalms. And for those brutes of sots and rakes who formerly learned how to grunt morally under the sway of Methodism and more recently again as a "Salvation Army," a penitential spasm may really be the relatively highest achievement of "humanity" to which they can be raised: that much may be conceded in all fairness. But what is offensive even in the most humane Englishman is his lack of music, speaking metaphorically (but not only metaphorically): in the movements of his soul and body he has no rhythm and dance, indeed not even the desire for rhythm and dance, for "music." Listen to him speak; watch the most beautiful Englishwomen *walk*—there are no more beautiful doves and swans in any country in the world—finally listen to them sing! But I am asking too much—

Schopenhauer attacked Hegel after his death in the strongest terms, in print. See Walter Kaufmann, *Hegel* (Garden City, N.Y., Doubleday, 1965), section 54. It is remarkable how completely Nietzsche emancipated himself from Schopenhauer's view of Hegel, considering Nietzsche's early enthusiasm for Schopenhauer.

253

There are truths that are recognized best by mediocre minds because they are most congenial to them; there are truths that have charm and seductive powers only for mediocre spirits: we come up against this perhaps disagreeable proposition just now, since the spirit of respectable but mediocre Englishmen—I name Darwin, John Stuart Mill, and Herbert Spencer—is beginning to predominate in the middle regions of European taste. Indeed, who would doubt that it is useful that *such* spirits should rule at times? It would be a mistake to suppose that the spirits of a high type that soar on their own paths would be particularly skillful at determining and collecting many small and common facts and then drawing conclusions from them: on the contrary, being exceptions, they are from the start at a disadvantage when it comes to the "rule." Finally, they have more to do than merely to gain knowledge—namely, to *be* something new, to *signify* something new, to *represent* new values. Perhaps the chasm between *know* and *can* is greater, also uncannier, than people suppose: those who can do things in the grand style, the creative, may possibly have to be lacking in knowledge—while, on the other hand, for scientific discoveries of the type of Darwin's a certain narrowness, aridity, and industrious diligence, something English in short, may not be a bad disposition.

Finally, we should not forget that the English with their profound normality have once before caused an over-all depression of the European spirit: what people call "modern ideas" or "the ideas of the eighteenth century" or also "French ideas"—that, in other words, against which the *German* spirit has risen with a profound disgust—was of English origin; there is no doubt of that. The French have merely been apes and mimes of these ideas; also their best soldiers; unfortunately, their first and most thoroughgoing *victims* as well: for over this damnable Anglomania of "modern ideas" the *âme française*[32] has in the end become so thin and emaciated

---

[32] French soul.

that today one recalls her sixteenth and seventeenth centuries, her profound and passionate strength, and her inventive nobility almost with disbelief. Yet we must hang on to this proposition of historical fairness with our very teeth, defending it against momentary appearances: European *noblesse*—of feeling, of taste, of manners, taking the word, in short, in every higher sense—is the work and invention of *France;* European vulgarity, the plebeianism of modern ideas, that of *England.*—[33]

254

Even now France is still the seat of the most spiritual and sophisticated culture in Europe and the foremost school of taste—but one has to know how to find this "France of taste." [34] Those who belong to it stay well hidden: it may be a small number in whom it lives—at that, perhaps human beings whose legs might be sturdier, some of them fatalists, somber and sick, some of them overly delicate and artificial, such as have the *ambition* to hide. One point they all have in common: they plug their ears against the raging stupidity and the noisy twaddle of the democratic bourgeois. Indeed, the foreground today is taken up by a part of France that has become stupid and coarse: recently, at Victor Hugo's funeral,[35] it celebrated a veritable orgy of bad taste and at the same time self-admiration. They have in common one other point as well: the good will to resist any spiritual Germanization—and a still better incapacity to succeed.

Perhaps Schopenhauer is even now more at home and in-

---

[33] Nietzsche's influence on French letters since the turn of the century has been second only to his influence on German literature and thought; his reputation in England has been negligible. The British writers of the first rank who were influenced greatly by him were Irish: Shaw, Yeats, and Joyce.

[34] Parts of this section were later included by Nietzsche, slightly revised, in *Nietzsche contra Wagner,* in the chapter "Where Wagner Belongs" (*Portable Nietzsche,* pp. 671f.). He also used section 256 in the same chapter of *Nietzsche contra Wagner* and in the following one, and sections 269 and 270 for the chapter "The Psychologist Speaks Up" (pp. 677ff.).

[35] Victor Hugo died May 22, 1885.

digenous in this France of the spirit, which is also a France of pessimism, than he ever was in Germany—not to speak of Heinrich Heine, who has long become part of the very flesh and blood of the subtler and more demanding lyric poets of Paris, or of Hegel, who today exerts an almost tyrannical influence through Taine, who is the *foremost* historian now living. But as for Richard Wagner: the more French music learns to form itself in accordance with the actual needs of the *âme moderne*,[36] the more it will "Wagnerize"— that one can predict—and it is doing enough of that even now.

Nevertheless, there are three things to which the French can still point with pride today, as their heritage and possession and an enduring mark of their ancient cultural superiority over Europe, in spite of all voluntary and involuntary Germanization and vulgarization of their taste. First, the capacity for artistic passions, for that devotion to "form" for which the phrase *l'art pour l'art* has been invented along with a thousand others: that sort of thing has not been lacking in France for the last three centuries and has made possible again and again, thanks to their reverence for the "small number," a kind of chamber music in literature for which one looks in vain in the rest of Europe.

The second thing on which the French can base a superiority over Europe is their old, manifold, *moralistic*[37] culture, as a result of which we find, on the average, even in the little *romanciers* of the newspapers and in chance *boulevardiers de Paris* a psychological oversensitivity and curiosity of which in Germany, for example, one simply has no idea (let alone the thing itself). For this the Germans lack a few centuries of moralistic work which, as mentioned, France did not spare herself; anyone who calls the Germans "naïve" on that account praises them for a defect. (By way of contrast to the German inexperience and innocence *in voluptate psychologica*,[38] which is none too distantly related to the tediousness of

---

[36] Modern soul.

[37] The negative overtones of "moralistic" in current English usage are out of place in this context; Nietzsche is plainly thinking of the French term *moraliste*.

[38] In the delight of psychology.

German company, and as the most consummate expression of a typically French curiosity and inventiveness for this realm of delicate thrills, one may consider Henri Beyle,[39] that remarkable anticipatory and precursory human being who ran with a Napoleonic tempo through *his* Europe, through several centuries of the European soul, as an explorer and discoverer of this soul: it required two generations to *catch up* with him in any way, to figure out again a few of the riddles that tormented and enchanted him, this odd epicurean and question mark of a man who was France's last great psychologist.)

There is yet a third claim to superiority. The French character contains a halfway successful synthesis of the north and the south which allows them to comprehend many things and to do things which an Englishman could never understand. Their temperament, periodically turned toward and away from the south, in which from time to time Provençal and Ligurian blood foams over, protects them against the gruesome northern gray on gray and the sunless concept-spooking and anemia—the disease of *German* taste against whose excesses one has now prescribed for oneself, with considerable resolution, blood and iron,[40] which means "great politics" (in accordance with a dangerous healing art which teaches me to wait and wait but so far has not taught me any hope.) Even now one still encounters in France an advance understanding and

---

[39] The great French novelist (1783-1842) who is better known by his pen name, Stendhal. Nietzsche's writings abound in tributes to him; e.g., section 39 above.

[40] Bismarck's famous phrase. On May 12, 1859, writing to the cabinet minister Schleinitz from St. Petersburg, Bismarck spoke of "an infirmity of Prussia that sooner or later we shall have to cure *ferro et igni*." In an evening session of the budget commission of the Prussian parliament, September 30, 1862, he said: "It is not by speeches and majority resolutions that the great questions of the time are decided—that was the mistake of 1848 and 1849—but by iron and blood." And on January 28, 1886, Bismarck said to the Parliament: "It is not my fault that at that time I was misunderstood. It was a matter of military questions, and I said: Place as great a military force as possible, in other words as much blood and iron as possible, in the hand of the king of Prussia, then he will be able to make the politics you desire; with speeches and riflemen's festivals and songs it cannot be made; it can be made only with blood and iron."

accommodation of those rarer and rarely contented human beings who are too comprehensive to find satisfaction in any fatherland-ishness and know how to love the south in the north and the north in the south—the born Midlanders, the "good Europeans."

It was for them that *Bizet* made music, this last genius to see a new beauty and seduction—who discovered a piece of *the south of music*.

255

Against German music all kinds of precautions seem to me to be indicated. Suppose somebody loves the south as I love it, as a great school of convalescence, in the most spiritual as well as the most sensuous sense, as an uncontainable abundance of sun and transfiguration by the sun that suffuses an existence that believes and glories in itself: well, such a person will learn to be somewhat on his guard against German music, because in corrupting his taste again it also corrupts his health again.

If such a southerner, not by descent but by *faith,* should dream of the future of music, he must also dream of the redemption of music from the north, and in his ears he must have the prelude of a more profound, more powerful, perhaps more evil and mysterious music, a supra-German music that does not fade away at the sight of the voluptuous blue sea and the brightness of the Mediterranean sky, nor does it turn yellow and then pale as all German music does —a supra-European music that prevails even before the brown sunsets of the desert, a music whose soul is related to palm trees and feels at home and knows how to roam among great, beautiful, lonely beasts of prey—

I could imagine a music whose rarest magic would consist in its no longer knowing anything of good and evil, only now and then some sailor nostalgia, some golden shadows and delicate weak-nesses would pass over it—an art that from a great distance would behold, fleeing toward it, the colors of a setting *moral* world that had almost become unintelligible—and that would be hospitable and profound enough to receive such late fugitives.—

256

Owing to the pathological estrangement which the insanity of nationality has induced, and still induces, among the peoples of Europe; owing also to the shortsighted and quick-handed politicians who are at the top today with the help of this insanity, without any inkling that their separatist policies can of necessity only be *entr'acte* policies; owing to all this and much else that today simply cannot be said, the most unequivocal portents are now being overlooked, or arbitrarily and mendaciously reinterpreted—that *Europe wants to become one*.

In all the more profound and comprehensive men of this century, the over-all direction of the mysterious workings of their soul was to prepare the way for this new *synthesis* and to anticipate experimentally the European of the future: only in their foregrounds or in weaker hours, say in old age, did they belong to the "fatherlandish"—they were merely taking a rest from themselves when they became "patriots." I am thinking of such human beings as Napoleon, Goethe, Beethoven, Stendhal, Heinrich Heine, Schopenhauer: do not hold it against me when I include Richard Wagner, too, with them, for one should not allow oneself to be led astray about him by his own misunderstandings—geniuses of his type rarely have the right to understand themselves. Even less, to be sure, by the indecent noise with which people in France now close themselves off against him and resist him: the fact remains nevertheless that the *late French romanticism* of the forties and Richard Wagner belong together most closely and intimately. In all the heights and depths of their needs they are related, fundamentally related: it is Europe, the one Europe, whose soul surges and longs to get further and higher through their manifold and impetuous art —where? into a new light? toward a new sun? But who could express precisely what all these masters of new means of language could not express precisely? What is certain is that the same storm and stress tormented them and that they *sought* in the same way, these last great seekers!

Literature dominated all of them up to their eyes and ears—

they were the first artists steeped in world literature—and most of them were themselves writers, poets, mediators and mixers of the arts and senses (as a musician, Wagner belongs among painters; as a poet, among musicians; as an artist in general, among actors); all of them were fanatics of *expression* "at any price"—I should stress Delacroix, who was most closely related to Wagner—all of them great discoverers in the realm of the sublime, also of the ugly and gruesome, and still greater discoverers concerning effects, display, and the art of display windows—all of them talents far beyond their genius—virtuosos through and through, with uncanny access to everything that seduces, allures, compels, overthrows; born enemies of logic and straight lines, lusting after the foreign, the exotic, the tremendous, the crooked, the self-contradictory; as human beings, Tantaluses of the will, successful plebeians who knew themselves to be incapable, both in their lives and works, of a noble tempo, a *lento*[41]—take Balzac, for example—unbridled workers, almost self-destroyers through work; antinomians and rebels against custom, ambitious and insatiable without balance and enjoyment; all of them broke and collapsed in the end before the Christian cross (with right and reason: for who among them would have been profound and original[42] enough for a philosophy of the *Antichrist?*)—on the whole, an audaciously daring, magnificently violent type of higher human beings who soared, and tore others along, to the heights—it fell to them to first teach their century—and it is the century of the *crowd!*—the concept "higher man"—

Let the German friends of Richard Wagner ponder whether there is in Wagner's art anything outright German, or whether it is not just its distinction that it derives from *supra-German* sources and impulses. Nor should it be underestimated to what extent Paris was indispensable for the development of his type, and at the decisive moment the depth of his instincts led him to Paris. His entire manner and self-apostolate could perfect itself only when he saw the model of the French socialists. Perhaps it will be found after a subtler comparison that, to the honor of Richard Wagner's Ger-

---

[41] Slow tempo.
[42] *Ursprünglich.*

man nature, his doings were in every respect stronger, more audacious, harder, and higher than anything a Frenchman of the nineteenth century could manage—thanks to the fact that we Germans
are still closer to barbarism than the French. Perhaps Wagner's
strangest creation is inaccessible, inimitable, and beyond the feelings of the whole, so mature, Latin race, not only today but forever: the figure of Siegfried, that *very free* man who may indeed be
much too free, too hard, too cheerful, too healthy, too *anti-
Catholic* for the taste of ancient and mellow cultured peoples. He
may even have been a sin against romanticism, this anti-romantic
Siegfried: well, Wagner more than atoned for this sin in his old and
glum days when—anticipating a taste that has since then become
political—he began, if not to walk, at least to preach, with his
characteristic religious vehemence, *the way to Rome.*

Lest these final words be misunderstood, I will enlist the assistance of a few vigorous rhymes which will betray to less subtle ears,
too, what I want—what I have against the "final Wagner" and his
Parsifal music:

—Is this still German?—
Out of a German heart, this sultry screeching?
a German body, this self-laceration?
German, this priestly affectation,
this incense-perfumed sensual preaching?
German, this halting, plunging, reeling,
this so uncertain bim-bam pealing?
this nunnish ogling, *Ave* leavening,
this whole falsely ecstatic heaven overheavening?
—Is this still German?—
You still stand at the gate, perplexed?
Think! What you hear is *Rome—Rome's faith without the text.*

PART NINE

---◆◆◆---

WHAT IS NOBLE [1]

---

[1] *Vornehm*. See section 212 above, especially the last paragraph.

Part Nine

257

Every enhancement of the type "man" has so far been the work of an aristocratic society—and it will be so again and again—a society that believes in the long ladder of an order of rank and differences in value between man and man, and that needs slavery in some sense or other. Without that *pathos of distance* which grows out of the ingrained difference between strata-—when the ruling caste constantly looks afar and looks down upon subjects and instruments and just as constantly practices obedience and command, keeping down and keeping at a distance—that other, more mysterious pathos could not have grown up either—the craving for an ever new widening of distances within the soul itself, the development of ever higher, rarer, more remote, further-stretching, more comprehensive states—in brief, simply the enhancement of the type "man," the continual "self-overcoming of man," to use a moral formula in a supra-moral sense.

To be sure, one should not yield to humanitarian illusions about the origins of an aristocratic society (and thus of the presupposition of this enhancement of the type "man"): truth is hard. Let us admit to ourselves, without trying to be considerate, how every higher culture on earth so far has *begun*. Human beings whose nature was still natural, barbarians in every terrible sense of the word, men of prey who were still in possession of unbroken strength of will and lust for power, hurled themselves upon weaker, more civilized, more peaceful races, perhaps traders or cattle raisers, or upon mellow old cultures whose last vitality was even then

---

2 *Stände: Stand* can mean—apart from position, state, condition—class, rank, profession, and *Stände* can mean the estates of the realm. Asked to indicate her *Stand* on a questionnaire, a German woman might write, even after World War II: *Strassenbahnschaffnerswitwe*, that is, "widow of a streetcar conductor."

flaring up in splendid fireworks of spirit and corruption. In the beginning, the noble caste was always the barbarian caste: their predominance did not lie mainly in physical strength but in strength of the soul—they were more *whole* human beings (which also means, at every level, "more whole beasts").

258

Corruption as the expression of a threatening anarchy among the instincts and of the fact that the foundation of the affects, which is called "life," has been shaken: corruption is something totally different depending on the organism in which it appears. When, for example, an aristocracy, like that of France at the beginning of the Revolution, throws away its privileges with a sublime disgust and sacrifices itself to an extravagance of its own moral feelings, that is corruption; it was really only the last act of that centuries-old corruption which had led them to surrender, step by step, their governmental prerogatives, demoting themselves to a mere *function* of the monarchy (finally even to a mere ornament and showpiece). The essential characteristic of a good and healthy aristocracy, however, is that it experiences itself *not* as a function (whether of the monarchy or the commonwealth) but as their *meaning* and highest justification—that it therefore accepts with a good conscience the sacrifice of untold human beings who, *for its sake,* must be reduced and lowered to incomplete human beings, to slaves, to instruments. Their fundamental faith simply has to be that society must *not* exist for society's sake but only as the foundation and scaffolding on which a choice type of being is able to raise itself to its higher task and to a higher state of *being*[3]—comparable to those sun-seeking vines of Java—they are called *Sipo Matador* —that so long and so often enclasp an oak tree with their tendrils until eventually, high above it but supported by it, they can unfold their crowns in the open light and display their happiness.

---

[3] Cf. the outlook of the heroes of the *Iliad.*

259

Refraining mutually from injury, violence, and exploitation and placing one's will on a par with that of someone else—this may become, in a certain rough sense, good manners among individuals if the appropriate conditions are present (namely, if these men are actually similar in strength and value standards and belong together in *one* body). But as soon as this principle is extended, and possibly even accepted as the *fundamental principle of society,* it immediately proves to be what it really is—a will to the *denial* of life, a principle of disintegration and decay.

Here we must beware of superficiality and get to the bottom of the matter, resisting all sentimental weakness: life itself is *essentially* appropriation, injury, overpowering of what is alien and weaker; suppression, hardness, imposition of one's own forms, incorporation and at least, at its mildest, exploitation—but why should one always use those words in which a slanderous intent has been imprinted for ages?

Even the body within which individuals treat each other as equals, as suggested before—and this happens in every healthy aristocracy—if it is a living and not a dying body, has to do to other bodies what the individuals within it refrain from doing to each other: it will have to be an incarnate will to power, it will strive to grow, spread, seize, become predominant—not from any morality or immorality but because it is *living* and because life simply *is* will to power. But there is no point on which the ordinary consciousness of Europeans resists instruction as on this: everywhere people are now raving, even under scientific disguises, about coming conditions of society in which "the exploitative aspect" will be removed—which sounds to me as if they promised to invent a way of life that would dispense with all organic functions. "Exploitation" does not belong to a corrupt or imperfect and primitive society: it belongs to the *essence* of what lives, as a basic organic function; it is a consequence of the will to power, which is after all the will of life.

If this should be an innovation as a theory—as a reality it is the *primordial fact* of all history: people ought to be honest with themselves at least that far.

260

Wandering through the many subtler and coarser moralities which have so far been prevalent on earth, or still are prevalent, I found that certain features recurred regularly together and were closely associated—until I finally discovered two basic types and one basic difference.

There are *master morality* and *slave morality*[4]—I add immediately that in all the higher and more mixed cultures there also appear attempts at mediation between these two moralities, and yet more often the interpenetration and mutual misunderstanding of both, and at times they occur directly alongside each other—even in the same human being, within a *single* soul.[5] The moral discrimination of values has originated either among a ruling group whose consciousness of its difference from the ruled group was accompanied by delight—or among the ruled, the slaves and dependents of every degree.

In the first case, when the ruling group determines what is "good," the exalted, proud states of the soul are experienced as conferring distinction and determining the order of rank. The noble human being separates from himself those in whom the opposite of such exalted, proud states finds expression: he despises them. It should be noted immediately that in this first type of morality the opposition of "good" and *"bad"* means approximately the same as "noble" and "contemptible." (The opposition of "good" and *"evil"* has a different origin.) One feels contempt for the cowardly, the

---

4 While the ideas developed here, and explicated at greater length a year later in the first part of the *Genealogy of Morals,* had been expressed by Nietzsche in 1878 in section 45 of *Human, All-Too-Human,* this is the passage in which his famous terms "master morality" and "slave morality" are introduced.

5 These crucial qualifications, though added immediately, have often been overlooked. "Modern" moralities are clearly mixtures; hence their manifold tensions, hypocrisies, and contradictions.

anxious, the petty, those intent on narrow utility; also for the suspicious with their unfree glances, those who humble themselves, the doglike people who allow themselves to be maltreated, the begging flatterers, above all the liars: it is part of the fundamental faith of all aristocrats that the common people lie. "We truthful ones"—thus the nobility of ancient Greece referred to itself.

It is obvious that moral designations were everywhere first applied to *human beings* and only later, derivatively, to actions. Therefore it is a gross mistake when historians of morality start from such questions as: why was the compassionate act praised? The noble type of man experiences *itself* as determining values; it does not need approval; it judges, "what is harmful to me is harmful in itself"; it knows itself to be that which first accords honor to things; it is *value-creating.* Everything it knows as part of itself it honors: such a morality is self-glorification. In the foreground there is the feeling of fullness, of power that seeks to overflow, the happiness of high tension, the consciousness of wealth that would give and bestow: the noble human being, too, helps the unfortunate, but not, or almost not, from pity, but prompted more by an urge begotten by excess of power. The noble human being honors himself as one who is powerful, also as one who has power over himself, who knows how to speak and be silent, who delights in being severe and hard with himself and respects all severity and hardness. "A hard heart Wotan put into my breast," says an old Scandinavian saga: a fitting poetic expression, seeing that it comes from the soul of a proud Viking. Such a type of man is actually proud of the fact that he is *not* made for pity, and the hero of the saga therefore adds as a warning: "If the heart is not hard in youth it will never harden." Noble and courageous human beings who think that way are furthest removed from that morality which finds the distinction of morality precisely in pity, or in acting for others, or in *désintéressement;* faith in oneself, pride in oneself, a fundamental hostility and irony against "selflessness" belong just as definitely to noble morality as does a slight disdain and caution regarding compassionate feelings and a "warm heart."

It is the powerful who *understand* how to honor; this is their art, their realm of invention. The profound reverence for age and tradition—all law rests on this double reverence—the faith and prejudice in favor of ancestors and disfavor of those yet to come are typical of the morality of the powerful; and when the men of "modern ideas," conversely, believe almost instinctively in "progress" and "the future" and more and more lack respect for age, this in itself would sufficiently betray the ignoble origin of these "ideas."

A morality of the ruling group, however, is most alien and embarrassing to the present taste in the severity of its principle that one has duties only to one's peers; that against beings of a lower rank, against everything alien, one may behave as one pleases or "as the heart desires," and in any case "beyond good and evil"— here pity and like feelings may find their place.[6] The capacity for, and the duty of, long gratitude and long revenge—both only among one's peers—refinement in repaying, the sophisticated concept of friendship, a certain necessity for having enemies (as it were, as drainage ditches for the affects of envy, quarrelsomeness, exuberance—at bottom, in order to be capable of being good *friends*): all these are typical characteristics of noble morality which, as suggested, is not the morality of "modern ideas" and therefore is hard to empathize with today, also hard to dig up and uncover.[7]

---

[6] The final clause that follows the dash, omitted in the Cowan translation, is crucial and qualifies the first part of the sentence: a noble person has no *duties* to animals but treats them in accordance with his feelings, which means, if he is noble, with pity.

The ruling masters, of course, are not always noble in this sense, and this is recognized by Nietzsche in *Twilight of the Idols,* in the chapter "The 'Improvers' of Mankind," in which he gives strong expression to his distaste for Manu's laws concerning outcastes (*Portable Nietzsche,* pp. 503-05); also in *The Will to Power* (ed. W. Kaufmann, New York, Random House, 1967), section 142. Indeed, in *The Antichrist,* section 57, Nietzsche contradicts outright his formulation above: "When the exceptional human being treats the mediocre more tenderly than himself and his peers, this is not mere courtesy of the heart—it is simply his *duty*."

More important: Nietzsche's obvious distaste for slave morality and the fact that he makes a point of liking master morality better does not imply that he endorses master morality. Cf. the text for note 5 above.

[7] Clearly, master morality cannot be discovered by introspection nor by the observation of individuals who are "masters" rather than "slaves." Both of these misunderstandings are widespread. What is called for is rather a rereading of, say, the *Iliad* and, to illustrate "slave morality," the New Testament.

It is different with the second type of morality, *slave morality*. Suppose the violated, oppressed, suffering, unfree, who are uncertain of themselves and weary, moralize: what will their moral valuations have in common? Probably, a pessimistic suspicion about the whole condition of man will find expression, perhaps a condemnation of man along with his condition. The slave's eye is not favorable to the virtues of the powerful: he is skeptical and suspicious, *subtly* suspicious, of all the "good" that is honored there—he would like to persuade himself that even their happiness is not genuine. Conversely, those qualities are brought out and flooded with light which serve to ease existence for those who suffer: here pity, the complaisant and obliging hand, the warm heart, patience, industry, humility, and friendliness are honored—for here these are the most useful qualities and almost the only means for enduring the pressure of existence. Slave morality is essentially a morality of utility.

Here is the place for the origin of that famous opposition of "good" and "evil": into evil one's feelings project power and dangerousness, a certain terribleness, subtlety, and strength that does not permit contempt to develop. According to slave morality, those who are "evil" thus inspire fear; according to master morality it is precisely those who are "good" that inspire, and wish to inspire, fear, while the "bad" are felt to be contemptible.

The opposition reaches its climax when, as a logical consequence of slave morality, a touch of disdain is associated also with the "good" of this morality—this may be slight and benevolent— because the good human being has to be *undangerous* in the slaves' way of thinking: he is good-natured, easy to deceive, a little stupid perhaps, *un bonhomme*.[8] Wherever slave morality becomes preponderant, language tends to bring the words "good" and "stupid" closer together.

One last fundamental difference: the longing for *freedom,* the instinct for happiness and the subtleties of the feeling of free-

---

[8] Literally "a good human being," the term is used for precisely the type described here.

dom belong just as necessarily to slave morality and morals as art-ful and enthusiastic reverence and devotion are the regular symp-tom of an aristocratic way of thinking and evaluating.

This makes plain why love *as passion*—which is our Euro-pean specialty—simply must be of noble origin: as is well known, its invention must be credited to the Provençal knight-poets, those magnificent and inventive human beings of the *"gai saber"* [9] to whom Europe owes so many things and almost owes itself.—

261

Among the things that may be hardest to understand for a noble human being is vanity: he will be tempted to deny it, where another type of human being could not find it more palpable. The problem for him is to imagine people who seek to create a good opinion of themselves which they do not have of themselves—and thus also do not "deserve"—and who nevertheless end up *believing* this good opinion themselves. This strikes him half as such bad taste and lack of self-respect, and half as so baroquely irrational, that he would like to consider vanity as exceptional, and in most cases when it is spoken of he doubts it.

He will say, for example: "I may be mistaken about my value and nevertheless demand that my value, exactly as I define it, should be acknowledged by others as well—but this is no vanity (but conceit or, more frequently, what is called 'humility' or 'modesty')." Or: "For many reasons I may take pleasure in the good opinion of others: perhaps because I honor and love them and all their pleasures give me pleasure; perhaps also because their good opinion confirms and strengthens my faith in my own good opinion; perhaps because the good opinion of others, even in cases

---

9 "Gay science": in the early fourteenth century the term was used to desig-nate the art of the troubadours, codified in *Leys d'amors*. Nietzsche subtitled his own *Fröhliche Wissenschaft* (1882), *"la gaya scienza,"* placed a quatrain on the title page, began the book with a fifteen-page "Prelude in German Rhymes," and in the second edition (1887) added, besides a Preface and Book V, an "Appendix" of further verses.

where I do not share it, is still useful to me or promises to become so—but all that is not vanity."

The noble human being must force himself, with the aid of history, to recognize that, since time immemorial, in all somehow dependent social strata the common man *was* only what he was *considered:* not at all used to positing values himself, he also attached no other value to himself than his masters attached to him (it is the characteristic *right of masters* to create values).

It may be understood as the consequence of an immense atavism that even now the ordinary man still always *waits* for an opinion about himself and then instinctively submits to that—but by no means only a "good" opinion; also a bad and unfair one (consider, for example, the great majority of the self-estimates and self-underestimates that believing women accept from their father-confessors, and believing Christians quite generally from their church).

In accordance with the slowly arising democratic order of things (and its cause, the intermarriage of masters and slaves), the originally noble and rare urge to ascribe value to oneself on one's own and to "think well" of oneself will actually be encouraged and spread more and more now; but it is always opposed by an older, ampler, and more deeply ingrained propensity—and in the phenomenon of "vanity" this older propensity masters the younger one. The vain person is delighted by *every* good opinion he hears of himself (quite apart from all considerations of its utility, and also apart from truth or falsehood), just as every bad opinion of him pains him: for he submits to both, he *feels* subjected to them in accordance with that oldest instinct of submission that breaks out in him.

It is "the slave" in the blood of the vain person, a residue of the slave's craftiness—and how much "slave" is still residual in woman, for example!—that seeks to *seduce* him to good opinions about himself; it is also the slave who afterwards immediately prostrates himself before these opinions as if he had not called them forth.

And to say it once more: vanity is an atavism.

262

A *species*[10] comes to be, a type becomes fixed and strong, through the long fight with essentially constant *unfavorable* conditions. Conversely, we know from the experience of breeders[11] that species accorded superabundant nourishment and quite generally extra protection and care soon tend most strongly toward variations of the type and become rich in marvels and monstrosities (including monstrous vices).

Now look for once at an aristocratic commonwealth—say, an ancient Greek *polis,*[12] or Venice—as an arrangement, whether voluntary or involuntary, for *breeding:* [13] human beings are together there who are dependent on themselves and want their species to prevail, most often because they *have to* prevail or run the terrible risk of being exterminated. Here that boon, that excess, and that protection which favor variations are lacking; the species needs itself as a species, as something that can prevail and make itself durable by virtue of its very hardness, uniformity, and simplicity of form, in a constant fight with its neighbors or with the oppressed who are rebellious or threaten rebellion. Manifold experience teaches them to which qualities above all they owe the fact that, despite all gods and men, they are still there, that they have always triumphed: these qualities they call virtues, these virtues alone they cultivate.[14] They do this with hardness, indeed they want hardness; every aristocratic morality is intolerant—in the education of youth, in their arrangements for women, in their marriage customs, in the relations of old and young, in their penal laws (which take into account deviants only)—they consider intolerance itself a virtue, calling it "justice."

In this way a type with few but very strong traits, a species of

---

[10] Throughout this section *Art* is rendered as species, and *Typus* as type. Elsewhere, *Art* is often translated as type.

[11] *Züchter.*

[12] City-state.

[13] *Züchtung.*

[14] *Züchtet sie gross.*

severe, warlike, prudently taciturn men, close-mouthed and closely linked (and as such possessed of the subtlest feeling for the charms and *nuances* of association), is fixed beyond the changing generations; the continual fight against ever constant *unfavorable* conditions is, as mentioned previously, the cause that fixes and hardens a type.

Eventually, however, a day arrives when conditions become more fortunate and the tremendous tension decreases; perhaps there are no longer any enemies among one's neighbors, and the means of life, even for the enjoyment of life, are superabundant. At one stroke the bond and constraint of the old discipline[15] are torn: it no longer seems necessary, a condition of existence—if it persisted it would only be a form of *luxury,* an archaizing *taste.* Variation, whether as deviation (to something higher, subtler, rarer) or as degeneration and monstrosity, suddenly appears on the scene in the greatest abundance and magnificence; the individual dares to be individual and different.

At these turning points of history we behold beside one another, and often mutually involved and entangled, a splendid, manifold, junglelike growth and upward striving, a kind of *tropical* tempo in the competition to grow, and a tremendous ruin and self-ruination, as the savage egoisms that have turned, almost exploded, against one another wrestle "for sun and light" and can no longer derive any limit, restraint, or consideration from their previous[16] morality. It was this morality itself that dammed up such enormous strength and bent the bow in such a threatening manner; now it is "outlived." The dangerous and uncanny point has been reached where the greater, more manifold, more comprehensive life transcends and *lives beyond* the old morality; the "individual" appears, obliged to give himself laws and to develop his own arts and wiles for self-preservation, self-enhancement, self-redemption.

All sorts of new what-fors and wherewithals; no shared formulas any longer; misunderstanding allied with disrespect; decay, cor-

---

[15] *Zucht.*

[16] *Bisherigen:* elsewhere *bisher* has always been rendered as "so far"; see Preface, note 1.

ruption, and the highest desires gruesomely entangled; the genius of the race overflowing from all cornucopias of good and bad; a calamitous simultaneity of spring and fall, full of new charms and veils that characterize young, still unexhausted, still unwearied corruption. Again danger is there, the mother of morals, great danger, this time transposed into the individual, into the neighbor and friend, into the alley, into one's own child, into one's own heart, into the most personal and secret recesses of wish and will: what may the moral philosophers emerging in this age have to preach now?

These acute observers and loiterers discover that the end is approaching fast, that everything around them is corrupted and corrupts, that nothing will stand the day after tomorrow, except *one* type of man, the incurably *mediocre*. The mediocre alone have a chance of continuing their type and propagating—they are the men of the future, the only survivors: "Be like them! Become mediocre!" is now the only morality that still makes sense, that still gets a hearing.

But this morality of mediocrity is hard to preach: after all, it may never admit what it is and what it wants. It must speak of measure and dignity and duty and neighbor love—it will find it difficult *to conceal its irony*.—

263

There is an *instinct for rank* which, more than anything else, is a sign of a *high* rank; there is a delight in the nuances of reverence that allows us to infer noble origin and habits. The refinement, graciousness, and height of a soul is tested dangerously when something of the first rank passes by without being as yet protected by the shudders of authority against obtrusive efforts and ineptitudes—something that goes its way unmarked, undiscovered, tempting, perhaps capriciously concealed and disguised, like a living touchstone. Anyone to whose task and practice it belongs to search out souls will employ this very art in many forms in order to determine the ultimate value of a soul and the unalterable, innate order of rank to which it belongs: he will test it for its *instinct of reverence.*

Différence engendre haine:[17] the baseness of some people suddenly spurts up like dirty water when some holy vessel, some precious thing from a locked shrine, some book with the marks of a great destiny, is carried past; and on the other hand there is a reflex of silence, a hesitation of the eye, a cessation of all gestures that express how a soul *feels* the proximity of the most venerable. The way in which reverence for the *Bible* has on the whole been maintained so far in Europe is perhaps the best bit of discipline and refinement of manners that Europe owes to Christianity: such books of profundity and ultimate significance require some external tyranny of authority for their protection in order to gain those millennia of *persistence* which are necessary to exhaust them and figure them out.

Much is gained once the feeling has finally been cultivated in the masses (among the shallow and in the high-speed intestines of every kind) that they are not to touch everything; that there are holy experiences before which they have to take off their shoes and keep away their unclean hands—this is almost their greatest advance toward humanity. Conversely, perhaps there is nothing about so-called educated people and believers in "modern ideas" that is as nauseous as their lack of modesty and the comfortable insolence of their eyes and hands with which they touch, lick, and finger everything; and it is possible that even among the common people, among the less educated, especially among peasants, one finds today more *relative* nobility of taste and tactful reverence than among the newspaper-reading *demi-monde* of the spirit, the educated.

264

One cannot erase from the soul of a human being what his ancestors liked most to do and did most constantly: whether they

---

[17] Difference engenders hatred.

were, for example, assiduous savers and appurtenances of a desk and cash box, modest and bourgeois in their desires, modest also in their virtues; or whether they lived accustomed to commanding from dawn to dusk, fond of rough amusements and also perhaps of even rougher duties and responsibilities; or whether, finally, at some point they sacrificed ancient prerogatives of birth and possessions in order to live entirely for their faith—their "god"—as men of an inexorable and delicate conscience which blushes at every compromise. It is simply not possible that a human being should *not* have the qualities and preferences of his parents and ancestors in his body, whatever appearances may suggest to the contrary. This is the problem of race.[18]

If one knows something about the parents, an inference about the child is permissible: any disgusting incontinence, any nook envy, a clumsy insistence that one is always right—these three things together have always constituted the characteristic type of the plebeian—that sort of thing must as surely be transferred to the child as corrupted blood; and with the aid of the best education one will at best *deceive* with regard to such a heredity.

And what else is the aim of education and "culture" today? In our very popularity-minded—that is, plebeian—age, "education" and "culture" *have* to be essentially the art of deceiving—about one's origins, the inherited plebs in one's body and soul. An educator who today preached truthfulness above all and constantly challenged his students, "be true! be natural! do not pretend!"—even such a virtuous and guileless ass would learn after a while to reach for that *furca* of Horace to *naturam expellere:* with what success? "Plebs" *usque recurret.*[19]—

---

[18] Here, as elsewhere, Nietzsche gives expression to his Lamarckian belief in the heredity of acquired characteristics, shared by Samuel Butler and Bernard Shaw but anathema to Nazi racists and almost universally rejected by geneticists. His Lamarckism is not just an odd fact about Nietzsche but symptomatic of his conception of body and spirit: he ridiculed belief in "pure" spirit but believed just as little in any "pure" body; he claimed that neither could be understood without the other. For a detailed discussion see Kaufmann, *Nietzsche,* Chapter 10.

[19] Horace's *Epistles,* I.10, 24: "Try with a pitchfork to drive out nature, she always returns."

265

At the risk of displeasing innocent ears I propose: egoism belongs to the nature of a noble soul—I mean that unshakable faith that to a being such as "we are" other beings must be subordinate by nature and have to sacrifice themselves. The noble soul accepts this fact of its egoism without any question mark, also without any feeling that it might contain hardness, constraint, or caprice, rather as something that may be founded in the primordial law of things: if it sought a name for this fact it would say, "it is justice itself." Perhaps it admits under certain circumstances that at first make it hesitate that there are some who have rights equal to its own; as soon as this matter of rank is settled it moves among these equals with their equal privileges, showing the same sureness of modesty and delicate reverence that characterize its relations with itself—in accordance with an innate heavenly mechanism understood by all stars. It is merely another aspect of its egoism, this refinement and self-limitation in its relations with its equals—every star is such an egoist—it honors *itself* in them and in the rights it cedes to them; it does not doubt that the exchange of honors and rights is of the nature of all social relations and thus also belongs to the natural condition of things.

The noble soul gives as it takes, from that passionate and irritable instinct of repayment that lies in its depth. The concept "grace" [20] has no meaning or good odor *inter pares;* [21] there may be a sublime way of letting presents from above happen to one, as it were, and to drink them up thirstily like drops—but for this art and gesture the noble soul has no aptitude. Its egoism hinders it: quite generally it does not like to look "up"—but either *ahead,* horizontally and slowly, or down: *it knows itself to be at a height.*

266

"Truly high respect one can have only for those who do not *seek* themselves."—Goethe to Rat Schlosser.

---

[20] *"Gnade."*
[21] Among equals.

267

The Chinese have a proverb that mothers even teach children: *siao-sin*—"make your heart *small!*" This is the characteristic fundamental propensity in late civilizations: I do not doubt that an ancient Greek would recognize in us Europeans of today, too, such self-diminution; this alone would suffice for us to "offend his taste."—

268

What, in the end, is common? [22]

Words are acoustical signs for concepts; concepts, however, are more or less definite image signs for often recurring and associated sensations, for groups of sensations. To understand one another, it is not enough that one use the same words; one also has to use the same words for the same species of inner experiences; in the end one has to have one's experience in *common*.

Therefore the human beings of *one* people understand one another better than those belonging to different peoples even if they employ the same language; or rather when human beings have long lived together under similar conditions (of climate, soil, danger, needs, and work), what *results*[23] from this is people who "understand [24] one another"—a people. In all souls an equal number of often recurring experiences has come to be predominant over experiences that come more rarely: on the basis of the former one understands the other, quickly and ever more quickly—the history of language is the history of a process of abbreviation—and on the basis of such quick understanding one associates, ever more closely.

The greater the danger is, the greater is the need to reach agreement quickly and easily about what must be done; not mis-

---

22 *Die Gemeinheit:* commonness; but it usually means vulgarity, meanness, baseness.
23 *Entsteht.*
24 *"Sich versteht."*

understanding one another in times of danger is what human beings simply cannot do without in their relations. In every friendship or love affair one still makes this test: nothing of that sort can
endure once one discovers that one's partner associates different
feelings, intentions, nuances, desires, and fears with the same
words. (Fear of the "eternal misunderstanding"—that is the benevolent genius which so often keeps persons of different sex from rash
attachments to which their senses and hearts prompt them—this
and *not* some Schopenhauerian "genius of the species"!)

Which group of sensations is aroused, expresses itself, and issues commands in a soul most quickly, is decisive for the whole order of rank of its values and ultimately determines its table of
goods. The values of a human being betray something of the *structure* of his soul and where it finds its conditions of life, its true need.

Assuming next that need has ever brought close to one another
only such human beings as could suggest with similar signs similar
requirements and experiences, it would follow on the whole that
easy communicability of need—which in the last analysis means
the experience of merely average and *common* experiences—must
have been the most powerful of all powers at whose disposal man
has been so far. The human beings who are more similar, more ordinary, have had, and always have, an advantage; those more se-
lect, subtle, strange, and difficult to understand, easily remain
alone, succumb to accidents, being isolated, and rarely propagate.
One must invoke tremendous counter-forces in order to cross this
natural, all too natural *progressus in simile,* the continual development of man toward the similar, ordinary, average, herdlike—
common!

269

The more a psychologist—a born and inevitable psychologist
and unriddler of souls—applies himself to the more exquisite cases
and human beings, the greater becomes the danger that he might
suffocate from pity.[25] He *needs* hardness and cheerfulness more

---

[25] Cf. *Zarathustra,* Part IV.

than anyone else. For the corruption, the ruination of the higher men, of the souls of a stranger type, is the rule: it is terrible to have such a rule always before one's eyes. The manifold torture of the psychologist who has discovered this ruination, who discovers this whole inner hopelessness of the higher man, this eternal "too late" in every sense, first in one case and then *almost* always through the whole of history—may perhaps lead him one day to turn against his own lot, embittered, and to make an attempt at self-destruction—may lead to his own "corruption."

In almost every psychologist one will perceive a telltale preference for and delight in association with everyday, well-ordered people: this reveals that he always requires a cure, that he needs a kind of escape and forgetting, away from all that with which his insights, his incisions, his "craft" have burdened his conscience. He is characterized by fear of his memory. He is easily silenced by the judgments of others; he listens with an immobile face as they venerate, admire, love, and transfigure where he has *seen*—or he even conceals his silence by expressly agreeing with some foreground opinion. Perhaps the paradox of his situation is so gruesome that precisely where he has learned the greatest pity coupled with the greatest contempt, the crowd, the educated, the enthusiasts learn the greatest veneration—the veneration for "great men" and prodigies for whose sake one blesses and honors the fatherland, the earth, the dignity of humanity, and oneself, and to whom one refers the young, toward whom one educates them—

And who knows whether what happened in all great cases so far was not always the same: that the crowd adored a god—and that the "god" was merely a poor sacrificial animal. Success has always been the greatest liar—and the "work" itself is a success; the great statesman, the conqueror, the discoverer is disguised by his creations, often beyond recognition; the "work," whether of the artist or the philosopher, invents the man who has created it, who is supposed to have created it; "great men," as they are venerated, are subsequent pieces of wretched minor fiction; in the world of historical values, counterfeit *rules*.

Those great poets, for example—men like Byron, Musset, Poe, Leopardi, Kleist, Gogol (I do not dare mention greater names, but I mean them) [26]—are and perhaps must be men of fleeting moments, enthusiastic, sensual, childish, frivolous and sudden in mistrust and trust; with souls in which they usually try to conceal some fracture; often taking revenge with their works for some inner contamination, often seeking with their high flights to escape into forgetfulness from an all-too-faithful memory; often lost in the mud and almost in love with it, until they become like the will-o'-the-wisps around swamps and *pose* as stars—the people may then call them idealists—often fighting against a long nausea, with a recurring specter of unbelief that chills and forces them to languish for *gloria* and to gobble their "belief in themselves" from the hands of intoxicated flatterers—what *torture* are these great artists and all the so-called higher men for anyone who has once guessed their true nature! [27]

It is easy to understand that *these* men should so readily receive from woman—clairvoyant in the world of suffering and, unfortunately, also desirous far beyond her strength to help and save —those eruptions of boundless and most devoted *pity* which the multitude, above all the venerating multitude, does not understand and on which it lavishes inquisitive and self-satisfied interpretations. This pity deceives itself regularly about its powers; woman would like to believe that love can achieve *anything*—that is her characteristic *faith*. Alas, whoever knows the heart will guess how poor, stupid, helpless, arrogant, blundering, more apt to destroy than to save is even the best and profoundest love!

It is possible that underneath the holy fable and disguise of

---

[26] The parenthesis is not found in the first two editions of 1886 and 1891, but it appears in all standard editions, including Schlechta's, although he purports to follow the original edition. When Nietzsche included this passage in *Nietzsche contra Wagner* in slightly revised form, the remark was set off by dashes instead of parentheses and read, "I do not mention far greater names, but I mean them" (*Portable Nietzsche*, p. 678). The third edition of *Beyond Good and Evil* (1894) has "far greater names."

According to the table comparing the page numbers of the different editions of *Beyond Good and Evil* in Vol. VII (1903) of the Grossoktav edition of the *Werke*, the third edition of *Beyond* was dated 1893, the fourth 1894, and the page numbers of both are the same; but the Princeton University Library has a copy of the *Dritte Auflage* (third edition) dated 1894.

[27] Another leitmotif of *Zarathustra*, Part IV.

Jesus' life there lies concealed one of the most painful cases of the martyrdom of *knowledge about love:* the martyrdom of the most innocent and desirous heart, never sated by any human love; *demanding* love, to be loved and nothing else, with hardness, with insanity, with terrible eruptions against those who denied him love; the story of a poor fellow, unsated and insatiable in love, who had to invent hell in order to send to it those who did not *want* to love him—and who finally, having gained kowledge about human love, had to invent a god who is all love, all *ability* to love—who has mercy on human love because it is so utterly wretched and unknowing. Anyone who feels that way, who *knows* this about love— *seeks* death.

But why pursue such painful matters? Assuming one does not have to.—

270

The spiritual haughtiness and nausea of every man who has suffered profoundly—it almost determines the order of rank *how* profoundly human beings can suffer—his shuddering certainty, which permeates and colors him through and through, that by virtue of his suffering he *knows more* than the cleverest and wisest could possibly know, and that he knows his way and has once been "at home" in many distant, terrifying worlds of which *"you* know nothing"—this spiritual and silent haughtiness of the sufferer, this pride of the elect of knowledge, of the "initiated," of the almost sacrificed, finds all kinds of disguises necessary to protect itself against contact with obtrusive and pitying hands and altogether against everything that is not its equal in suffering. Profound suffering makes noble; it separates.

One of the most refined disguises is Epicureanism, and a certain ostentatious courage of taste which takes suffering casually and resists everything sad and profound. There are "cheerful people" who employ cheerfulness because they are misunderstood on its account—they *want* to be misunderstood. There are "scientific men" who employ science because it creates a cheerful appearance, and because being scientific suggests that a human being is superficial—they *want* to seduce others to this false inference. There are free, insolent spirits who would like to conceal and deny that they are broken, proud, incurable hearts (the cynicism of Hamlet—the case of Galiani);[28] and occasionally even foolishness is the mask for an unblessed all-too-certain knowledge.

From which it follows that it is characteristic of more refined humanity to respect "the mask" and not to indulge in psychology and curiosity in the wrong place.

271

What separates two people most profoundly is a different sense and degree of cleanliness. What avails all decency and mutual usefulness and good will toward each other—in the end the fact remains: "They can't stand each other's smell!"

The highest instinct of cleanliness places those possessed of it in the oddest and most dangerous lonesomeness, as saints: for precisely this is saintliness—the highest spiritualization of this instinct. Whether one is privy to someone's indescribable abundance of pleasure in the bath, or whether one feels some ardor and thirst that constantly drives the soul out of the night into the morning and out of the dim and "dark moods" into what is bright, brilliant, profound, and refined—just as such a propensity *distinguishes*—it is a noble propensity—it also *separates*.

The saint's pity is pity with the *dirt* of what is human, all too human. And there are degrees and heights where he experiences even pity itself as a pollution, as dirty—

272

Signs of nobility: never thinking of degrading our duties into duties for everybody; not wanting to delegate, to share, one's own responsibility; counting one's privileges and their exercise among one's *duties*.

---

[28] The parenthesis is not found in the first four editions (see note 26 above), but in most subsequent editions, including Schlechta's. In *Nietzsche contra Wagner* we read, instead of the parenthesis: "—the case of Hamlet."

273

A human being who strives for something great considers everyone he meets on his way either as a means or as a delay and obstacle—or as a temporary resting place. His characteristic high-grade *graciousness* toward his fellow men becomes possible only once he has attained his height and rules. Impatience and his consciousness that until then he is always condemned to comedy—for even war is a comedy and conceals, just as every means conceals the end—spoil all of his relations to others: this type of man knows solitude and what is most poisonous in it.

274

The problem of those who are waiting.—It requires strokes of luck and much that is incalculable if a higher man in whom the solution of a problem lies dormant is to get around to action in time —to "eruption," one might say. In the average case it does *not* happen, and in nooks all over the earth sit men who are waiting, scarcely knowing in what way they are waiting, much less that they are waiting in vain. Occasionally the call that awakens—that accident which gives the "permission" to act—comes too late, when the best youth and strength for action has already been used up by sitting still; and many have found to their horror when they "leaped up" that their limbs had gone to sleep and their spirit had become too heavy. "It is too late," they said to themselves, having lost their faith in themselves and henceforth forever useless.

Could it be that in the realm of the spirit "Raphael without hands," taking this phrase in the widest sense, is perhaps not the exception but the rule? [29]

---

[29] An allusion to an oft-quoted sentence from Lessing's *Emilia Galotti,* Act I, Scene 4: "Or do you think, my Prince, that Raphael would not have been the greatest artistic [literally: painterly] genius if he had been born by some misfortune without hands?"

This section reminds us forcefully that Nietzsche is not proposing any easy bifurcation of mankind: not only are appearances misleading, as he points out again and again, but he considers the belief in opposite values an

Genius is perhaps not so rare after all—but the five hundred *hands* it requires to tyrannize the *kairos,* "the right time," seizing chance by its forelock.

275

Anyone who does not *want* to see what is lofty in a man looks that much more keenly for what is low in him and mere foreground —and thus betrays himself.

276

In all kinds of injury and loss the lower and coarser soul is better off than the nobler one: the dangers for the latter must be greater; the probability that it will come to grief and perish is actually, in view of the multiplicity of the conditions of its life, tremendous.

In a lizard a lost finger is replaced again; not so in man.

277

—Bad enough! The same old story! When one has finished building ones' house, one suddenly realizes that in the process one has learned something that one really needed to know in the worst way—before one began. The eternal distasteful "too late!"

The melancholy of everything *finished!* [30]—

278

Wanderer, who are you? I see you walking on your way without scorn, without love, with unfathomable eyes; moist and sad like

---

inveterate prejudice (see, e.g., section 2) and insists on a scale of subtle shades, degrees, and nuances.

[30] This section may signal the approaching end of the book. And the immediately following sections, being less continuous than the preceding, may also have been placed here from a sense of "where else?"—the end being at hand. In a sense, to be sure, they belong in Part IX, "What Is Noble," for they deal with the feelings of the uncommon man who lives apart; but they seem more personal.

a sounding lead that has returned to the light, unsated, from every depth—what did it seek down there?—with a breast that does not sigh, with a lip that conceals its disgust, with a hand that now reaches only slowly: who are you? what have you done? Rest here: this spot is hospitable to all—recuperate! And whoever you may be: what do you like now? what do you need for recreation? Name it: whatever I have I offer to you!

"Recreation? Recreation? You *are* inquisitive! What are you saying! But give me, please——"

What? What? Say it!

"Another mask! A second mask!" [31]—

279

Men of profound sadness betray themselves when they are happy: they have a way of embracing happiness as if they wanted to crush and suffocate it, from jealousy: alas, they know only too well that it will flee.

280

"Too bad! What? Isn't he going—back?"

Yes, but you understand him badly when you complain. He is going back like anybody who wants to attempt a big jump.—

281

—"Will people believe me? But I demand that they should believe me: I have always thought little and badly of myself, only on very rare occasions, only when I had to, always without any desire for 'this subject,' more than ready to digress from 'myself'; always without faith in the result, owing to an unconquerable mistrust of the *possibility* of self-knowledge which went so far that even in the concept of 'immediate knowledge,' which theoreticians permit themselves, I sensed a *contradictio in adjecto:* this whole

---

[31] See sections 30, 40, 289, and 290.

fact is almost the most certain thing I do know about myself. There must be a kind of aversion in me to *believing* anything definite about myself.

"Does this perhaps point to a riddle? Probably; but fortunately none for my own teeth.

"Perhaps it betrays the species to which I belong?

"But not to me—and of that I am glad."

282

—"But whatever happened to you?"

"I don't know," he said hesitantly; "perhaps the Harpies flew over my table."

Nowadays it happens occasionally that a mild, moderate, reticent person suddenly goes into a rage, smashes dishes, upends the table, screams, raves, insults everybody—and eventually walks off, ashamed, furious with himself—where? what for? To starve by himself? To suffocate on his recollection?

If a person has the desires of a high and choosy soul and only rarely finds his table set and his food ready, his danger will be great at all times; but today it is extraordinary. Thrown into a noisy and plebeian age with which he does not care to eat out of the same dishes, he can easily perish of hunger and thirst or, if eventually he "falls to" after all—of sudden nausea.

Probably all of us have sat at tables where we did not belong; and precisely the most spiritual among us, being hardest to nourish, know that dangerous dyspepsia which comes of a sudden insight and disappointment about our food and our neighbors at the table—the *after-dinner nausea*.

283

It involves subtle and at the same time noble self-control, assuming that one wants to praise at all, if one always praises only where one does *not* agree: for in the other case one would after all praise oneself, which offends good taste. Still this kind of self-control furnishes a neat occasion and provocation for constant misunderstandings. To be in a position to afford this real luxury of taste and morality, one must not live among dolts of the spirit but rather among people whose misunderstandings and blunders are still amusing owing to their subtlety—or one will have to pay dearly for it!

"He praises me: *hence* he thinks I am right"—this asinine inference spoils half our life for us hermits, for it leads asses to seek our neighborhood and friendship.

284

To live with tremendous and proud composure; always beyond—. To have and not to have one's affects, one's pro and con, at will; to condescend to them, for a few hours; to *seat* oneself on them as on a horse, often as on an ass—for one must know how to make use of their stupidity as much as of their fire. To reserve one's three hundred foregrounds; also the dark glasses; for there are cases when nobody may look into our eyes, still less into our "grounds." And to choose for company that impish and cheerful vice, courtesy. And to remain master of one's four virtues: of courage, insight, sympathy, and solitude.[32] For solitude is a virtue for us, as a sublime bent and urge for cleanliness which guesses how all contact between man and man—"in society"—involves inevitable uncleanliness. All community makes men—somehow, somewhere, sometime "common."

---

[32] But see section 227: "Honesty, supposing that this is our virtue . . ." And *Dawn,* section 556 (quoted in full): "*The good four.—Honest* with ourselves and whoever *else* is our friend; *courageous* with the enemy; *magnanimous* with the vanquished; *courteous*—always: thus the four cardinal virtues want us." Plato's four cardinal virtues had been wisdom, courage, temperance, and justice (*Republic* 427ff.). In German, the four terms in the *Dawn* are: *redlich, tapfer, grossmütig, höflich;* the four above: *Mut, Einsicht, Mitgefühl, Einsamkeit. Mut* and *Tapferkeit* are synonyms and mean courage. Honesty and insight are clearly related but not synonymous, and this is also true of magnanimity and sympathy. (The literal meaning of sympathy and *Mitgefühl* is the same and neither is restricted to suffering; both mean feeling with others what they feel.) The inclusion of sympathy among the four virtues is noteworthy, particularly as it occurs in "What Is Noble" in *Beyond Good and Evil.*

285

The greatest events and thoughts—but the greatest thoughts are the greatest events—are comprehended last: the generations that are contemporaneous with them do not *experience* such events —they live right past them. What happens is a little like what happens in the realm of stars. The light of the remotest stars comes last to men; and until it has arrived man *denies* that there are—stars there. "How many centuries does a spirit require to be comprehended?"—that is a standard, too; with that, too, one creates an order of rank and etiquette that is still needed—for spirit and star.[33]

286

"Here the vision is free, the spirit exalted." [34]

But there is an opposite type of man that is also on a height and also has free vision—but looks *down*.

287

—What is noble? What does the word "noble" still mean to us today? What betrays, what allows one to recognize the noble human being, under this heavy, overcast sky of the beginning rule of the plebs that makes everything opaque and leaden?

---

[33] Cf. *Zarathustra*, Part II: "the greatest events—they are not our loudest but our stillest hours. Not around the inventors of new noise, but around the inventors of new values does the world revolve; it revolves *inaudibly*" ("On Great Events," p. 243); and "Thoughts that come on doves' feet guide the world" ("The Stillest Hour," p. 258). The implications for Nietzsche's alleged bifurcation of humanity should not be overlooked: We are in no position to tell who among our contemporaries is great.

[34] Goethe's *Faust*, lines 11989f. This aphorism makes little sense unless one recognizes the quotation and knows that Doctor Marianus thus leads up to his apostrophe to the queen of heaven.— One may wonder whether it could possibly be noble to insist so often that one is looking *down*; but at least Nietzsche does not purport to speak of himself.

It is not actions that prove him—actions are always open to many interpretations, always unfathomable—nor is it "works." Among artists and scholars today one finds enough of those who betray by their works how they are impelled by a profound desire for what is noble; but just this need *for* what is noble is fundamentally different from the needs of the noble soul itself and actually the eloquent and dangerous mark of its lack. It is not the works, it is the *faith* that is decisive here, that determines the order of rank —to take up again an ancient religious formula in a new and more profound sense: some fundamental certainty that a noble soul has about itself, something that cannot be sought, nor found, nor perhaps lost.

The noble soul has reverence for itself.[35]

288

There are human beings who have spirit in an inevitable way; they may turn and twist as they please and hold their hands over their giveaway eyes (as if a hand did not give away secrets!)—in the end it always will out that they have something they conceal, namely spirit. One of the subtlest means for keeping up the deception at least as long as possible and of successfully appearing more stupid than one is—which in ordinary life is often as desirable as an umbrella—is called *enthusiasm,* if we include what belongs with it; for example, virtue. For as Galiani, who should know, says: *vertu est enthousiasme.*

289

In the writings[36] of a hermit one always also hears something of the echo of the desolate regions, something of the whispered

---

[35] Cf. Aristotle's *Nicomachean Ethics* (1169a): "The good man ought to be a lover of self, since he will then act nobly, and so both benefit himself and his fellows; but the bad man ought not to be a lover of self, since he will follow his base passions, and so injure both himself and his neighbours" (Rackham translation). Cf. also the long note for section 212 above.

[36] "Footsteps" in the Cowan translation depends on misreading *Schritten* instead of *Schriften.*

tones and the furtive look of solitude; in his strongest words, even
in his cry, there still vibrates a new and dangerous kind of silence
—of burying something in silence. When a man has been sitting
alone with his soul in confidential discord and discourse, year in
and year out, day and night; when in his cave—it may be a labyrinth or a gold mine—he has become a cave bear or a treasure dig-
ger or a treasure guard and dragon; then even his concepts eventually acquire a peculiar twilight color, an odor just as much of depth
as of must, something incommunicable and recalcitrant that blows
at every passerby like a chill.

The hermit does not believe that any philosopher—assuming
that every philosopher was first of all a hermit—ever expressed his
real and ultimate opinions in books: does one not write books precisely to conceal what one harbors? [37] Indeed, he will doubt
whether a philosopher could *possibly* have "ultimate and real"
opinions, whether behind every one of his caves there is not, must
not be, another deeper cave—a more comprehensive, stranger,
richer world beyond the surface, an abysmally deep ground behind every ground, under every attempt to furnish "grounds." [38]
Every philosophy is a foreground philosophy—that is a hermit's
judgment: "There is something arbitrary in his stopping *here* to
look back and look around, in his not digging deeper *here* but laying
his spade aside; there is also something suspicious about it." Every
philosophy also *conceals* a philosophy; every opinion is also a hide-
out, every word also a mask.

290

Every profound thinker is more afraid of being understood
than of being misunderstood. The latter may hurt his vanity, but
the former his heart, his sympathy, which always says: "Alas, why
do *you* want to have as hard a time as I did?"

---

[37] *Um zu verbergen, was man bei sich birgt.* See sections 30 and 40 above.
[38] *Ein Abgrund hinter jedem Grunde, unter jeder "Begründung."*

291

Man, a manifold, mendacious, artificial, and opaque animal, uncanny to the other animals less because of his strength than because of his cunning and shrewdness, has invented the good conscience to enjoy his soul for once as *simple;* and the whole of morality is a long undismayed forgery which alone makes it at all possible to enjoy the sight of the soul. From this point of view much more may belong in the concept of "art" than is generally believed.

292

A philosopher—is a human being who constantly experiences, sees, hears, suspects, hopes, and dreams extraordinary things; who is struck by his own thoughts as from outside, as from above and below, as by *his* type of experiences and lightning bolts; who is perhaps himself a storm pregnant with new lightnings; a fatal human being around whom there are constant rumblings and growlings, crevices, and uncanny doings. A philosopher—alas, a being that often runs away from itself, often is afraid of itself—but too inquisitive not to "come to" again—always back to himself.

293

A man who says, "I like this, I take this for my own and want to protect it and defend it against anybody"; a man who is able to manage something, to carry out a resolution, to remain faithful to a thought, to hold a woman, to punish and prostrate one who presumed too much; a man who has his wrath and his sword and to whom the weak, the suffering, the hard pressed, and the animals, too, like to come[39] and belong by nature, in short a man who is by nature a *master*—when such a man has pity, well, *this* pity has value. But what good is the pity of those who suffer. Or those who, worse, *preach* pity.

---

[39] *Gern zufallen:* literally, they like to fall to him or to his lot.

Almost everywhere in Europe today we find a pathological sensitivity and receptivity to pain; also a repulsive incontinence in lamentation, an increase in tenderness that would use religion and philosophical bric-a-brac to deck itself out as something higher—there is a veritable cult of suffering. The *unmanliness* of what is baptized as "pity" in the circles of such enthusiasts is, I should think, what always meets the eye first.

This newest kind of bad taste should be exorcized vigorously and thoroughly; and I finally wish that one might place around one's heart and neck the good amulet *"gai saber"*—"gay science," to make it plain to the plain.[40]

294

The Olympian vice.— In despite of that philosopher who, being a real Englishman, tried to bring laughter into ill repute among all thinking men—"laughing is a bad infirmity of human nature, which every thinking mind will strive to overcome" (Hobbes)[41]—

---

[40] *Um es den Deutschen zu verdeutlichen.* Cf. section 260. note 9.

[41] Translated into English from Nietzsche's German. Though the words appear in quotation marks, there seem to be only five passages in which Hobbes discusses laughter—never in quite these words. (Two of these are found in the Latin works and add nothing to the quotations that follow.) Hobbes explained laughter by invoking the will to power, albeit without using that term.

The first and longest discussion is found in *Human Nature* (1640), Chapter IX.13: "There is a passion that hath no name; but the sign of it is that distortion of the countenance which we call *laughter*, which is always *joy*. . . . Whatsoever it be that moveth to laughter, it must be *new* and *unexpected*. Men laugh often, especially such as are greedy of applause from every thing they do well, at their *own* actions performed never so little beyond their own expectations; as also at their own *jests*: and in this case it is manifest, that the passion of laughter proceedeth from a *sudden conception* of some *ability* in himself that laugheth. Also men laugh at the *infirmities* of others, by comparison wherewith their own abilities are set off and illustrated. Also men laugh at *jests*, the *wit* whereof always consisteth in the elegant *discovering* and conveying to our minds some *absurdity* of *another:* and in this case also the passion of laughter proceedeth from the *sudden* imagination of our own odds and eminency. . . . For when a jest is broken upon ourselves, or friends of whose dishonour we participate, we never laugh thereat. I may therefore conclude, that the passion of laughter is nothing else but *sudden glory* arising from some sudden *conception* of some *eminency* in ourselves, by comparison with the *infirmity* of others, or

I should actually risk an order of rank among philosophers depending on the rank of their laughter—all the way up to those capable of *golden* laughter. And supposing that gods, too, philosophize, which has been suggested to me by many an inference—I

---

with our own formerly: for men laugh at the follies of themselves past . . . Besides, it is vain glory, and an argument of little worth, to think the infirmity of another, sufficient matter for his triumph."

The parallel passage in the *Leviathan* (1651), Part I, Chapter 6, p. 27, which is much shorter, ends: "And it is incident most to them, that are conscious of the fewest abilities in themselves; who are forced to keep themselves in their own favour, by observing the imperfections of other men. And therefore much Laughter at the defects of others is a signe of Pusillanimity. For of great minds, one of the proper workes is, to help and free others from scorn; and compare themselves onely with the most able."

Finally, in "The Answer of Mr. Hobbes to Sir William Davenant's Preface before Gondibert" (Paris, Jan. 10, 1650; reprinted in *The English Works of Thomas Hobbes,* vol. IV, 1840) Hobbes says (pp. 454f.): "Great persons, that have their minds employed on great designs, have not leisure enough to laugh, and are pleased with the contemplation of their own power and virtues, so as they need not the infirmities and vices of other men to recommend themselves to their own favour by comparison, as all men do when they laugh."

Hobbes is evidently thinking quite literally of laughter while for Nietzsche laughter represents an attitude toward the world, toward life, and toward oneself. In *The Gay Science* (1882) he had written: "Laughter means: to rejoice at another's expense [*schadenfroh sein*], but with a good conscience" (section 200). And still earlier, in *Human, All-Too-Human* (1878): "Descending below the animals.— When man neighs with laughter, he surpasses all animals by his vulgarity" (section 553). But in the second volume of the same work (1879) we find an aphorism (section 173): "*Laughing and smiling.*— The more joyous and certain his spirit becomes, the more man unlearns loud laughter; instead a more spiritual smile constantly wells up in him. . . ." And in a note of that period (*Musarion* edition, IX, 413): "Everything *sudden* pleases if it does no *harm;* hence wit. . . . For a tension is thus released. . . ." And another note (same page): "Caricature is the beginning of art. That something *signifies,* delights. That whatever signifies, should mock and be laughed at, delights still more. Laughing at something is the first sign of a higher psychic life (as in the fine arts)."

In spite of the title *The Gay Science,* Nietzsche's celebration of laughter is encountered first and foremost in *Zarathustra.* To cite all the relevant passages (*Portable Nietzsche* pp. 248, 272, 294, 310, 341, 342, 427) would be pointless, but the three most significant should be mentioned.

"Not by wrath does one kill but by laughter. Come, let us kill the spirit of gravity!" ("On Reading and Writing," p. 153).

"As yet he has not learned laughter or beauty. Gloomy this hunter returned from the woods of knowledge. . . . But I do not like these tense souls. . . . As yet his knowledge has not learned to smile. . . . Gracefulness

should not doubt that they also know how to laugh the while in a superhuman and new way—and at the expense of all serious things. Gods enjoy mockery: it seems they cannot suppress laughter even during holy rites.

295

The genius of the heart, as that great concealed one possesses it, the tempter god[42] and born pied piper of consciences whose voice knows how to descend into the netherworld of every soul; who does not say a word or cast a glance in which there is no consideration and ulterior enticement; whose mastery includes the knowledge of how to seem—not what he is but what is to those who follow him one *more* constraint to press ever closer to him in order to follow him ever more inwardly and thoroughly—the genius of the heart who silences all that is loud and self-satisfied, teaching it to listen; who smooths rough souls and lets them taste a new desire—to lie still as a mirror, that the deep sky may mirror itself in them—the genius of the heart who teaches the doltish and rash hand to hesitate and reach out more delicately; who guesses the concealed and forgotten treasure, the drop of graciousness and sweet spirituality under dim and thick ice, and is a divining rod for every grain of gold that has long lain buried in the dungeon of much mud and sand; the genius of the heart from whose touch everyone walks away richer, not having received grace and sur-

---

is part of the graciousness of the great-souled. . . . Verily, I have often laughed at the weaklings who thought themselves good because they had no claws" ("On Those Who Are Sublime," pp. 228-31, one of the most important chapters in Nietzsche's writings).

"What has so far been the greatest sin here on earth? Was it not the word of him who said, 'Woe unto those who laugh here'? . . . He did not love enough: else he would also have loved us who laugh. But he hated and mocked us: howling and gnashing of teeth he promised us. . . . Laughter I have pronounced holy; you higher men, *learn* to laugh!" ("On the Higher Man," sections 16 and 20, pp. 405-408).

For Nietzsche laughter becomes less a physical phenomenon than a symbol of joyous affirmation of life and of the refusal to bow before the spirit of gravity.

[42] Cf. section 42, note: *Versucher-Gott* could also mean "god of experimenters."

prised, not as blessed and oppressed by alien goods, but richer in himself, newer to himself than before, broken open, blown at and sounded out by a thawing wind, perhaps more unsure, tenderer, more fragile, more broken, but full of hopes that as yet have no name, full of new will and currents, full of new dissatisfaction and undertows——but what am I doing, my friends? [43]

Of whom am I speaking to you? Have I forgotten myself so far that I have not even told you his name? Unless you have guessed by yourselves who this questionable spirit and god is who wants to be *praised* in such fashion. For just as happens to everyone who from childhood has always been on his way and in foreign parts, many strange and not undangerous spirits have crossed my path, too, but above all he of whom I was speaking just now, and he again and again—namely, no less a one than the god *Dionysus,* that great ambiguous one and tempter god to whom I once offered, as you know, in all secrecy and reverence, my first-

---

[43] Some of the features of this portrait bring to mind Socrates. In this connection section 212 might be reread; also the beginning of section 340 of *The Gay Science: "The dying Socrates.*— I admire the courage and wisdom of Socrates in everything he did, said—and did not say. This mocking and enamored monster and pied piper of Athens, who made the most arrogant youths tremble and sob, was not only the wisest talker who ever lived: he was just as great in his silence. . . ."

The image of the pied piper recurs in the first sentence of the present section—and the Preface to *Twilight of the Idols* where Nietzsche calls himself "an old psychologist and pied piper" (*Portable Nietzsche,* p. 466). With the praise of Socrates' greatness "in his silence" compare Nietzsche's comment on *Beyond Good and Evil* in *Ecce Homo,* where he praises the book for "the subtlety of its form, of its intent, of its art of *silence,*" all of which he contrasts with *Zarathustra.*

Finally, the section on the genius of the heart should be compared with the words of the Platonic Socrates, on the last page of the *Theaetetus:* "Supposing you should ever henceforth try to conceive afresh, Theaetetus, if you succeed your embryo thoughts will be the better as a consequence of today's scrutiny; and if you remain barren, you will be gentler . . . having the good sense not to fancy you know what you do not know. For that, and no more, is all that my art can effect; nor have I any of that knowledge possessed by all the great and admirable men of our own day or of the past. But this midwife's art is a gift from heaven; my mother had it for women, and I for young men of a generous spirit and for all in whom beauty dwells" (F. M. Cornford translation).

born—as the last, it seems to me, who offered him a *sacrifice:* for I have found no one who understood what I was doing then.[44]

Meanwhile I have learned much, all too much, more about the philosophy of this god, and, as I said, from mouth to mouth— I, the last disciple and initiate of the god Dionysus—and I suppose I might begin at long last to offer you, my friends, a few tastes of this philosophy, insofar as this is permitted to me? In an undertone, as is fair, for it concerns much that is secret, new, strange, odd, uncanny.

Even that Dionysus is a philosopher, and that gods, too, thus do philosophy, seems to me to be a novelty that is far from innocuous and might arouse suspicion precisely among philosophers. Among you, my friends, it will not seem so offensive, unless it comes too late and not at the right moment; for today, as I have been told, you no longer like to believe in God and gods. Perhaps I shall also have to carry frankness further in my tale than will always be pleasing to the strict habits of your ears? Certainly the god in question went further, very much further, in dialogues of this sort and was always many steps ahead of me.

Indeed, if it were permitted to follow human custom in according to him many solemn pomp-and-virtue names, I should have to give abundant praise to his explorer and discoverer courage, his daring honesty, truthfulness, and love of wisdom. But such a god has no use whatever for all such venerable junk and pomp. "Keep that," he would say, "for yourself and your likes and

---

[44] Although "first-born" is plural in the original (*Erstlinge*), the primary reference is certainly to *The Birth of Tragedy.* From the Preface added to the new edition of 1886 (the same year that saw the publication of *Beyond Good and Evil*) it is plain that by now Nietzsche felt that he himself had not fully understood in 1872 what he was doing.

More important: the Dionysus of his later works is no longer the Dionysus of *The Birth of Tragedy.* In the early work, Dionysus stands for uncontrolled, frenzied, intoxicated passion and is contrasted with Apollo; in the later works, Dionysus stands for controlled and creatively employed passion—the mature Goethe is now called Dionysian (*Twilight,* section 49, *Portable Nietzsche,* pp. 553f.)—and is contrasted with "the Crucified" (end of *Ecce Homo*) and the extirpation of the passions and the denial of this world.

whoever else has need of it! I—have no reason for covering my nakedness."

One guesses: this type of deity and philosopher is perhaps lacking in shame?

Thus he once said: "Under certain circumstances I love what is human"—and with this he alluded to Ariadne who was present[45] —"man is to my mind an agreeable, courageous, inventive animal that has no equal on earth; it finds its way in any labyrinth. I am well disposed towards him: I often reflect how I might yet advance him and make him stronger, more evil, and more profound than he is."

"Stronger, more evil, and more profound?" I asked startled. "Yes," he said once more; "stronger, more evil, and more profound; also more beautiful"—and at that the tempter god smiled with his halcyon smile as though he had just paid an enchanting compliment. Here we also see: what this divinity lacks is not only a sense of shame—and there are also other good reasons for conjecturing that in several respects all of the gods could learn from us humans. We humans are—more humane.[46]—

296

Alas, what are you after all, my written and painted thoughts! It was not long ago that you were still so colorful, young, and malicious, full of thorns and secret spices—you made me sneeze and laugh—and now? You have already taken off your novelty, and some of you are ready, I fear, to become truths: they already look so immortal, so pathetically decent, so dull! And has it ever been different? What things do we copy, writing and painting, we mandarins with Chinese brushes, we immortalizers of things that *can* be written—what are the only things we are able to paint? Alas, always only what is on the verge of withering and losing its fragrance! Alas, always only storms that are passing, ex-

---

[45] There is a large literature, much of it inordinately pretentious and silly, about Nietzsche's conception of Ariadne. For a very brief explanation, see Kaufmann's *Nietzsche,* Chapter 1, section II.

[46] *"Wir Menschen sind—menschlicher. . . ."*

hausted, and feelings that are autumnal and yellow! Alas, always only birds that grew weary of flying and flew astray and now can be caught by hand—by *our* hand! We immortalize what cannot live and fly much longer—only weary and mellow things! And it is only your *afternoon,* you, my written and painted thoughts, for which alone I have colors, many colors perhaps, many motley caresses and fifty yellows and browns and greens and reds: but nobody will guess from that how you looked in your morning, you sudden sparks and wonders of my solitude, you my old beloved— *wicked* thoughts!

From High Mountains

━━━◆◉◆━━━

AFTERSONG

TRANSLATOR'S NOTE

"Aus hohen Bergen. Nachgesang." In the original edition this title occupies a right-hand page by itself, facing section 296, and the poem begins on the next right-hand page. The asterisks at the beginning and end of the poem are found in the original edition.

My translation, though relatively faithful, is not entirely literal; and this is one reason for furnishing the original text, too—in fairness to both author and reader. There is another reason: fairness to the translator; for the poem is not one of Nietzsche's best. (The five dots occurring four times in the German text do not mark an omission but are among Nietzsche's characteristic punctuation devices: sometimes they are used to indicate that a thought breaks off or that something remains unsaid; here they plainly suggest a long pause.)

More of Nietzsche's verse, also with the original and translation on facing pages, is included in *Twenty German Poets: A Bilingual Collection*.[1] One of those poems, "To the Mistral: A Dancing Song," has a somewhat similar rhyme scheme but strikes me as a much better poem than "From High Mountains."

I confess that I do not admire the present poem—except for one magnificent line which defies translation:

Nur wer sich wandelt, bleibt mit mir verwandt.

My version does not capture the play on words but tries to communicate the meaning: "One has to change to stay akin to me." Or: "Only those who change remain related to me." This rendering is far from perfect but it at least rectifies the misreading of the line in L. A. Magnus' translation of the poem appended to Helen Zimmern's version of *Beyond Good and Evil:* "None but new kith are native of my land!"

---

[1] Edited, translated, and introduced by Walter Kaufmann (New York, Modern Library, 1963).

Nietzsche had sent an earlier version[2] of this poem to Heinrich von Stein, with the comment: "This is for you, my dear friend, to remember Sils Maria and in gratitude for your letter, *such* a letter." [3] In his reply the "dear friend" gave expression to his Wagner worship and asked Nietzsche to participate by letter in his weekly discussions with two friends about articles in the *Wagner-Lexicon*.[4] The poem seems sentimental to me, but Nietzsche did know loneliness as few men have ever known it.

W.K.

[2] In that version the order of the second and third stanzas was reversed, as was that of the seventh and eighth, and the tenth and eleventh. Moreover, the wording was slightly different in several places, and the last two stanzas were missing entirely.

[3] *Friedrich Nietzsches Gesammelte Briefe* (Friedrich Nietzsche's collected letters) vol. III (2nd ed., Leipzig, 1905), pp. 243-45, end of November 1884, from Nizza. Heinrich von Stein's letter is printed in *ibid.*, pp. 240-42.

[4] *Ibid.*, pp. 245ff.

Aus hohen Bergen.

NACHGESANG.

       *   *   *

  *   *   *   *   *   *

Oh Lebens Mittag! Feierliche Zeit!
       Oh Sommergarten!
Unruhig Glück im Stehn und Spähn und Warten:—
Der Freunde harr' ich, Tag und Nacht bereit,
Wo bleibt ihr Freunde? Kommt! 's ist Zeit! 's ist Zeit!

War's nicht für euch, dass sich des Gletschers Grau
       Heut schmückt mit Rosen?
Euch sucht der Bach, sehnsüchtig drängen, stossen
Sich Wind und Wolke höher heut in's Blau,
Nach euch zu spähn aus fernster Vogel-Schau.

Im Höchsten ward für euch mein Tisch gedeckt:—
       Wer wohnt den Sternen
So nahe, wer des Abgrunds grausten Fernen?
Mein Reich—welch Reich hat weiter sich gereckt?
Und meinen Honig—wer hat ihn geschmeckt? . . . . .

—Da *seid* ihr, Freunde!—Weh, doch *ich* bin's nicht,
       Zu dem ihr wolltet?
Ihr zögert, staunt—ach, dass ihr lieber grolltet!
Ich—bin's nicht mehr? Vertauscht Hand, Schritt, Gesicht?
Und was ich bin, euch Freunden—bin ich's nicht?

Ein Andrer ward ich? Und mir selber fremd?
       Mir selbst entsprungen?
Ein Ringer, der zu oft sich selbst bezwungen?
Zu oft sich gegen eigne Kraft gestemmt,
Durch eignen Sieg verwundet und gehemmt?

From High Mountains

AFTERSONG

* * *

* * * * * *

O noon of life! O time to celebrate!
O summer garden!
Restlessly happy and expectant, standing,
Watching all day and night, for friends I wait:
Where are you, friends? Come! It is time! It's late!

The glacier's gray adorned itself for you
Today with roses;
The brook seeks you, and full of longing rises
The wind, the cloud, into the vaulting blue
To look for you from dizzy bird's-eye view.

Higher than mine no table has been set:
Who lives so near
The stars or dread abysses half as sheer?
My realm, like none, is almost infinite,
And my sweet honey—who has tasted it?——

—There you are, friends!—Alas, the man you sought
You do not find here?
You hesitate, amazed? Anger were kinder!
I—changed so much? A different face and gait?
And what I am—for you, friends, I am not?

Am I another? Self-estranged? From me—
Did I elude?
A wrestler who too oft himself subdued?
Straining against his strength too frequently,
Wounded and stopped by his own victory?

Ich suchte, wo der Wind am schärfsten weht?
   Ich lernte wohnen,
Wo Niemand wohnt, in öden Eisbär-Zonen,
Verlernte Mensch und Gott, Fluch und Gebet?
Ward zum Gespenst, das über Gletscher geht?

—Ihr alten Freunde! Seht! Nun blickt ihr bleich,
   Voll Lieb' und Grausen!
Nein, geht! Zürnt nicht! Hier—könntet *ihr* nicht hausen:
Hier zwischen fernstem Eis- und Felsenreich—
Hier muss man Jäger sein und gemsengleich.

Ein *schlimmer* Jäger ward ich!—Seht, wie steil
   Gespannt mein Bogen!
Der Stärkste war's, der solchen Zug gezogen— —:
Doch wehe nun! Gefährlich ist *der* Pfeil,
Wie *kein* Pfeil,—fort von hier! Zu eurem Heil! . . . . .

Ihr wendet euch?—Oh Herz, du trugst genung,
   Stark blieb dein Hoffen:
Halt *neuen* Freunden deine Thüren offen!
Die alten lass! Lass die Erinnerung!
Warst einst du jung, jetzt—bist du besser jung!

Was je uns knüpfte, Einer Hoffnung Band,—
   Wer liest die Zeichen,
Die Liebe einst hineinschrieb, noch, die bleichen?
Dem Pergament vergleich ich's, das die Hand
Zu fassen *scheut,*—ihm gleich verbräunt, verbrannt.

Nicht Freunde mehr, das sind—wie nenn' ich's doch?—
   Nur Freunds-Gespenster!
Das klopft mir wohl noch Nachts an Herz und Fenster,
Das sieht mich an und spricht: ,,wir *waren's* doch?"—
—Oh welkes Wort, das einst wie Rosen roch!

Oh Jugend-Sehnen, das sich missverstand!
   Die *ich* ersehnte,
Die ich mir selbst verwandt-verwandelt wähnte,
Dass *alt* sie wurden, hat sie weggebannt:
Nur wer sich wandelt, bleibt mit mir verwandt.

Oh Lebens Mittag! Zweite Jugendzeit!
   Oh Sommergarten!
Unruhig Glück im Stehn und Spähn und Warten!

I sought where cutting winds are at their worst?
          I learned to dwell
Where no one lives, in bleakest polar hell,
Unlearned mankind and god, prayer and curse?
Became a ghost that wanders over glaciers?

—My ancient friends! Alas! You show the shock
          Of love and fear!
No, leave! Do not be wroth! You—can't live here—
Here, among distant fields of ice and rock—
Here one must be a hunter, chamois-like.

A wicked archer I've become.—The ends
          Of my bow kiss;
Only the strongest bends his bow like this.
No arrow strikes like that which my bow sends:
Away from here—for your own good, my friends!——

You leave?—My heart: no heart has borne worse hunger;
          Your hope stayed strong:
Don't shut your gates; new friends may come along.
Let old ones go. Don't be a memory-monger!
Once you were young—now you are even younger.

What once tied us together, one hope's bond—
          Who reads the signs
Love once inscribed on it, the pallid lines?
To parchment I compare it that the hand
Is loath to touch—discolored, dark, and burnt.

No longer friends—there is no word for those—
          It is a wraith
That knocks at night and tries to rouse my faith,
And looks at me and says: "Once friendship was—"
—O wilted word, once fragrant as the rose.

Youth's longing misconceived inconstancy.
          Those whom I deemed
Changed to my kin, the friends of whom I dreamed,
Have aged and lost our old affinity:
One has to change to stay akin to me.

O noon of life! Our second youthful state!
          O summer garden!
Restlessly happy and expectant, standing,

Der Freunde harr' ich, Tag und Nacht bereit,
Der *neuen* Freunde! Kommt! 's ist Zeit! 's ist Zeit!

* * *

Dies Lied ist aus,—der Sehnsucht süsser Schrei
    Erstarb im Munde:
Ein Zaubrer that's, der Freund zur rechten Stunde,
Der Mittags-Freund—nein! fragt nicht, wer es sei—
Um Mittag war's, da wurde Eins zu Zwei . . . . .

Nun feiern wir, vereinten Siegs gewiss,
    Das Fest der Feste:
Freund *Zarathustra* kam, der Gast der Gäste!
Nun lacht die Welt, der grause Vorhang riss,
Die Hochzeit kam für Licht und Finsterniss . . . . .

* * *   * *

* *

Looking all day and night, for friends I wait:
For new friends! Come! It's time! It's late!

*   *

*   *

This song is over—longing's dulcet cry
   Died in my mouth:
A wizard did it, friend in time of drought,
The friend of noon—no, do not ask me who—
At noon it was that one turned into two——

Sure of our victory, we celebrate
   The feast of feasts:
Friend Zarathustra came, the guest of guests!
The world now laughs, rent are the drapes of fright,
The wedding is at hand of dark and light——

*   *   *   *

*   *   *   *

*   * *   *

*   *

INDEX

A

actors, 7, 9, 97, 205
admiration, 118
Aeschylus, 224
affability, 93
affect, 13n, 85, 117, 187, 192, 198, 258, 260, 284; will as, 19, 19n, 36
Alcibiades, 200
"all too human," **TP**, **NP**, 204, 271
America, 44
anarchists, 188, 202; anarchism, 248
Anglomania, 253
Antichrist, 256
anti-Semitism, 248n, 251. See also Jews
Apollo, 295n
Aquinas, Thomas, 13n, 19n
Ariadne, 295, 295n
aristocracies, 258, 259; faith of, 260; aristocratic: feeling, 58; morals, 46; society, 257, 262; spirit, 239; values, 32
Aristophanes, 28, 231, 232; Aristophanean derision, 223
Aristotle, **TP**, 211n, 212n, 239n, 287n; Aristotelianism of morals, 198; Aristotelian presuppositions, 188
art(s), 33, 59, 188, 198, 223, 224, 240, 246, 255, 256, 260, 291; artists, 11, 31, 59, 110, 137, 188, 192, 200, 204, 209, 210, 213, 225, 240, 269, 287
asceticism, 61; ascetics, 229
Asia (Asiatic), **NP**, 52, 56, 188, 208, 238

atheism, 53, 209
Atkins, Samuel D., 28n
atomism, 12, 12n, 17
Augustine, 12n, 50, 200
Austria, 251, 251n

B

Bacon, Francis, 252
bad, the, 190, 260. See also beyond good and evil; evil
Baldwin, James Mark, 13n, 19n
Balzac, Honoré de, 204, 256
Bayle, Pierre, 28
Beethoven, Ludwig van, 245, 256
Being, lap of, 2
Benebelungen, 251n
Bentham, Jeremy, 228
Berkeley, George, 36
Berlin wit and sand, 244
Bertram, Ernst, 200n, 250n
Beyle, Henri, 39, 254, 256
beyond good and evil, **TP**, 40n, 44, 56, 153, 241n, 250n, 255, 260. See also good
Bible, **TP**, 28, 52, 247, 263
bieder; Biederkeit, 244
Bismarck, Otto von, 241n, 251n, 254n
Bizet, Georges, 254
"blood," concept of, 213, 213n
Borgia, Cesare, 197, 197n
Boscovich, Ruggiero Giuseppe, 12, 12n
Bradley, F. H., **TP**
Brahmins, 61
Brandes, Georg, **TP**, **NPn**

breeding, 262
Bruno, Giordano, 25
Buddha, 56; Buddhism, 61, 202
Burckhardt, Jacob, **TP**
Butler, Samuel, 264n
Byron, Lord, 245, 269

C

Caesar, Julius, 200; Caesarian culti-
    vator, 207
Cagliostro, Alessandro, 194, 205
cant, 228
Carlyle, Thomas, 252
Catholicism, 48; Catholics, 251n;
    Roman catholicity, 46; anti-Cath-
    olicism, 256
Catiline, Lucius Sergius, 194
causa sui, 15, 21
cause and effect, 21, 47
Celts, 48
certainty, 1, 10; "immediate," 16,
    17, 34; uncertainty, 1
Chimaera, 190n
China, 32; Chinese, 267, 296; Mo-
    zart's Chinese touches, 245
Christianity (Christian, Christians),
    NP, 11, 12, 46, 48, 49, 52, 54,
    56, 61, 62, 104, 104n, 168, 188,
    189, 191, 200, 202, 203, 210, 223,
    229, 252, 256, 261, 263; Christian-
    ecclesiastical pressure of millennia,
    NP; spiritual men of, 62. *See also*
    religion
Cicero, 13n, 19n, 247.
Circe, 208, 229
cleanliness, 74, 74n, 271, 284
cogito, "I think," "it thinks," 16, 17,
    54
cognition, 192
Comte, Auguste, 48
conscience, 98, 208, 208n; good, 214,
    291; and science, 45, 45n
cooking, 234
Copernicus, Nicholas, 12
Cornford, F. M., **TP**
corruption, 258, 269
Corsica, 208
costume(s), 223; lie-costumes, 208
Cowan, Marianne, **TP**, 1n, 204n,
    205n, 208n, 260n, 289n

criminal, 109–10; criminals, pun-
    ishment of, 201
Cromwell, Oliver, 46
cruelty in higher culture, 229; in re-
    ligion, 55; in tragedy, 229
cultivation (cultivate), **NPn**, 61, 203,
    213, 239, 262, 263; Caesarian cul-
    tivator, 207; of new ruling class in
    Europe, 251; of tyrants, 242;
    species-cultivating, 4
culture, evolution of higher, 257
cynicism, 26

D

danger, dangerous, dangers, 28, 29,
    39, 40, 42, 44, 45, 62, 103, 195,
    198, 201, 205, 207, 208, 212, 220,
    224, 228, 238, 239, 242, 245, 282;
    as mother of morals, 262; danger-
    ous maybes, 2; undangerous, 260
Dante Alighieri, **TP**, 236
Danto, Arthur C., 56n
Darwin, Charles, 253; Darwinists,
    14
Davenant, Sir William, 294n
deception, 2, 9, 31, 34, 36, 264
Delacroix, Ferdinand Victor Eugène,
    256
democracy, democratic, democrats,
    NP, 202–204, 210, 238n, 239; dem-
    ocratic bourgeoisie, 254; demo-
    cratic enlightenment, **NP**; demo-
    cratic taste, 44; Europe's demo-
    cratic movement, 242; splinter
    wills in, 208
Demosthenes, 247
Descartes, René, 2n, 54, 191
devil, 129
Diderot, Denis, 28
Dionysiokolakes, Dionysus, 7, 7n,
    295, 295n
discipline, 188, 203, 219, 225, 252,
    262; critical, 210; of science, 230
disappointment, 99
disinterest, 220; disinterested knowl-
    edge, 207
distance, pathos of, 257
dogmatism, dogmatists, dogmatizing,
    NP, 43, 43n, 211
Don Quixote, 25n

Dostoevsky, Feodor Mikhailovich, **TP**

dreams, 193
drives. 6, 23, 36, 158, 189, 201
Dühring, Eugen, 204, 204n
dumpf, 241n
duty. 226

E

ego, 16, 17
Egypt, **NP**, 28
Elector of Brandenburg, 251n
Electra, 209n
Empedocles, 204
England, **TP**, 208, 228, 251n, 252, 253, 253n
English, **TP, TPn,** 4n, 8n, 189, 224, 228, 251–54, 294; nobility, 251; women, **TP**
enthusiasm, 288
Epicurus, 7, 7n; Epicurean, 200; god, 62; philosophy, 61; spirit; 62; Epicureanism, 270
d'Épinay, Mme, 26n, 222
equality, 30, 201, 259; "equal before God," 62; of rights, 44, 212, 219, 238, 265
Eros, 168
Eternal-Feminine/Masculine, 236
eternal recurrence, 56, 56n
Europe, **TPn, NP**, 10–12, 44, 47, 52, 62, 186, 189, 199, 202, 208, 209, 212, 222, 224, 228, 231, 232, 239, 241, 242, 244, 245, 251, 254, 256, 260. 263, 293; what Europe owes to the Jews, 250
European(s), 62, 188, 200, 201, 202, 209, 214, 223, 224, 242, 245, 253, 254, 259, 267; "evolving European," 242; good Europeans, **NP, NPn,** 241, 243, 254; morality, 203; music, 255; problem, 251; races, 62; spirit, 188, 253; soul, 254, 256; theism, 53
evil, 39, 195, 201, 250n, 260; good and, 149, 153, 202, 241n, 250n, 255, 260. *See also* beyond good and evil; good and evil
existentialism, **TP**, 21n, 43n
exploitation, 259

F

faculties, Kant's concept of, 11
faith, 1n, 2, 36, 46, 55, 58, 180, 186, 191, 202, 203, 205, 223, 231, 239, 241. 250n, 264, 269, 287; in opposite values, 2; of former times, 10; of governesses, 34, 34n; of aristocrats, 260; Christian, 46
falseness, falsification, 4, 34, 59, 191, 230
familiarity, 182
fatherlandishness, 241, 245, 254, 256
fear, 192, 209, 229, 232, 239, 269; in religion, 49, 59; of eternal misunderstanding, 268; of the neighbor, 201, 201n
Fichte, Johann Gottlieb, 244
Flaubert, Gustave, 218
Florentine, 223
Förster, Bernhard, **TP**
France, 48, 208, 210, 218, 241n, 253, 254, 256, 258; "France of taste," 254
French, **TP,** 4n, 48, 209, 244, 248, 254, 256; character, 254; "French ideas," 253; anti-French stupidity, 251
French Revolution, 38, 46, 191, 239, 244, 245, 258
Frederick II (medieval German emperor), 200, 200n; Frederick II (the Great), 209, 209n; Frederickianism, 209
Frederick William I, 209n
Freud, Sigmund, **TP**, 68n, 189n, 289n, 231n
friends, friendship, **TP,** 27, 40, 195, 217, 260, 268, 283

G

Galiani, Abbé Ferdinand, 26, 26n, 222, 228, 270, 288
gāngāsrotagati, 27, 27n
Ganges River, 27n
Gast, Peter, **TPn,** 8n
Gemüt, gemütlich, 244n
genius, 248, 274, 274n; of the heart, 295; "of the species," 268

Geoffrin, Marie-Thérèse, 26n
German, Germans, **TP, NP,** 11, 28,
  56, 58, 126, 126n, 192, 193, 204,
  209, 239, 240, 245–48, 250n, 251,
  252, 254, 255, 256; honesty, 244;
  music, 255; "profundity of," 244;
  skepticism, 209; soul, 48, 240, 244;
  spirit, 11, 209, 251–53; taste, 28,
  39, 244, 254; Germanomania, 251
Germany, **TP,** 28, 47, 58, 204, 208,
  209, 210, 241n, 247, 251, 254
Gillispie, Charles C., 12n
God, 10, 21, 26, 34n, 37, 50, 53, 55,
  56n, 57–60, 101, 121, 129, 150,
  164, 186, 188, 191, 198, 199, 202,
  203, 205, 205n, 207, 219, 223, 237,
  244, 248, 295; "equal before," 62;
  love of, 67
god(s), 2, 7, 40, 44, 46, 55, 56n,
  62, 65a, 66, 80, 144, 188, 202n,
  218, 227, 262, 264, 269, 294, 295,
  295n; on the cross, 46
Goethe, Johann Wolfgang von, 28,
  198, 198n, 209, 209n, 231n, 232n,
  236, 238n, 241n, 244, 244n, 252,
  256, 266, 286, 295n; *Faust,* 244n,
  286n; *Werther,* 245
Gogol, Nikolai Vasilievich, 269
good, the, **NPn,** 23, 35n, 39, 43, 135,
  148, 190, 191, 194, 202, 204, 223,
  250n, 260, 261, 268; common, 43;
  good will, 208
good conscience, 291, definition of,
  214
good and evil, 4, 147, 147n, 149, 159,
  198, 201, 202, 207, 209, 250n, 260;
  "good" and "wicked" drives, 23
good taste, 224
gratitude, 49, 49n, 58, 62, 74, 74n,
  207, 260
Great Britain, *see* England
great men, 269; man who strives for
  the great, 273
greatness, concept of, 212
greatness of soul, 212; Aristotle's
  portrait of, 212n
Greece, 7, 49, 260
Greek(s), 28, 30, 49, 52, 121, 238,
  248, 248n, 267; philosophy, 20;
  polis, 262
Grossoktav edition, 65an, 269n
Gundolf, Friedrich, 200n

Guyon, Jeanne-Marie Bouvier de, 50,
  50n

H

Hafiz, 198
Hamlet, 62n, 208, 208n, 270, 270n
Hampshire, Stuart N., 12n
happiness, 103, 193, 198, 212, 279
Harpies, 282
Hartmann, Eduard von, 204, 204n
Hauptstück, 1n
Hegel, Georg Wilhelm Friedrich
  TP, 43n, 204, 204n, 210, 211, 244,
  252, 252n, 254; Hegelianism, **TP**
Heine, Heinrich, 254, 256
Helvétius, Claude Adrien, 228, 228n
Heraclitus, 204
Hercules (constellation), 243
herd, 191, 199, 201–03, 212, 228
  242; instincts, 201, 202
heredity, 264
hermit, 289
"higher men," 61, 62, 72, 173, 182,
  212, 221, 228, 256, 269, 274, 286
historical sense, 204, 224
Hobbes, Thomas, 252, 294, 294n
Homer, 224, 228, 238; *Iliad,* 191n,
  258n, 260n
honesty, 26, 31, 34, 227, 230, 250n,
  284n; German, 244
Horace, *Odes,* 251n; *Epistles,* 264n
Hugo, Victor, 254, 254n
Hume, David, 209n, 252

I

Ibsen, Henrik, **TP,** 213n; *An Enemy
  of the People,* **TP,** 213n
immoral, immorality, 6, 32, 95, 201,
  221, 226, 228, 259
independence, 29, 41
Indian(s), 20, 30, 52; Wars, 208
Indo-Germanic peoples, 20
Innocent XII, 50n
Inquisition, 50n
insanity and nationality, 256
instinct(s), 3, 10, 13, 22, 26, 36, 44,
  55, 58, 59, 62, 83, 145, 189, 191,
  201, 202, 206, 207, 209, 212, 218,
  224, 233, 238, 239, 251, 258; of
  cleanliness, 271; of obedience, 199;

for rank, 263; religious, 53, 58;
    instinctive activities, 3
intimacy, 167
irony, 212
Italians, 247, 251
Italy, 208

J

Jack the Dreamer, 208n
Japanese, 229
Jaspers, Karl, 40n, 250n
Java, 258
Jean Paul, *see* Richter, J. P. F.
Jesuitism, Jesuits, **NP,** 48, 206
Jesus, 164, 269
Jews, Jewish, **TP, TPn,** 52, 164, 195,
    248, 248n, 250n, 251, 251n; Jew-
    ess, **TPn;** "Wandering Jew," 251
Joyce, James, 208n, 253n
judgments, 4, 4n, 11, 32, 43, 191,
    205, 219; synthetic *a priori,* 11
justice, 9, 201, 213, 262, 265

K

Kant, Immanuel, 1n, 4n, 5, 11, 54,
    187, 188, 209n, 210, 210n, 211,
    211n, 220n, 252; the great Chinese
    of Königsberg, 210; table of cate-
    gories, 11, 44
Kantorowicz, Ernst, 200n
Kierkegaard, Soren, **TP,** 40n
kindness, 184
Kleist, Heinrich von, 269
knowledge, 2, 6, 25, 26, 64, 65, 71,
    101, 152, 171, 191, 192, 204, 205,
    208 210, 229, 231, 253, 270; about
    love, 269; absolute, 16; and cogni-
    tion, 192; "disinterested," 207;
    self-, 32, 231, 281; will to, 24
Kotzebue, August Friedrich Ferdi-
    nand von, 244, 244n
Kundry, 47
kūrmagati, 27, 27n

L

laisser aller, 188
Lamarck, Jean-Baptiste, 213n, 264n
Lambert, Anne-Thérèse de, 235

last man, 225n
laughter, 223, 294, 294n
Leibniz, Gottfried Wilhelm von, 207
leisure, 189
Leopardi, Giacomo, 269
Lessing, Gotthold Ephraim, **TP,** 28;
    Emilia Galotti, 274n
Levy, Oscar, **TP**
literature, French, 254; German, 246
Locke, John, 20, 252, 252n
love, 142; of God, 67; as passion,
    260, 269; self-, 287n; sexual, 114;
    Christians' love of men, 104
Luther, Martin, 46, 50; Luther's
    Bible, 247
lying, 180, 183, 192

M

Macbeth, 229n
Machiavelli, Niccolò, 28, 28n; *The
    Prince,* 28
McTaggart, J. M. E., **TP**
madness, 156
Magnus, L. A., **A**
man, enhancement of, 257
mandūkagati, 27, 27n
Manu's laws, 260n
Marianus, Doctor, 286n
Marlowe, Christopher, 209n
marriage, 123
Marschner, Heinrich, 245
mask(s), **NP,** 4, 5, 25, 30n, 40, 40n,
    47, 204, 221, 225, 230, 270, 278,
    289
master(s), 6, 46, 198, 202, 204, 207,
    212, 230, 241, 241n, 246, 261,
    293; master and slave morality,
    40n, 212n, 260, 260n, 261
mediocrity, 201, 206, 218, 242, 262;
    truths of mediocre minds, 253
Mendelssohn, Felix, 245, 248n
Mephistopheles, 209n, 244
metaphysicians, metaphysics, meta-
    physical, 2, 6, 16, 21, 229, 230;
    faith of, 2; "need," 12
Methodism, 252
Michelet, Jules, 209
Mill, John Stuart, 253
Molière, 11
Molinos, Miguel, 50n
Montaigne, Michel Eyquem de, 208

"monumentalistic" historiography, 200n

Moore, G. E., **TP**

morality, moral, morals, 4–6, 9, 23, 25, 26, 32, 34, 39, 46, 47, 55, 56, 64, 95, 108, 143, 164, 186–203, 204, 208, 211, 212, 215–18, 221, 223, 228, 250, 252, 254, 255, 257, 260, 262, 291; aristocratic, 46; definition of, 19; extra-moral period, 32; higher, 202; of mediocrity, 262; of self-denial, 33; moral judgments, 219; pre-moral period, 32; rational foundation of, 186; as timidity, 198, 201

Moses, 60n

Mozart, Wolfgang Amadeus, 245

Münchhausen, Baron, 21

Musarion edition, 65an, 186n, 227n, 294n

music, 106, 239, 254; French, 254; German, 245, 255. *See also* Wagner

Muslims, 20, 30

Musset, Alfred de, 269

mysticism, mystics, 5, 11, 40, 50, 50n, 204, 220

N

Napoleon, 199, 209, 232, 244, 244n, 245, 256; Napoleonic tempo, 254; Napoleon's mother, 239

Naumann, C. G., **TP**

nausea, 203, 203n, 224, 263, 269, 270, 282

Nausicaa, 96

Nazis, 251n, 264n

Necker, Mme, 26n

New Testament, 52, 212n, 260n, 287n. *See also* Bible; Old Testament

niaiserie, 3, 3n; *allemande*, 11; *religieuse*, 48

Nietzsche: Works: *The Antichrist*, **NPn**, 208n, 210n, 260n; *The Birth of Tragedy*, 208n, 240n, 295n; *The Case of Wagner*, 240n; *The Dawn*, 195n, 201n, 284n; *Ecce Homo*, 209n, 221n, 227n, 251n, 295n; editions, **TP**, 65an *see also* Gross-

oktav edition; Musarion edition); *Friedrich Nietzsches Briefe an Mutter und Schwester*, **TP**; *Friedrich Nietzsches Briefe an Peter Gast*, **TP**; *Friedrich Nietzsches Briefwechsel mit Franz Overbeck*, **TP**; *Friedrich Nietzsches Gesammelte Briefe*, **An**; *The Gay Science* (*Die fröhliche Wissenschaft*), 209n, 260n, 294n, 295n; *Genealogy of Morals*, 54n, 260n; *Human, All-Too-Human*, **TPn**, **NPn**, 195n, 260n, 294n; *Nietzsche contra Wagner*, 240n, 254n, 269, 269n, 270n; *Schopenhauer as Educator*, 227n; *Thus Spoke Zarathustra*, **TP**, 26n, 41n, 56n, 202n, 225n, 269n, 285n, 294n, 295n, "To the Mistral: A Dancing Song," **An**; *Twilight of the Idols*, 21n, 209n, 260n, 295n; "Untimely Meditation," 200n; *Werke in drei Bänden*, **TP** (*see also* Schlechta); *The Will to Power*, 260n

noble, nobility, 49, 61, 62, 190, 201, 206, 212, 212n, 213, 224; posterity, 38; signs of, 272; what is noble, 257–96.

O

obedience, 187, 188, 199

Odysseus, 96, 230

Oedipus, 1, 230

Oehler, Richard, 251n

Ogden, C. K., 4n

Old Testament, 52. *See also* Bible; New Testament

opposite(s), 2, 9, 47, 56, 58, 200, 212; men, 44; values, 2, 274n

Orient, the, 46

Oriental(s), 50, 238

Overbeck, Franz, **TP**

Ovid, 227n

P

Paneth, Doctor, **TPn**

Pascal, Blaise, 45, 46, 62, 229

Passmore, John, 34n

pathos of distance, 257
Pericles, 238
Persians, 30
perspective, 10, 11, 34, 188, 201, 250n; for Plato, NP; frog perspective, 2
Petronius, 28
Pharisaism, 135
philosophy, philosophers, TP, NP, 1–23, 25, 26, 34, 39, 47, 54, 56, 59, 61, 62, 186, 190, 191, 204, 205, 207–213, 220, 225, 228, 229, 241, 252, 262, 269, 289, 292–95; drive to knowledge in, 6; English, 252; German, 11, 20; good philosophers, 39, 39n; Greek, 20; Indian, 20; martyrdom of the philosopher, 25; new species of philosophers, 42–44, 61, 203, 210, 211; philosophers of the dangerous, 2; philosophical concepts, 20; philosophical laborers versus philosophers, 211
Phoenicians, 229; Phoenicianism, 46
physics, 14
physiology, 15
pia fraus, 105, 105n
pity, 29, 30, 62, 82, 171, 199, 201, 202, 204, 206, 222, 225, 239, 260, 269, 293; saint's, 271
Plato, Platonism, TP, NP, 7, 7n, 14, 28, 105n, 106, 190, 190n, 191, 204, 211n, 284n; Theaetetus, 295n
"plebs," 264, 287
Podach, E. F., TP, 9n
Poe, Edgar Allan, 269
poets, 161, 188, 269
Poles, 251n
positivism, 10, 204, 210
possession, 194
praise, 122, 170, 283; self-praise, 204, 204n
Praxiteles, 224n
prejudice(s), 1–23, 32, 34, 44, 199, 224, 242, 274n; moral, 23
pride, 9, 11, 21, 43, 46, 58, 73a, 111, 186, 211, 213, 229, 230, 270
Protagoras, 4n
Protestant(s), Protestantism, 48, 50, 58
Provençal knight-poets, 260

Prussia(n), 209, 254n; "pluck," 244; stupidity, 251
psychology, 23, 45, 47, 196, 218, 222, 229, 269, 270
punishing, 201, 201n
Puritanism, 61, 188, 216, 228, 229

Q

Quietism, 50n

R

races, 48, 61, 188, 189, 200, 208, 224, 242, 244, 251, 252, 256, 262; European, 62; Latin, 48, 256; Nazi race views, 251n; problem of, 264, 264n; spirit of, 48
rank, order of, 30, 39n, 52n, 59, 61, 194, 203, 204, 206, 212, 213, 219, 221, 224, 228, 257, 260, 263, 265, 268, 270, 285, 287, 294
Raphael, 224n; "Raphael without hands," 274, 274n
reality, 36
religion, 45–62, 198, 202, 205, 206, 216, 222, 229, 293; as sovereign, 62; for education and cultivation, 61; religious cruelty, 55; religious neurosis, 47. See also Christianity
Renan, Ernest, 48
reputation, 92
resentment, 49n, 58n, 73An
rhetoric, 247
Richter, Johann Paul Friedrich, 244, 244n, 245
Rilke, Rainer Maria, 201n
Roland, Mme, 233
Roman(s), 50n, 201, 229, 248, 248n; logic, 48; Rome, 46, 256
romanticism, 245, 250, 256
rhyme and rhythm, 188
Roosevelt, F. D., 201n
Ross, W. D., 34n
Rousseau, Jean-Jacques, 245
Russell, Bertrand, TP
Russia, 208, 227; Russian(s), 208, 208n; Russian Empire, 251
Ryle, Gilbert, 34n

S

Sabbath, 189
Saccheti, Franco, 147
sacrifice(s), 55, 220, 229, 229n, 230, 265; Christian faith as a, 46
Sainte-Beuve, Charles-Augustin de, 48
Saint-Évremond, Charles de, 224
saints, 30, 47, 50, 51, 271
Salis, Frl. von, TP
Salvation Army, 47, 252
Sand, George, 233
Sand, Karl Ludwig, 244, 244n
Sartre, Jean-Paul, TP, 21n, 109n, 203n
Schelling, Friedrich Wilhelm Joseph von, 11, 252
Schiller, Johann Christophe Friedrich von, 245; *Die Piccolomini,* 237n; "Shakespeare's Shadow," 239n; *Wilhelm Tell,* 229n
Schlechta, Karl, TP, 65n, 99n, 186n, 237n, 269n, 270n
Schlosser, Rat, 266
Schmeitzner, Ernst, TP, 5n
scholars, 39, 45, 58, 137, 204–14, 220, 239, 250n, 287; German, 58, 244; interests of, 6
Schopenhauer, Arthur, TP, 16, 19, 36, 47, 56, 186, 186n, 204, 204n, 227, 252, 252n, 254, 256; Schopenhauerian "genius of the species," 268
Schumann, Robert, 245
science, scientists, NP, 6, 14, 21, 23, 26, 127, 192, 198, 204, 205, 210, 230, 237; and conscience, problem of, 45, 45n; "being scientific," 208, 232; nature's conformity to law, 22; "science of morals," 186; scientific average man, 206; scientific men, 80, 211, 270
self-love, 287n
self-preservation, 13
semi-barbarism, 224
sensuality, 120, 155
sexual love, 114; sexuality, 75
Shakespeare, William, 224; "Shakespeare's Shadow," 239n. *See also Hamlet; Macbeth*

shame, 40, 65, 167, 231, 295
Shaw, George Bernard, 253n, 264n; *Major Barbara,* 202n
Shelley, Percy Bysshe, 245
siao-sin, 267
Siegfried, 256
Sipo Matador, 258
skepticism, skeptics, 46, 48, 54, 208, 208n, 209, 209n, 210, 211
slave(s), slavery, 44, 46, 50, 188, 195, 207, 225, 239, 242, 257, 258, 260, 261; slave morality, 212n, 260, 260n, 261; slave rebellion in morals, 195, 195n
socialists, 202, 203, 251n, 256
Socrates, NP, 80, 190, 191, 202, 208, 212, 295n; Socratism, 190
solitude, 44, 61
soul, 12, 19, 20, 30–32, 44, 45, 47, 52, 54, 58, 61, 62, 79, 188, 193, 203, 204, 207, 212, 225, 240, 245, 252, 254, 256, 257, 260, 263, 264, 268, 269, 271, 276, 291; democratic instincts of, 22; French, 253; German, 48, 240, 244; immortal, 10, 12; in true love, 142, 142n; "modern," 224; noble, 265, 287; soul superstition, NP
Spain, 208
Spaniards, 229
Spencer, Herbert, 253
Spinoza, Baruch, 5, 13, 13n, 25, 198, 205n, 211n
spirit(s), TPn, NP, 6, 46, 48, 52, 56–58, 74, 75, 87, 90, 122, 184, 186, 193, 199, 201, 203, 204, 207, 209, 210, 214, 216, 218–20, 223–25, 229, 230, 235, 238, 239, 241, 252–254, 263, 264n, 274, 285, 286, 288; "basic will of the," 229, 230; Epicurean, 62; free, 24–44, 61, 87, 105, 188, 203, 211, 213, 227, 230, 250n, 270; German 11, 209, 251–253; objective, 207–208
spiritual, spirituality, spiritualization, NPn, 26, 45, 57, 61, 188, 194, 198, 201, 209, 213, 227, 229, 252; spiritual *fatum,* 231; spiritual haughtiness, 270; malice spiritualized, 219; spiritual Germanization, 254

Staël, Mme de, 209n, 232. 233
Stände, 257n
Stefan George Circle, 200n
Stein, Heinrich von, **A, An**
Stendhal, *see* Beyle
Stoa, Stoicism, Stoics, 8, 9, 188, 189,
    198, 207, 227
style, tempo of, 28
sublimation, 58, 189, 189n, 209
suffering 62, 202, 225, 229, 251, 270,
    284n, 293
suicide, 157
superstition, **NP**, 32, 47; of logicians,
    17
Swabians, 244
Sybel, Heinrich von, 251, 251n
sympathy, 284, 284n
synthesis, 256

T

Tacitus, 195
Taine, Hippolyte, 254
talent, 130, 151
Tartuffery, 5, 24, 228, 249
Täusche-Volk, 244
teleology, 13, 14
tempo, 27, 27n, 28, 28n, 246, 246n
Teutonic stupidity, 251
theology, 204
thinking, concept of, 16, 17, 19, 213
Tiberius, 55
tragedy, 229, 239, 239n; sense of the
    tragic, 155
translations, 28
Treitschke, Henrich von, 251, 251n
truth, truthfulness, **NP**, 1–5, 9–11,
    16, 25, 34, 35, 39, 43–45, 48, 59,
    81, 128, 134, 166, 177, 202, 210,
    211, 220, 229, 230–32, 261, 264;
    mediocre, 253

U

untruth, 1, 3; as a condition of life,
    4; the will to, 24, 59
Ural-Altaic languages, 20
utilitarianism, utilitarians, utility,
    174, 188, 196, 191, 201, 204, 206,
    225, 228, 260, 261

V

Vaihinger, Hans, 4n
values(s), 1, 2, 4, 32, 34, 43, 46, 62,
    186, 191, 203, 206, 208, 211, 212,
    250n, 253, 260 261, 268, 274n;
    aristocratic, 32; Christian value
    judgments, 189; inversion of, 195;
    one's own, 261; of a soul, 263;
    value-creating, 260, 285n
vanity, 143, 176, 261
Vedanta, **NP**, 54
Venice, 262
Versuch, Versucher, Versuchung,
    42n, 210n
Vinci, Leonardo da, 200
virtues, 30, 39, 132, 199, 201, 207,
    208, 212–39, 241, 249, 251, 260,
    262, 262n, 288; four virtues, 284,
    284n
Voltaire, 26, 28, 35, 224; Voltairian
    bitterness, 216

W

Wagner, Richard, 41n, 47, 203n, 240,
    244, 245, 254, 254n, 256, **A**; *Meis-
    tersinger*, 240; *Nietzsche contra
    Wagner*, 269n; *Parsifal*, 256, *Tris-
    tan and Isolde*, 229; Wagnerienne,
    229; "Wagnerize," 254
war, 273
Wars of Liberation, 244
Weber, Karl Maria von, 245
Wesen, 45n
Whither and For What of man, the,
    211
will, 1, 19, 21, 24, 36, 44, 47, 51, 61,
    62, 117, 188, 201, 203, 208, 209,
    211, 212, 229, 230, 239, 242; as
    affect, 19, 19n, 36; freedom of, 18,
    19, 21, 44, 53, 208, 213; sickness
    of, 208; will to stupidity, 107; will
    to the denial of life, 259; "unfree
    will," 21; will to untruth, 24, 59
will to power, 22, 23, 40n, 44, 51,
    186, 198, 211, 227, 241n, 257,
    259, 294n; exploitation as a conse-
    quence of, 259; life as, 13, 36; of

the spirit, 229, 230; spiritual, 9
Winkel, 41n
Wittgenstein, Ludwig, 28n
woman, women, **TP,** 84–86, 114–15,
   127, 131, 139, 144–45, 147–48,
   194, 204, 207, 231–39, 261, 269
Wotan, 260

Y

Yeats, William Butler, 253n
youth, 31, 44, 260

Z

Zimmern, Helen, **TP, A**

VINTAGE POLITICAL SCIENCE
AND SOCIAL CRITICISM

V-428   ABDEL-MALEK, ANOUAR   *Egypt: Military Society*
V-365   ALPEROVITZ, GAR   *Atomic Diplomacy*
V-286   ARIES, PHILIPPE   *Centuries of Childhood*
V-334   BALTZELL, E. DIGBY   *The Protestant Establishment*
V-335   BANFIELD & WILSON   *City Politics*
V-198   BARDOLPH, RICHARD   *The Negro Vanguard*
V-185   BARNETT, A. DOAK   *Communist China and Asia*
V-87   BARZUN, JACQUES   *God's Country and Mine*
V-705   BAUER, INKELES, AND KLUCKHOHN   *How the Soviet System Works*
V-270   BAZELON, DAVID   *The Paper Economy*
V-42   BEARD, CHARLES A.   *The Economic Basis of Politics* and *Related Writings*
V-59   BEAUFRE, GEN. ANDRÉ   *NATO and Europe*
V-60   BECKER, CARL L.   *Declaration of Independence*
V-17   BECKER, CARL L.   *Freedom and Responsibility in the American Way of Life*
V-228   BELOFF, MAX   *The United States and the Unity of Europe*
V-199   BERMAN, H. J. (ed.)   *Talks on American Law*
V-352   BERNSTEIN, PETER L.   *The Price of Prosperity,* Revised Edition
V-211   BINKLEY, WILFRED E.   *President and Congress*
V-81   BLAUSTEIN & WOOCK (eds.)   *Man Against Poverty: World War III—Articles and Documents on the Conflict between the Rich and the Poor*
V-513   BOORSTIN, DANIEL J.   *The Americans: The Colonial Experience*
V-358   BOORSTIN, DANIEL J.   *The Americans: The National Experience*
V-414   BOTTOMORE, T. B.   *Classes in Modern Society*
V-44   BRINTON, CRANE   *The Anatomy of Revolution*
V-37   BROGAN, D. W.   *The American Character*
V-234   BRUNER, JEROME   *The Process of Education*
V-196   BRYSON, L., et al.   *Social Change in Latin America Today*
V-30   CAMUS, ALBERT   *The Rebel*
V-33   CARMICHAEL AND HAMILTON   *Black Power: The Politics of Liberation in America*
V-98   CASH, W. J.   *The Mind of the South*
V-429   DE CASTRO, GERASSI, & HOROWITZ (eds.)   *Latin American Radicalism: A Documentary Report on Left and Nationalist Movements*
V-272   CATER, DOUGLASS   *The Fourth Branch of Government*
V-290   CATER, DOUGLASS   *Power in Washington*
V-420   CORNUELLE, RICHARD C.   *Reclaiming the American Dream*
V-311   CREMIN, LAWRENCE A.   *The Genius of American Education*
V-67   CURTIUS, ERNEST R.   *The Civilization of France*
V-234   DANIELS, R. V.   *A Documentary History of Communism*
V-235   (Two volumes)
V-237   DANIELS, ROBERT V.   *The Nature of Communism*
V-252   DAVID, et al.   *The Politics of National Party Conventions*
V-746   DEUTSCHER, ISAAC   *The Prophet Armed*

V-747   DEUTSCHER, ISAAC   *The Prophet Unarmed*

V-748   DEUTSCHER, ISAAC   *The Prophet Outcast*

V-333   ELLIS, CLYDE T.   *A Giant Step*

V-390   ELLUL, JACQUES   *Technological Society*

V-379   EMERSON, T. I.   *Toward A General Theory of the First Amendment*

V-47   EPSTEIN & FORSTER   *The Radical Right: Report on the John Birch Society and Its Allies*

V-353   EPSTEIN & FORSTER   *Report on the John Birch Society 1966*

V-422   FALL, BERNARD B.   *Hell in a Very Small Place: The Siege of Dien Bien Phu*

V-423   FINN, JAMES   *Protest: Pacifism and Politics*

V-225   FISCHER, LOUIS (ed.)   *The Essential Gandhi*

V-707   FISCHER, LOUIS   *Soviets in World Affairs*

V-424   FOREIGN POLICY ASSOCIATION, EDITORS OF   *A Cartoon History of United States Foreign Policy—Since World War I*

V-413   FRANK, JEROME D.   *Sanity and Survival: Psychological Aspects of War and Peace*

V-382   FRANKLIN & STARR (eds.)   *The Negro in 20th Century America*

V-224   FREYRE, GILBERTO   *New World in the Tropics*

V-368   FRIEDENBERG, EDGAR Z.   *Coming of Age in America*

V-416   FRIENDLY AND GOLDFARB   *Crime and Publicity*

V-378   FULBRIGHT, J. WILLIAM   *The Arrogance of Power*

V-264   FULBRIGHT, J. WILLIAM   *Old Myths and New Realities* and Other Commentaries

V-354   FULBRIGHT, J. WILLIAM (intro.)   *The Vietnam Hearings*

V-328   GALENSON, WALTER   *A Primer on Employment & Wages*

V-461   GARAUDY, ROGER   *From Anathema to Dialogue: A Marxist Challenge to the Christian Churches*

V-434   GAVIN, JAMES M.   *Crisis Now*

V-475   GAY, PETER   *The Enlightenment: The Rise of Modern Paganism*

V-277   GAY, PETER   *Voltaire's Politics*

V-406   GETTLEMAN & MERMELSTEIN   *The Great Society Reader: The Failure of American Liberalism*

V-174   GOODMAN, P. & P.   *Communitas*

V-325   GOODMAN, PAUL   *Compulsory Mis-education* and *The Community of Scholars*

V-32   GOODMAN, PAUL   *Growing Up Absurd*

V-417   GOODMAN, PAUL   *People or Personnel* and *Like a Conquered Province*

V-247   GOODMAN, PAUL   *Utopian Essays and Practical Proposals*

V-357   GOODWIN, RICHARD N.   *Triumph or Tragedy:* Reflections on Vietnam

V-248   GRUNEBAUM, G. E., VON   *Modern Islam:* The Search for Cultural Identity

V-430   GUEVARA, CHE   *Guerrilla Warfare*

V-389   HAMILTON, WALTON   *The Politics of Industry*

V-69   HAND, LEARNED   *The Spirit of Liberty*

V-319   HART, H. L. A.   *Law, Liberty and Morality*

V-427   HAYDEN, TOM   *Rebellion in Newark: Official Violence and Ghetto Response*

V-404   HELLER, WALTER (ed.)   *Perspectives on Economic Growth*

V-283   HENRY, JULES   *Culture Against Man*

V-465   HINTON, WILLIAM   *Fanshen: A Documentary of Revolution in a Chinese Village*

V-95   HOFSTADTER, RICHARD   *The Age of Reform*

V-9   HOFSTADTER, RICHARD   *The American Political Tradition*

V-317   HOFSTADTER, RICHARD   *Anti-Intellectualism in American Life*

V-385   HOFSTADTER, RICHARD   *Paranoid Style in American Politics*

V-749   HOWE, IRVING (ed.)   *Basic Writings of Trotsky*

V-201   HUGHES, H. STUART   *Consciousness and Society*

V-241   JACOBS, JANE   *Death & Life of Great American Cities*

V-433   JACOBS, PAUL   *Prelude to Riot: A View of Urban America from the Bottom*

V-332   JACOBS & LANDAU (eds.)   *The New Radicals*

V-369   KAUFMANN, WALTER (ed.)   *The Birth of Tragedy and The Case of Wagner*

V-401   KAUFMANN, WALTER (ed.)   *On the Genealogy of Morals and Ecce Homo*

V-337   KAUFMANN, WALTER (tr.)   *Beyond Good and Evil*

V-470   KEY, V. O., JR.   *The Responsible Electorate: Rationality in Presidential Voting 1936–1960*

V-361   KOMAROVSKY, MIRRA   *Blue-Collar Marriage*

V-152   KRASLOW AND LOORY   *The Secret Search for Peace in Vietnam*

V-341   KIMBALL & McCLELLAN   *Education and the New America*

V-215   LACOUTURE, JEAN   *Ho Chi Minh*

V-327   LACOUTURE, JEAN   *Vietnam: Between Two Truces*

V-367   LASCH, CHRISTOPHER   *The New Radicalism in America*

V-399   LASKI, HAROLD J. (ed.)   *Harold J. Laski on The Communist Manifesto*

V-287   LA SOUCHÈRE, ÉLÉNA DE   *An Explanation of Spain*

V-426   LEKACHMAN, ROBERT   *The Age of Keynes*

V-280   LEWIS, OSCAR   *The Children of Sánchez*

V-421   LEWIS, OSCAR   *La Vida: A Puerto Rican Family in the Culture of Poverty—San Juan and New York*

V-370   LEWIS, OSCAR   *Pedro Martínez*

V-284   LEWIS, OSCAR   *Village Life in Northern India*

V-392   LICHTHEIM, GEORGE   *The Concept of Ideology and Other Essays*

V-474   LIFTON, ROBERT JAY   *Revolutionary Immortality: Mao Tse-Tung and the Chinese Cultural Revolution*

V-384   LINDESMITH, ALFRED   *The Addict and The Law*

V-267   LIPPMANN, WALTER   *The Essential Lippmann*

V-204   LOMAX, LOUIS   *Thailand: The War that Is, The War that Will Be*

V-469   LOWE, JEANNE R.   *Cities in a Race with Time: Progress and Poverty in America's Renewing Cities*

V-407   MACK, RAYMOND   *Our Children's Burden: Studies of Desegregation in Ten American Communities*

V-193   MALRAUX, ANDRÉ   *Temptation of the West*

V-324   MARITAIN, JACQUES   *Existence and the Existent*

V-386   McPHERSON, JAMES   *The Negro's Civil War*

V-102   MEYERS, MARVIN   *The Jacksonian Persuasion*

V-273   MICHAEL, DONALD N.   *The Next Generation*

V-19   MILOSZ, CZESLAW   *The Captive Mind*

V-411   MINOGUE, KENNETH R.   *The Liberal Mind*

V-316   MOORE, WILBERT E.   *The Conduct of the Corporation*

V-251   MORGENTHAU, HANS J.   *Purpose of American Politics*

V-703   MOSELY, PHILIP E.   *The Kremlin and World Politics:* Studies in Soviet Policy and Action (Vintage Original)

V-57   MURCHLAND, BERNARD (ed.)   *The Meaning of the Death of God*

V-274   MYRDAL, GUNNAR   *Challenge to Affluence*

V-337   NIETZSCHE, FRIEDRICH   *Beyond Good and Evil*

V-369   NIETZSCHE, FRIEDRICH   *The Birth of Tragedy and The Case of Wagner*

V-401   NIETZSCHE, FRIEDRICH   *On the Genealogy of Morals and Ecce Homo*

V-285   PARKES, HENRY B.   *Gods and Men*

V-72   PEN, JAN   *Primer on International Trade*

V-46   PHILIPSON, M. (ed.)   *Automation:* Implications for the Future (Vintage Original)

V-258   PIEL, GERARD   *Science in the Cause of Man*

V-128   PLATO   *The Republic*

V-309   RASKIN & FALL (eds.)   *The Viet-Nam Reader*

V-719   REED, JOHN   *Ten Days That Shook the World*

V-192   REISCHAUER, EDWIN O.   *Beyond Vietnam: The United States and Asia*

V-212   ROSSITER, CLINTON   *Conservatism in America*

V-267   ROSSITER & LARE (eds.)   *The Essential Lippmann*

V-472   ROSZAK, THEODORE (ed.)   *The Dissenting Academy*

V-288   RUDOLPH, FREDERICK   *The American College and University*

V-408   SAMPSON, RONALD V.   *The Psychology of Power*

V-435   SCHELL, JONATHAN   *The Military Half*

V-431   SCHELL, JONATHAN   *The Village of Ben Suc*

V-403   SCHRIEBER, DANIEL   *Profile of a School Dropout*

V-375   SCHURMANN AND SCHELL (eds.)   *The China Reader: Imperial China,* I

V-376   SCHURMANN & SCHELL (eds.)   *The China Reader: Republican China,* II

V-377   SCHURMANN & SCHELL (eds.)   *The China Reader: Communist China,* III

V-394   SEABURY, PAUL   *Power, Freedom and Diplomacy*

V-220   SHONFIELD, ANDREW   *Attack on World Poverty*

V-359   SILVERT, et al.   *Expectant Peoples*

V-432   SPARROW, JOHN   *After the Assassination: A Positive Appraisal of the Warren Report*

V-388   STAMPP, KENNETH   *The Era of Reconstruction 1865-1877*

V-253   STAMPP, KENNETH   *The Peculiar Institution*

V-244   STEBBINS, RICHARD P.   *U. S. in World Affairs, 1962*

V-374   STILLMAN & PFAFF   *Power and Impotence*

V-439   STONE, I. F.   *In a Time of Torment*

V-53   SYNGE, J. M.   *The Aran Islands* and Other Writings

V-231   TANNENBAUM, FRANK   *Slave & Citizen:* The Negro in the Americas

V-312   TANNENBAUM, FRANK   *Ten Keys to Latin America*

V-322   THOMPSON, E. P.   *The Making of the English Working Class*

V-749   TROTSKY, LEON   *Basic Writings of Trotsky*

V-206   WALLERSTEIN, IMMANUEL   *Africa:* The Politics of Independence (Vintage Original)

V-405   WASSERMAN & SWITZER   *The Vintage Guide to Graduate Study*

V-298	WATTS, ALAN W.	*The Way of Zen*
V-145	WARREN, ROBERT PENN	*Segregation*
V-323	WARREN, ROBERT PENN	*Who Speaks for the Negro?*
V-729	WEIDLE, W.	*Russia:* Absent & Present
V-249	WIEDNER, DONALD L.	*A History of Africa:* South of the Sahara
V-313	WILSON, EDMUND	*Apologies to the Iroquois*
V-208	WOODWARD, C. VANN	*Burden of Southern History*

A free catalogue of VINTAGE BOOKS *will be sent at your request. Write to* Vintage Books, 457 Madison Avenue, New York, New York 10022.

VINTAGE WORKS OF SCIENCE
AND PSYCHOLOGY

V-286   ARIES, PHILIPPE   *Centuries of Childhood*

V-292   BATES, MARSTON   *The Forest and the Sea*

V-129   BEVERIDGE, W. I. B.   *The Art of Scientific Investigation*

V-291   BIEBER, I., AND OTHERS   *Homosexuality*

V-320   BERNSTEIN, JEREMY   *The Analytical Engine*

V-336   BOHR, NIELS   *Essays on Atomic Physics*

V-11   BRILL, A. A., M.D.   *Lectures on Psychoanalytic Psychiatry*

V-168   BRONOWSKI, J.   *The Common Sense of Science*

V-169   BROWN, NORMAN O.   *Life Against Death*

V-419   BROWN, NORMAN O.   *Love's Body*

V-160   BUCHHEIM, ROBERT W. (ed.)   *The New Space Handbook* (revised)

V-172   CHADWICK, JOHN   *The Decipherment of Linear B*

V-338   CHURCH, JOSEPH   *Language and the Discovery of Reality*

V-410   CHURCH, JOSEPH (ed.)   *Three Babies: Biographies of Cognitive Development*

V-156   DUNBAR, FLANDERS, M.D.   *Your Child's Mind and Body*

V-157   EISELEY, LOREN   *The Immense Journey*

V-390   ELLUL, JACQUES   *The Technological Society*

V-348   EVANS, JEAN   *Three Men*

V-413   FRANK, JEROME D.   *Sanity and Survival: Psychological Aspects of War and Peace*

V-236   FREEMAN & MARCH   *The New World of Physics*

V-132   FREUD, SIGMUND   *Leonardo da Vinci: A Study in Psychosexuality*

V-14   FREUD, SIGMUND   *Moses and Monotheism*

V-124   FREUD, SIGMUND   *Totem and Taboo*

V-396   GILSON, ETIENNE   *The Christian Philosophy of Saint Augustine*

V-195   GRODDECK, GEORG   *The Book of the It*

V-404   HELLER, WALTER (ed.)   *Perspectives on Economic Growth*

V-283   HENRY, JULES   *Culture Against Man*

V-397   HERSKOVITS, MELVILLE J.   *The Human Factor in Changing Africa*

V-150   HOOPER, ALFRED   *Makers of Mathematics*

V-268   JUNG, C. G.   *Memories, Dreams, Reflections*

V-436   KAUFMANN, WALTER   *Nietzsche: Philosopher, Psychologist, Antichrist*

V-437   KAUFMANN, WALTER (ed.)   *The Will to Power*

V-361   KOMAROVSKY, MIRRA   *Blue-Collar Marriage*

V-74   KÖHLER, WOLFGANG   *The Mentality of Apes*

V-226   KROEBER & KLUCKHOLN   *Culture*

V-151   KUHN, HERBERT   *On the Track of Prehistoric Man*

V-164   KUHN, THOMAS S.   *The Copernican Revolution*

V-426   LEKACHMAN, ROBERT   *The Age of Keynes*

V-105   LESLIE, CHARLES (ed.)   *Anthropology of Folk Religion* (A Vintage Original)

V-97   LESSER, SIMON   *Fiction and the Unconscious*

V-280   LEWIS, OSCAR   *The Children of Sánchez*

V-421   LEWIS, OSCAR   *La Vida: A Puerto Rican Family in the Culture of Poverty—San Juan and New York*

V-370   LEWIS, OSCAR   *Pedro Martínez*

V-284   LEWIS, OSCAR   *Village Life in Northern India*

V-384   LINDESMITH, ALFRED   *The Addict and The Law*

V-76   LINTON, RALPH   *The Tree of Culture*

V-407   MACK, RAYMOND   *Our Children's Burden: Studies of Desegregation in Ten American Communities*

V-209   MARCUSE, HERBERT   *Eros and Civilization*

V-437   NIETZSCHE, FRIEDRICH   *The Will to Power*

V-462   PIAGET, JEAN   *Six Psychological Studies*

V-258   PIEL, GERARD   *Science in the Cause of Man*

V-70   RANK, OTTO   *The Myth of the Birth of the Hero* and Other Essays

V-99   REDLICH, FRITZ, M.D. and BINGHAM, JUNE   *The Inside Story:* Psychiatry and Everyday Life

V-395   ROKEACH, MILTON   *The Three Christs of Ypsilanti*

V-301   ROSS, NANCY WILSON (ed.)   *The World of Zen*

V-464   SARTRE, JEAN-PAUL   *Search for a Method*

V-289   THOMAS, ELIZABETH MARSHALL   *The Harmless People*

V-310   THORP, EDWARD O.   *Beat the Dealer*, Revised

V-109   THRUELSEN & KOBLER (eds.)   *Adventures of the Mind, I*

V-68   *Adventures of the Mind, II*

V-239   *Adventures of the Mind, III*

V-299   WATTS, ALAN W.   *The Joyous Cosmology:* Adventures in the Chemistry of Consciousness

V-466   WATTS, ALAN W.   *The Wisdom of Insecurity*

V-418   AUDEN, W. H.   *The Dyer's Hand*
V-398   AUDEN, W. H.   *The Enchafèd Flood*
V-22   BARZUN, JACQUES   *The Energies of Art*
V-93   BENNETT, JOAN   *Four Metaphysical Poets*
V-269   BLOTNER & GWYNN (eds.)   *Faulkner at the University*
V-259   BUCKLEY, JEROME H.   *The Victorian Temper*
V-51   BURKE, KENNETH   *The Philosophy of Literary Form*
V-75   CAMUS, ALBERT   *The Myth of Sisyphus*
V-171   CRUTTWELL, PATRICK   *The Shakespearean Moment*
V-471   DUVEAU, GEORGES   *1848: The Making of a Revolution*
V-4   EINSTEIN, ALFRED   *A Short History of Music*
V-261   ELLIS-FERMOR, UNA   *Jacobean Drama:* An Interpretation
V-177   FULLER, EDMUND   *Man in Modern Fiction*
V-13   GILBERT, STUART   *James Joyce's Ulysses*
V-363   GOLDWATER, ROBERT   *Primitivism in Modern Art,* Revised Edition
V-114   HAUSER, ARNOLD   *Social History of Art,* v. I
V-115   HAUSER, ARNOLD   *Social History of Art,* v. II
V-116   HAUSER, ARNOLD   *Social History of Art,* v. III
V-117   HAUSER, ARNOLD   *Social History of Art,* v. IV
V-438   HELLER, ERICH   *The Artist's Journey into the Interior and Other Essays*
V-20   HYMAN, S. E.   *The Armed Vision*
V-38   HYMAN, S. E. (ed.)   *The Critical Performance*
V-41   JAMES, HENRY   *The Future of the Novel*
V-12   JARRELL, RANDALL   *Poetry and the Age*
V-88   KERMAN, JOSEPH   *Opera as Drama*
V-260   KERMODE, FRANK   *The Romantic Image*
V-83   KRONENBERGER, LOUIS   *Kings and Desperate Men*
V-167   LA ROCHEFOUCAULD   *Maxims*
V-90   LEVIN, HARRY   *The Power of Blackness*
V-296   MACDONALD, DWIGHT   *Against the American Grain*
V-55   MANN, THOMAS   *Essays*
V-720   MIRSKY, D. S.   *A History of Russian Literature*
V-344   MUCHNIC, HELEN   *From Gorky to Pasternak*
V-118   NEWMAN, ERNEST   *Great Operas,* Volume I
V-119   NEWMAN, ERNEST   *Great Operas,* Volume II
V-107   NEWMAN, ERNEST   *Wagner as Man and Artist*
V-383   O'BRIEN, CONOR CRUISE   *Writers and Politics*
V-161   PICASSO, PABLO   *Picasso & the Human Comedy*
V-372   PRITCHETT, V. S.   *The Living Novel and Later Appreciations*
V-24   RANSOM, JOHN CROWE   *Poems and Essays*
V-412   SAARINEN, ALINE B.   *The Proud Possessors*
V-89   SCHORER, MARK   *William Blake*
V-108   SHAHN, BEN   *The Shape of Content*
V-275   SHAPIRO, KARL   *In Defense of Ignorance*
V-415   SHATTUCK, ROGER   *The Banquet Years,* Revised
V-366   SHATTUCK, ROGER   *Proust's Binoculars*
V-186   STEINER, GEORGE   *Tolstoy or Dostoevsky*
V-278   STEVENS, WALLACE   *The Necessary Angel*
V-39   STRAVINSKY, IGOR   *The Poetics of Music*

V-100	SULLIVAN, J. W. N. *Beethoven:* His Spiritual Development
V-243	SYPHER, WYLIE (ed.) *Art History:* An Anthology of Modern Criticism
V-266	SYPHER, WYLIE *Loss of the Self*
V-229	SYPHER, WYLIE *Rococo to Cubism*
V-166	SZE, MAI-MAI *The Way of Chinese Painting*
V-179	THOMSON, VIRGIL *Music Reviewed 1940-1954* (Vintage Original)
V-214	THOMSON, VIRGIL *The State of Music*
V-162	TILLYARD, E. M. W. *Elizabethan World Picture*
V-35	TINDALL, WILLIAM YORK *Forces in Modern British Literature*
V-82	TOYE, FRANCIS *Verdi:* His Life and Works
V-62	TURNELL, MARTIN *The Novel in France*
V-194	VALÉRY, PAUL *The Art of Poetry*
V-347	WARREN, ROBERT PENN *Selected Essays*
V-122	WILENSKI, R. H. *Modern French Painters,* Volume I (1863-1903)
V-123	WILENSKI, R. H. *Modern French Painters,* Volume II (1904-1938)
V-218	WILSON, EDMUND *Classics & Commercials*
V-181	WILSON, EDMUND *The Shores of Light*
V-360	WIMSATT & BROOKS *Literary Criticism*

V-715   ANDREYEV, LEONID *The Seven That Were Hanged* and Other Stories

V-158   AUDEN, W. H., & ISHERWOOD, C. *Two Plays:* The Dog Beneath the Skin *and* The Ascent of F6

V-342   BECKSON, KARL (ed.) *Aesthetes and Decadents*

V-80   BEERBOHM, MAX *Seven Men* and Two Others

V-271   BEDIER, JOSEPH *Tristan and Iseult*

V-93   BENNETT, JOAN *Four Metaphysical Poets*

V-321   BOLT, ROBERT *A Man for All Seasons*

V-21   BOWEN, ELIZABETH *The Death of the Heart*

V-48   BOWEN, ELIZABETH *The House in Paris*

V-79   BOWEN, ELIZABETH *Stories*

V-294   BRADBURY, RAY *The Vintage Bradbury* (A Vintage Original)

V-303   BRYHER *Roman Wall*

V-743   BUNIN, IVAN *The Gentleman from San Francisco* and Other Stories

V-207   CAMUS, ALBERT *Caligula & 3 Other Plays*

V-2   CAMUS, ALBERT *The Stranger*

V-223   CAMUS, ALBERT *The Fall*

V-245   CAMUS, ALBERT *The Possessed,* a play

V-281   CAMUS, ALBERT *Exile and the Kingdom*

V-28   CATHER, WILLA *Five Stories*

V-200   CATHER, WILLA *My Mortal Enemy*

V-140   CERF, BENNETT (ed.) *Famous Ghost Stories*

V-203   CERF, BENNETT (ed.) *Four Contemporary American Plays*

V-127   CERF, BENNETT (ed.) *Great Modern Short Stories*

V-326   CERF, CHRISTOPHER (ed.) *The Vintage Anthology of Science Fantasy*

V-293   CHAUCER, GEOFFREY *The Canterbury Tales,* a prose version in Modern English

V-142   CHAUCER, GEOFFREY *Troilus and Cressida*

V-753   CHEKHOV, ANTON *The Image of Chekhov:* 40 Stories

V-723   CHERNYSHEVSKY, N. G. *What Is to Be Done?*

V-146   CLARK, WALTER VAN T. *The Ox-Box Incident*

V-155   CONRAD, JOSEPH *Three Great Tales: The Nigger of the Narcissus, Heart of Darkness, Youth*

V-138   COZZENS, JAMES GOULD *S.S. San Pedro* and *Castaway*

V-10   CRANE, STEPHEN *Stories and Tales*

V-205   DINESEN, ISAK *Winter's Tales*

V-721   DOSTOYEVSKY, FYODOR *Crime and Punishment*

V-722   DOSTOYEVSKY, FYODOR *The Brothers Karamazov*

V-188   ESCHENBACH, W. VON *Parzival*

V-254   FAULKNER, WILLIAM *As I Lay Dying*

V-139   FAULKNER, WILLIAM *The Hamlet*

V-339   FAULKNER, WILLIAM *The Reivers*

V-381   FAULKNER, WILLIAM *Sanctuary*

V-5   FAULKNER, WILLIAM *The Sound and the Fury*

V-184   FAULKNER, WILLIAM *The Town*

V-351   FAULKNER, WILLIAM *The Unvanquished*

V-262   FAULKNER, WILLIAM *The Wild Palms*

V-149   FAULKNER, WILLIAM *Three Famous Short Novels: Spotted Horses, Old Man, The Bear*

V-282   FAULKNER, WILLIAM *The Mansion*

V-709	FEDIN, KONSTANTIN	*Early Joys*
V-130	FIELDING, HENRY	*Tom Jones*
V-45	FORD, FORD MADOX	*The Good Soldier*
V-187	FORSTER, E. M.	*A Room with a View*
V-7	FORSTER, E. M.	*Howards End*
V-40	FORSTER, E. M.	*The Longest Journey*
V-61	FORSTER, E. M.	*Where Angels Fear to Tread*
V-752	FRIEDBERG, MAURICE (ed.)	*Russian Short Stories:* A Bilingual Collection, Volume I
V-219	FRISCH, MAX	*I'm Not Stiller*
V-8	GIDE, ANDRÉ	*The Immoralist*
V-96	GIDE, ANDRÉ	*Lafcadio's Adventures*
V-27	GIDE, ANDRÉ	*Strait Is the Gate*
V-66	GIDE, ANDRÉ	*Two Legends*
V-467	GINSBURG, MIRRA (ed.)	*The Dragon: Fifteen Stories*
V-304	GOLD, HERBERT	*The Man Who Was Not With It*
V-473	GOODMAN, PAUL	*Adam and His Works: Collected Stories of Paul Goodman*
V-402	GOODMAN, PAUL	*Hawkweed*
V-300	GRASS, GÜNTER	*The Tin Drum*
V-425	GRAVES, ROBERT	*Claudius the God*
V-182	GRAVES, ROBERT	*I, Claudius*
V-217	GRAVES, ROBERT	*Sergeant Lamb's America*
V-717	GUERNEY, B. G. (ed.)	*An Anthology of Russian Literature* in the Soviet Period
V-255	HAMMETT, DASHIELL	*The Maltese Falcon* and *The Thin Man*
V-15	HAWTHORNE, NATHANIEL	*Short Stories*
V-476	HOROWITZ, ISRAEL	*First Season*
V-227	HOWES, BARBARA (ed.)	*23 Modern Stories*
V-307	HUMES, H. L.	*The Underground City*
V-305	HUMPHREY, WILLIAM	*Home From the Hill*
V-727	ILF AND PETROV	*The Twelve Chairs*
V-295	JEFFERS, ROBINSON	*Selected Poems*
V-380	JOYCE, JAMES	*Ulysses*
V-716	KAMEN, ISAI (ed.)	*Great Russian Stories*
V-134	LAGERKVIST, PÄR	*Barabbas*
V-240	LAGERKVIST, PÄR	*The Sibyl*
V-23	LAWRENCE, D. H.	*The Plumed Serpent*
V-71	LAWRENCE, D. H.	*St. Mawr* and *The Man Who Died*
V-706	LEONOV, LEONID	*The Thief*
V-170	MALAMUD, BERNARD	*The Magic Barrel*
V-136	MALRAUX, ANDRÉ	*The Royal Way*
V-180	MANN, THOMAS	*Buddenbrooks*
V-3	MANN, THOMAS	*Death in Venice*
V-86	MANN, THOMAS	*The Transposed Heads*
V-36	MANSFIELD, KATHERINE	*Stories*
V-137	MAUGHAM, SOMERSET	*Of Human Bondage*
V-78	MAXWELL, WILLIAM	*The Folded Leaf*
V-91	MAXWELL, WILLIAM	*They Came Like Swallows*
V-221	MAXWELL, WILLIAM	*Time Will Darken It*
V-306	MICHENER, JAMES A.	*Hawaii*
V-144	MITFORD, NANCY	*The Pursuit of Love*
V-197	MORGAN, F. (ed.)	*Hudson Review Anthology*
V-718	NABOKOV, V. (tr.)	*The Song of Igor's Campaign*
V-29	O'CONNOR, FRANK	*Stories*

V-49	O'HARA, JOHN	*Butterfield 8*
V-276	O'NEILL, EUGENE	*Six Short Plays*
V-18	O'NEILL, EUGENE	*The Iceman Cometh*
V-165	O'NEILL, EUGENE	*Three Plays:* Desire Under the Elms, Strange Interlude, and Mourning Becomes Electra
V-125	O'NEILL & OATES (eds.)	*Seven Famous Greek Plays*
V-478	PARONE, EDWARD (ed.)	*Collision Course*
V-753	PAYNE, ROBERT (tr.)	*The Image of Chekhov: 40 Stories*
V-466	PLATH, SYLVIA	*The Colossus: and Other Poems*
V-714	PUSHKIN, ALEXANDER	*The Captain's Daughter*
V-24	RANSOM, JOHN CROWE	*Poems and Essays*
V-731	REEVE, F. (ed.)	*Russian Plays,* Volume I
V-732	REEVE, F. (ed.)	*Russian Plays,* Volume II
V-297	RENAULT, MARY	*The King Must Die*
V-16	SARTRE, JEAN-PAUL	*No Exit* and Three Other Plays
V-65	SARTRE, JEAN-PAUL	*The Devil & the Good Lord* and Two Other Plays
V-238	SARTRE, JEAN-PAUL	*The Condemned of Altona*
V-441	SHAKESPEARE, WILLIAM	*Antony and Cleopatra* (Arden Edition)
V-443	SHAKESPEARE, WILLIAM	*King Henry IV, Part I* (Arden Edition)
V-444	SHAKESPEARE, WILLIAM	*King Henry IV, Part II* (Arden Edition)
V-445	SHAKESPEARE, WILLIAM	*King Lear* (Arden Edition)
V-446	SHAKESPEARE, WILLIAM	*Macbeth* (Arden Edition)
V-440	SHAKESPEARE, WILLIAM	*Measure for Measure* (Arden Edition)
V-447	SHAKESPEARE, WILLIAM	*The Merchant of Venice* (Arden Edition)
V-442	SHAKESPEARE, WILLIAM	*Othello* (Arden Edition)
V-448	SHAKESPEARE, WILLIAM	*The Tempest* (Arden Edition)
V-330	SHOLOKHOV, MIKHAIL	*And Quiet Flows the Don*
V-331	SHOLOKHOV, MIKHAIL	*The Don Flows Home to the Sea*
V-85	STEVENS, WALLACE	*Poems*
V-141	STYRON, WILLIAM	*The Long March*
V-63	SVEVO, ITALO	*Confessions of Zeno*
V-178	SYNGE, J. M.	*Complete Plays*
V-346	TERTZ, ABRAM	*The Makepiece Experiment*
V-750	TERTZ, ABRAM	*The Trial Begins* and *On Socialist Realism*
V-131	THACKERAY, W. M.	*Vanity Fair*
V-713	TOLSTOY, LEO	*The Kreutzer Sonata*
V-154	TRACY, HONOR	*Straight and Narrow Path*
V-477	TRAINER, DAVID	*The Undertaking and Other Plays*
V-202	TURGENEV, IVAN	*Torrents of Spring*
V-711	TURGENEV, IVAN	*The Vintage Turgenev* Volume I: *Smoke, Fathers and Sons, First Love*
V-712	TURGENEV, IVAN	Volume II: *On the Eve, Rudin, A Quiet Spot, Diary of a Superfluous Man*
V-257	UPDIKE, JOHN	*Olinger Stories: A Selection*
V-308	UPDIKE, JOHN	*Rabbit, Run*
V-467	ZAMYATIN, YEVGENY	*The Dragon: Fifteen Stories*
V-751	ZOSHCHENKO, MIKHAIL	*Nervous People* and Other Stories

A free catalogue of VINTAGE BOOKS *will be sent at your request. Write to* Vintage Books, 457 Madison Avenue, New York, New York 10022.